MIDDLE EAST
1940 — 1942
A STUDY IN AIR POWER

PALESTINE

TO THE EDITOR OF THE TIMES

Sir,—The statement of the late Chief Rabbi and his Ecclesiastical Court, which Dr. Lazarus quotes, calls for some criticism. To say that "the Divine promise that the Holy Land will for ever remain Israel's inheritance" implies that the Jews and the Jews alone have the right to look upon the land as their own. But the Pentateuch, to which the declaration appeals, does not warrant this interpretation. The first explicit promise of Palestine to the descendants of Abraham was at Shechem in Genesis xii, 7, in the words "unto thy seed will I give this land." The promise is repeated in xiii, 15, and xvii, 8. In the latter text Abraham made a covenant with God through circumcision, and all the land of Canaan was promised to him as "an everlasting possession."

It is generally supposed that these promises were made to Jews. But this is quite wrong. When the promise of perpetual possession was made the only child of Abraham was Ishmael, for Isaac had not been born. Therefore, if the word rendered "everlasting" in the English Bible and "for ever" in the late Chief Rabbi's declaration is to be taken literally, it is perfectly clear that the Arabs, Christian and Muslim, who trace their descent from Ishmael have the prior claim to possess the land.

I am, Sir, yours faithfully,
ALFRED GUILLAUME, Davidson Professor of Old Testament Studies in the University of London.
King's College, Strand, W.C.2, March 11.

By the Same Author

History
THE DUKE
PALMERSTON
MR. CHURCHILL
THE TWO MARSHALS
    (Bazaine—Petain)
THE SECOND EMPIRE
THE HUNDRED DAYS
THE HUNDRED YEARS
THE HUNDREDTH YEAR

Essays
IDYLLS OF THE QUEEN
BONNET AND SHAWL
THE MISSING MUSE
THE LIBERATORS
MEN OF LETTERS
MEN OF AFFAIRS
MEN OF WAR
STILL LIFE

Correspondence
THE QUEEN AND MR. GLADSTONE
GLADSTONE AND PALMERSTON

Americana
THE OTHER AMERICAS
INDEPENDENCE DAY
ARGENTINE TANGO
CONQUISTADOR

Air Chief Marshal
SIR ARTHUR TEDDER, G.C.B.

From a drawing by H. A. Freeth

MIDDLE EAST
1940 — 1942
A STUDY IN AIR POWER
By PHILIP GUEDALLA

I know the stride of the figure of a man, the carriage of a woman, the spread of a hawk.—MERTISEN, 2180 B.C.

On the desarts of Africa round the Fallen Angels the Guardian Prince of Albion burns in his nightly tent.—W. BLAKE, 1795 A.D.

HODDER AND STOUGHTON
LIMITED LONDON

MIDDLE EAST 1940-1942
First printed September 1944

Made and Printed in Great Britain for HODDER AND STOUGHTON LTD., London
by T. AND A. CONSTABLE LTD., Printers, Edinburgh

To

The R.A.F.

who wrote this book

CONTENTS

PORTRAITS

DECORATIONS BY GEOFF JONES

MAPS

(Crown Copyright Reserved)

PRELUDE

THE ASSEMBLING AND MANIPULATION of British air power in the Middle East (an area that often seems to run from somewhere near Gibraltar to the gates of India) is one of the great stories of the war. Perhaps it is the greatest on our side, as it is certainly the most significant in the use of the air weapon. Beginning with the gay impromptu of the days when young gentlemen in antique aircraft took on fantastic odds with cheerful gallantry and one officer described our system as "*Per ardua ad hoc*," it passed through the unpleasing epoch when British commanders in the Middle East had on their hands an average of four wars in three continents and juggled their small resources between the Western Desert, Abyssinia, Greece, Iraq, and Syria. These distractions overcome, their duties settled down to a duel with the *Luftwaffe* for control of the sky over Africa and the Mediterranean; and there is not the slightest doubt who won it.

Those operations are the first in which a complete Air Force has been brought to bear on every problem of air warfare. For the tendency to separatism between Fighter, Bomber, Coastal, and Army Co-operation Commands at home, encouraged by the static warfare conducted in the European sky from fixed bases, was quite out of place in Africa. Every problem was present—the attack and defence of sea-routes in the Mediterranean, the defence of Egypt (an island in the sand, as truly as Britain is an island in the sea), and the supreme requirements of military victory in a succession of land campaigns—and each of them was solved by a single Air Force working in internal harmony and in close partnership with the Eighth Army and the Royal Navy. This major achievement is the first of its kind in our military history; and I suspect that it will be studied as a classic in the art of war.

When the Air Ministry asked a complete beginner to write the story of the air war in the Middle East and to start by flying over the terrain, the novice answered cheerfully that he had never been off the ground except on a bicycle and that he hoped they did not mind. It appeared that they did not mind, unless he did; and as the feeling seemed to be mutual, the affair proceeded.

A determined student of other forms of war, the apprentice then enquired where he could find the principles of air warfare conveniently stated by some Mahan or Clausewitz of the fourth dimension. The reply was that there was nothing of the sort. In that case he concluded that he would have to improvise one for himself; and facilities for his education were generously afforded at Bomber, Fighter, Coastal, and Army Co-operation Commands, where busy people found time to tell him what they were about. When this stage of his initiation was concluded, the matter passed into other hands.

He is not likely to forget the winter afternoon when he stood in a new R.A.F. uniform, waiting to cross the tarmac of a Home Counties aerodrome and to climb into the Flying Fortress which was to take Tedder to the Mediterranean Air Command and himself for his first flight. As great personages had very naturally come to see the Air Chief Marshal off, the rash historian could not escape a private feeling that the firing-party was a shade excessive for his own modest execution; and one look at the exalted rank of his fellow-passengers convinced him that it would be just as well not to inaugurate his new career as a staff officer by being ignominiously ill over his betters. But presently he saw the little homes of Metroland go smoothly by beneath him and reassuringly discovered the unrivalled joys of sailing serenely across country at a lordly elevation. That eventful afternoon was the first of a long series of flights, which has since taken him 20,000 miles over three continents in pursuit of the people, places, and papers on which this book is founded.

A historian is normally familiar with the process of reconstructing past events from documents; and the present writer has often sought to render these more vivid to himself and others by visiting the places where they happened. But the persons who took part in them have habitually been uncommunicative, safely recumbent underneath their monuments and quite incapable of comment on his version of their performances. In the present case, however, the leading figures were all present, highly talkative, and uniformly disinclined to preserve a monumental dignity. (I cannot think of anyone more likely than Sir Arthur Tedder to make disrespectful comments on his neighbours in

Westminster Abbey.) That was the fascinating thing about an undertaking which confronted me with the living people in addition to the papers and the places. He was the liveliest of them by a long way; and he gave ungrudging aid to my education in the methods of air warfare from that first evening, when we discovered that we had both been reading History at the same time in different universities and he disclosed his merciful escape from the peaceful destiny of editing Pepys' papers in a Cambridge college.

After that we soared into Africa; and whilst he laboured at the problem of creating an inter-Allied Air Command, I pursued knowledge in his Headquarters at Algiers. Few environments were less congenial to pure research than the busy anteroom, in which my laboratory consisted of a large armchair and the adjacent area of floor, where practically all his callers tripped over my papers. But I learnt a lot there, before I left for Cairo to learn more. (That was a memorable journey, too, when we went rather higher than it is altogether comfortable to fly in an old pair of dress-socks, and I was largely kept alive by draughts of the rich beverage which fully justified Kinglake's pronouncement that "the love of tea is a glad source of fellow-feeling between the Englishman and the Asiatic"—and, for that matter, between a chilly British passenger and an Australian air-crew.)

Cairo was the next stage of my education, which proceeded for some weeks in that strange city—half East, half West, and wholly Cairene—whose aspect is reminiscent in equal parts of the newer quarters of Buenos Aires and the older portions of the Arabian Nights, with something Late Victorian about its strong, pervading sense that Lord Kitchener is always somewhere close at hand and that General Gordon has only just gone up the river to Khartoum. Nothing, surely, could be purer Kipling than that classic of Nineteenth Century militarism, the Kasr-el-Nil Barracks, which I never passed without a feeling that Mulvaney, Ortheris, and Learoyd might stroll out to take the air at any moment. Not far away I worked for some weeks in the dim recesses of R.A.F. Headquarters, Middle East; and as Mr. Gibbon wrote indulgently that "the captain of the Hampshire grenadiers (the reader may smile) has not been useless to the historian of the Roman empire," I hope the Squadron Leader (Temporary) had his uses too. He was more proud than he can say to wear its uniform in the months when he belonged to the R.A.F., to share its loyalties, and to feel himself a part, however loosely attached, of that incomparable Service. But deep down in his civilian heart he knew that there were other Services and that they did not invariably view one another with historical detachment. Nelson once wrote to Jervis that "the Army is, as usual, well dressed and powdered . . . but, as you well know, great exertions belong exclusively to the Navy." And had not the thoughtful Gleig, surveying Service relations in the Peninsula, observed that "perhaps I need not tell the reader, that between the infantry and cavalry in the British army, a considerable degree of jealousy exists; the former description of force regarding the latter as little better than useless, the latter regarding the former as extremely vulgar and ungenteel"? I will not venture to identify the modern heirs of these conflicting (and unjust) prejudices. But there are still noticeable traces of them; and as victory depends on a wise balance of sea, land, and air forces, I have done my best to make this narrative impartial.

The next stage in its preparation was to survey the ground, since one can hardly write about a war without seeing where it was fought; and it became my business to get acquainted with the Western Desert. I knew a little about deserts already. Rides across the baking *hammada* of Figuig, hot afternoons in the M'Zab, and a brief holiday acquaintance with Touggourt had already taught me something of the Sahara. Cairo was full of people saying that you simply *must* go to the Desert, because the air is like champagne (I observed that most of them were still in Cairo when I got back); and as one cannot learn much about deserts by flying over them or reading a map, which comes to the same thing, I took a 15-cwt. truck to make closer contact and spent the best part of ten days driving 750 miles from Cairo to Tobruk. I think I know a little of the Desert now; and there must have been something a trifle wrong with my first magnum of Desert air, because it was full of sediment. We drove out of Alexandria straight into the yellow, grinning teeth of a sand-storm; and as there was a good deal to be said for camping near a water-point, we lay all night in a pale nightmare of wind-driven sand beside a little railway station named Alamein. That was when I began to think that perhaps the management was apt to overdo the local colour and that it might be a little late in life for starting my career as a Boy Scout. For the historian had never spent a night outside a house in all his life; and the Western Desert hardly seemed the place for conducting this experiment.

But my companions pulled me through. Staff officer, driver, cook, and corporal-illustrator, we were an oddly diverse party from the Home Counties, Yorkshire, Scotland, and Australia. They tolerated my invariable tendency to go away and read a book, when there was any work to do; and they helped me to share Kinglake's discovery that "the first night of your first campaign (though you be but a peaceful campaigner) is a glorious time in your life." We could even overlook our driver's strange affection for a stretcher that he had once found at Tobruk, although he imparted a slightly macabre air to our encampment by insisting upon sleeping in it. For— Kinglake's *Eothen* again—"I always liked the men who attended me on these Eastern travels, for they were all of them brave, cheery-hearted fellows."

We rumbled steadily towards Tobruk across the melancholy plateau, where the sea-wind is less like champagne than a cold bath (Balaklava helmets are what you really want in the Sahara after dark) and my undressing tended to consist of taking off my braces and putting on another sweater. As the sheer edge of Libya climbed up the sky in front of us, we discovered that the Desert is a good deal harder than Hollywood has led its patrons to believe, especially since the explosives industry of two continents has devoted its best energies to blowing large holes in it, on most of which we bounced.

The odd thing about a modern battlefield on the morning after (it looks rather like Hampstead Heath after a demoniac Bank Holiday that has left behind wrecked lorries, crashed aircraft, and burnt-out tanks instead of paper bags) is the interminable mileage of silent telephone wires trailing on the ground, which once buzzed with excited voices. An old man in Brussels once told me of an equal triviality in the litter of Napoleonic battles, which had left the field of Waterloo a sea of cartridge-paper, drifted feet deep about the heavy fighting at La Haye Sainte and Hougomont. These are the details that romantic painters overlook; and we picked a cautious way among them, careful of uncharted mines, across the brown emptiness of Sidi Rezegh and the flat *hinterland* behind Tobruk. By that time I began to know the Desert moderately well, the limitless horizons and the odd proportions of the landscape—about one-sixth earth to five-sixths sky—"that eternal coastline—that fixed horizon . . . that daily, daily scene," which Kinglake once evoked drawing "deep Ionian curses" from Greek warriors at the siege of Troy and I watched performing the same exasperating function for our own fighting men. And I had tasted something of their waterless existence, which inspired the best deal that I ever did on the lecture platform. For when a Desert squadron asked if the new arrival could stand up and tell the troops what life was like in England now, a grimy visitor responded that he was ready to oblige, if his hosts would reciprocate with enough warm water for one thorough wash. The lecturer had once toured the Middle West at the noble rates prevailing before the Wall Street crash of 1929. But no reward was ever richer than that small canvas bucket of hot water at Gambut last March.

Then we came down, as thirsty men had come before us, to the green slopes of Cyrenaica and saw the red earth and the white houses of Benghazi. There was a delicious interlude of ease at Rommel's late headquarters in a little seaside pension, backed by the green and grey of the coast range at Apollonia, where a Turkish minaret looks at a Roman temple. They let me sleep in what, as other travellers boast about Queen Elizabeth, I always shall insist was Rommel's bedroom; and when we stole a chilly bathe, my companions plunged me into dark reflections for at least half a day by expressing a respectful hope that they would be able to run into the sea as fast when they were my age.

The next stop was Tripoli, where a white Turkish town is heaped along a headland and the Spanish Mole put out to sea with interruptions by the R.A.F. It was pleasant to explore the late Marshal Balbo's palace, a large construction replete with domes, horseshoe arches, flood-lit fountains, and flower-gardens in a style that may be termed Moss Brothers Mauresque. This Drury Lane magnificence cried aloud for an entrance of Princess Badroulboudour and the young ladies of the chorus. But there were still no signs of them, when I left for Malta.

That was a memorable sight as well. For it was worth coming a long way to circle over the grey cliffs of Malta and the blue clover-leaf of the Grand Harbour, and to see swarms of English wasps taking off to sting Sicily, and to walk about the little streets with their shattered buildings and their unbroken pride. Once the gate-keeper of Christendom, Malta had been the hinge on which British victory in Africa had turned; and as the door swung slowly open, the view from Malta in the spring of 1943 was well worth having.

Then I left Cairo northward-bound for a swift inspection of the scenes of R.A.F. activity in Syria; and this paper, which had been started in the Desert one forlorn evening at El Adem, was continued in Beyrout. It was somehow easier to think in full view of the blue Levant. A morning flight along the edge of Sinai and the brown cliffs of Palestine had been a sound lesson in Biblical geography. Tall cypresses among the red roofs of Beyrout, backed by green and purple hills and the white Syrian sierra, made a perfect décor; and I investigated the architectural frivolity of Vichy headquarters (once accommodated in an ex-Casino with an admirable view of the race-course). My duty to observe R.A.F. targets took me across the passes of the Lebanon to Damascus, where the bare, brown mountain looks down on the green orchards and the broad water-courses of the last oasis before the Desert closes in again. There, in a gentle haze of green, lines of tall poplars, brooding cypresses, and the eternal vigilance of minarets kept guard over the city; and perhaps I was not stretching duty too far by stopping for a look at Baalbek on the way. But there was really no excuse for my drive through Palestine, except that I had got to catch the plane for Iraq, and it seemed to start from somewhere near Jerusalem.

Reverting to a truck (when I was not in aircraft, I was generally to be found in trucks), I left Beyrout early and drove along the low Phoenician shore, where Tyre and Sidon used to be and the dim blue of the seaward horizon had once beckoned them to Carthage, to the Pillars of Hercules, and the open sea beyond. Palestine appeared at lunch-time; and all through that enchanted afternoon we seemed to have the country to ourselves. We drove the length of Armageddon and took the long curves of mountain-roads, until we swept over the last ridge of all and saw Jerusalem—domes, minarets, and cubes of modern buildings—facing us across the valley in the evening light. For we had come down on the City from the north, as the Crusaders came; and I sat there with my driver, staring.

My next business lay five hundred miles due east on the far side of the Arabian Desert, spacious home of more bad prose than any other region of the earth's surface. Literary Frenchmen, acquainted with the Algerian Sahara, love to term their desert's colour peau de lion. But here was something that looked less like a lion skin than a moth-eaten hearthrug. A dark, volcanic desert splashed with the paler brown of drifted sand, it was a sombre sight, heavy with Doughty's discarded adjectives and Lawrence's rejected similes, until it turned to the rusty red of the Iraqi Desert. There, between the lake and the great curve of the Euphrates, a sumptuous R.A.F. station, where young gentlemen had lived the "gay and lordly life" once admired (and enjoyed) by Mr. Winston Churchill in the Bangalore cantonments, offers the paradox of Habbaniya—tree-lined roads with English names and the innocence of garden flowers with the Desert waiting just round the corner and hyenas yelping outside a tall iron boundary fence. That English acre at the most vital point between the Nile and India had been unbelievably held against attack in 1941; and it is disturbing to think what might have happened to the war, if Habbaniya had fallen. After that I moved on to Baghdad and rose one step higher in the ascending scale of my pedigree bedrooms. For the pilgrim, who had slept in Rommel's, was promoted to the more gracious apartment (it had an admirable river view) of Rashid Ali's first and favourite wife.

Baghdad was a swift panorama of tiled and towered mosques along a gleaming waterfront, ending with the incredible Hegira of my return to Cairo. For it is stimulating to get up by the Tigris (with the Golden Mosque full in the light of early morning), to breakfast by the Euphrates, swoop across the forbidding desert of Arabia, lunch by the Jordan (where the mauve and purple of the hills round the Dead Sea was pure Holman Hunt), and to take tea by the Nile.

There was still one theatre of war to be surveyed; and as I faced southward for East Africa, the slender land of Egypt (irreverently termed by Kipling "a country which is not a country, but a longish strip of market-garden") slipped beneath our feet, until we saw the jagged mountains stand up behind Port Sudan. That seaside resort was sliding and dancing in the noonday heat; and somewhere down the coast the empty shell of Suakin lay beside its beach, faintly echoing the distant roar of old campaigns. For on the desert brown of the coast plain, between the Red Sea creaming in unlikely greens on island reefs and a horizon stormy with angry mountains, there were places named Handub and Trinkitat and Tokar and El Teb. "Val Baker, El Teb"—Kipling had once called up the old names from the churning paddle-wheels of a Nile steamer—"Tokar—Tamai—Tamanieb and Osman Digna! . . . Eighty-five—the Suakim–Berber Railway begun and quite as really abandoned. Korti—Abu Klea—the Desert Column. . . . Then—the smooth glide over deep water continues—another Suakim expedition with a great deal of Osman Digna and renewed attempts to build the Suakim–Berber Railway. 'Hashin,' say the paddle-wheels, slowing all of a sudden—'MacNeill's Zareba—the 15th Sikhs and another native regiment—Osman Digna in great pride and power, and Wady Halfa a frontier town. Tamai, once more; another Siege of Suakim; Gemaiza; Handub; Trinkitat, and Tokar—1887.'"

The old names that came back to Kipling thirty years ago drummed in my ears that afternoon, as the aircraft headed inland to climb over the steep edge of Eritrea. My business, however, lay with more immediate events, where British forces had challenged the sheer precipice of Keren and triumphed over Nature reinforced by Italians. There was a strange look of Rio in the rock formations, almost unbelievably precipitous, on which perspiring men had scaled the unscalable three times a day as a matter of routine and achieved a classic of mountain warfare in a climate congenial to camels; and Rio recurred in the strange, thrusting rock-fingers outside Kassala, where the Red Sea mountains subside into the brown levels of the Sudan.

The battlefields were all behind me now. I had seen what I came out to see, met the people, read the papers, formed my own opinions, and surveyed the ground over which the air war in the Middle East had been fought. I had watched the R.A.F. at work from the Home Counties to Baghdad and even (being a fair linguist) learnt to speak its language. That accomplishment, however, must be restricted. For, as Raleigh wrote at the opening of his noble volume on *The War in the Air*, "the writer of this history has endeavoured to make his narrative intelligible to those who, like himself, are outsiders, and, with that end in view, he has avoided, as far as possible, the masonic dialect of the service." But a command of it enabled me to understand much that might have been concealed; and, my lesson learnt, all that remains now is to write the book.   P. G.

KHARTOUM, *May*, 1943.

B

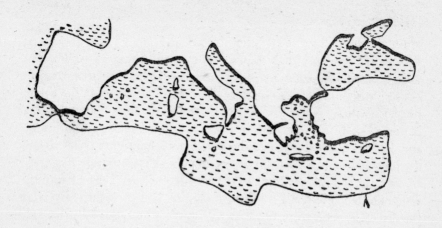

Chapter I

THE BOARD

TWO THOUSAND MILES FROM END TO END, the Mediterranean danced in the sunshine of June, 1940. The blue water
fingered innumerable beaches from Algiers to the Lebanon, looked
into little bays, and felt its way past islands. From the narrows, where
the last pulse of the Atlantic tides died in the Straits between the edge
of Spain and the dim bulk of Africa, it slowly broadened into the wide
arena of the Western Basin. There, in a great pentagon of sea, it
spread between North Africa, the coasts of France and Spain, and the
long Italian shore. Narrowing again, the sea-way passed between
the tip of Tunis and the flank of Sicily, until the channel opened on
the great triangle of the Central Mediterranean. To the south, mile
after mile, waves broke along the low African shore; and in the north,
Italy leaned towards the mountains of Albania across the straits beyond
Otranto. Eastward again a vestibule of water led between Greek
headlands and the upward thrust of Africa above Benghazi into the
spaces of the Eastern Mediterranean. Its northern half, flanked by
the shores of Greece and Turkey and studded with Aegean islands,
drew towards the guarded gateway of the Dardanelles; and to the
south it broadened into the great oblong of the Levant, where the
folded hills of Syria looked out across the red roofs of Beyrout and the
orange groves of Tyre. At its furthest corner Africa and Asia met in
the unpleasant wilderness of Sinai, and Port Said lay beside the broad,

ruled entrance of the Canal that joined Europe with the East. In the south the low Egyptian coastline faded into the western haze. At Alexandria blue and khaki figures sat eternally along an endless sea-wall between the long marine horizon and the brown apartment houses, whose angular modernity faces the blue sea and the white breakers with a distant look of Rio; and as the flags fluttered at the masthead of British warships or hung limp on Greek custom-houses and Turkish quays, further to the west French guns looked out to sea, the long Italian coast slept in the sun, and war crept slowly nearer.

For war had not yet come to the Mediterranean. The war was still four hundred miles away, where a sagging line of French divisions faced the Germans from the Eastern frontier to the English Channel. A German rush had carried Norway and cleared the Low Countries; and that week, as England held her breath, it converged upon a tired army round a single blazing port in Flanders. The French were failing visibly; and as the British reeled after Dunkirk, their spokesman promised (and could promise) little more than a continuation of the fight on the beaches, on the landing-grounds, in the fields and in the streets of a beleaguered island. If they would not surrender, it might be time to take the war a little further south, to cut their sea-way to the East by Suez, to disintegrate their Empire while their hands were full at home. For it was threaded on a slender cord that ran through the Mediterranean past Malta and, by way of Egypt, to the gates of India and (still more vital) to the oil of Persia and Iraq. If that were cut, the rest was simple; and it should not be difficult to cut it, if Italy would act.

Three times in the past ninety years Italian shrewdness had divined the winning side in European wars and rallied to it. This perspicacity was the foundation of Italian power; and in June, 1940, it did not seem difficult for Italy to choose the winning side again. The French were plainly beaten; and that circumstance should simplify the conquest of Nice, Savoy, and Corsica. But Italy had larger views. For the new Rome required an empire; Abyssinia was not enough; and Egypt was a noble province that would fill the unwholesome gap between the wastes of Libya and the high valleys of Italian East Africa. The gains were obvious; the losses, it might be hoped, would be insignificant; and as the June days went by and Mussolini made his choice, the long shape of Italy shadowed the Mediterranean.

Gibraltar held the western gateway. British uniforms went up

and down the narrow street or stood behind the hooded guns, deep
in the tunnelled Rock; and the ships lay at anchor in its shadow.
Eastward-bound, they slid past the point and headed for the open sea.
The narrows opened on a corridor flanked by the watching mountains
of Andalusia and the Riff coast; and as Spain had seen enough fighting
in three years of civil war, the watchers on the shore were neutral
and likely to remain so. But as the vestibule grew wider, a friendly
coast appeared to southward, where the long Algerian littoral ran for
six hundred miles and the tricolour flew over white towns between
the mountains and the sea.

The sea was broader now. Two hundred miles beyond Gibraltar
the Spanish sea-board tilted back to flank the Western Basin of the
Mediterranean. Framed between Italy and Spain, its broad expanses,
once Nelson's classic cruising-ground, were in Allied control. For
France lay along its northern shore from the Pyrenees to the Alps and
faced Algeria across four hundred miles of sea, where south-bound
ships steamed from Marseilles to the white arches of Algiers; and
Allied shipping for the East could move with safety in the shelter of
the Algerian shore. But as it drew level with the first dunes of Tunisia,
the channel narrowed. For Sardinia was not much above a hundred
miles from the edge of Africa. Further east the passage grew still
narrower, where traffic moved for close on two hundred miles through
the Sicilian Channel. The friendly coast of Tunis faced Sicily across
eighty miles of water; and it was plain that the masters of Italian policy
had power to cut the Mediterranean in two.

Full in the throat of the Sicilian Channel, sixty miles from Italian
territory and eight hundred from the nearest British base, a limestone
island lay in the midsummer glare. Pale stone walls enclosed the tiny
fields of Malta; the long roll of the island landscape rose to brown,
Spanish-looking townships, topped by a distant dome; and in Valletta
the stern magnificence of military architecture had made a sort of
Venice grown to manhood, with the broad sea for its lagoon and
house-bound creeks alive with the strange prows of *dghaisas* instead
of gondolas on dark canals. But Malta was a lonely speck in the blue
sea that summer, half-way between Gibraltar and Port Said. Armed
for attack, it might obstruct the movement of Italian forces from the
Continent to Tripoli. But a cautious strategy had withdrawn the
British fleet to Alexandria; and it seemed too near the Italian mainland
for use as an air base. This caution even rendered its defence precarious.

For it could only be supplied by sea; and though French beaches in Tunisia were no more than two hundred miles away, British fleets at Alexandria and Gibraltar were four times as remote. So long as British fleets were based there, Malta had been the doorkeeper of the East. But once they were banished by the uncomfortable proximity of Italian aircraft, it became a lonely sentinel on an untravelled road.

The sea-way to the East by Suez ran past Sicily; and if it was true (as high authority pronounced) that the passage of a convoy, however heavily escorted, within a hundred miles of the metropolitan air force of a first-class Power was not a feasible operation of war, the Italians could bar the way. That was the worst of the Suez Canal. For however admirable it might be for shipping that arrived there, its arrival was highly doubtful, if it had first to traverse the Sicilian Channel within fighter-range of shore-based Italian aircraft. Indeed, the Italian position was still more menacing. Students of ancient history were well aware that "a sea power occupying both Sicily and the North of Africa will go far towards gaining command of the Mediterranean"; and though Professor Holland Rose (*The Mediterranean in the Ancient World*, 1933) was writing of the Punic Wars, truths founded on geography were apt to be unchanging. For, as Mahan wrote, "geography underlies strategy" (*Naval Strategy*, 1911). He prescribed that "in considering any theatre of actual or possible war, or of a prospective battlefield, the first and most essential thing is to determine what position, or chain of positions by their natural and inherent advantages affect control of the greatest part of it"; and if war was coming to the Mediterranean, the chain of Italian positions on both sides of the sea were of primary importance. At the moment a large proportion of North Africa was in French hands. But the whole coast from Tripoli to the Egyptian frontier was now Italian; and Mussolini was uncomfortably astride the road to Suez.

For the south shore of the Central Mediterranean was formed by Libya, on which Herodotus had once pronounced the cautious judgment that "it seems to me that Libya is not to compare for goodness of soil with either Asia or Europe." (An equal reticence once led Lord Salisbury to describe large areas of the Sudan as "light sandy soil.") Indeed, a close inspection seems to favour the ancient tourist's division of the habitable world into "Europe, Asia, and Libya." Few regions of the earth's surface are less attractive than the late Vilayet of Tripoli, seized by Italian aggression from the Turks in 1911 and consisting largely of several distinct varieties of desert. A mood of classical grandiloquence now termed it Libya; and in the capital, close to its western edge, Marshal Balbo presided in an edifice of pantomime magnificence, where the woodwork was uniformly shoddy and the grey silk walls of the Governor-General's office were illuminated through an appalling lampshade. In a packing-case downstairs a framed and painted allegory recalled the triumph of his trans-Atlantic flight with a quantity of eagles brooding and in motion, avoiding awkwardness in the Latin text commemorative of his exploit by draping a large eagle's wing across his destination's final syllable in case Chicago was not felt to be sufficiently Ciceronian; and in a drawer the latest volume of *Gli Annali dell' Africa Italiana* portrayed in sumptuous typography and admirable photographs the Roman triumphs of road-making, with which the astonished uplands of Abyssinia were now incorporated in a nobler system. On its cover a full-length statue of Caesar lifted an impressive hand above the bold mis-statement that the empire knew no bounds.

This was untrue of Libya, bounded with precision on three sides by the sea, Tunisia, and Egypt. True, its southern border groped with some uncertainty towards the French Sahara and the less appetising portions of the Sudan. But as this region was entirely waterless, it did not greatly matter. Turkey had not prized its African dependency, which was largely used as a place of exile for officials who had failed to give satisfaction; and even in Italian occupation there was much to confirm this unfavourable estimate. At one extremity the streets of Tripoli were huddled at the water's edge, where an impressive mole prolonged the Spanish fort to form the best harbour on the coast between Tunis and Alexandria. There were shops in the arcades of the new town; and a shady promenade along the front competed with a noble square in the lee of the old citadel, where a Roman wolf had looked down from his Venetian pillar to admire the Duce in the act of brandishing a sword of superhuman size in token of his benevolent intentions towards Islam. But inland the town died away into a sea of ochre dunes, where the hedges faded into tall bent until the slow surge of the Desert submerged everything except where the dainty buildings of the airport fifteen miles away were bright with bougainvillea.

For Libya was unmistakably a desert land. On the north the sea broke for miles along a long brown shore; and inland the midsummer sun of 1940 drove down on the brown immensities of the Sahara. It is the misfortune of Africa that, too wet in some parts, it is far too dry in others. While the centre of the continent exhibits swamps the size of counties and great lakes as big as Scotland framed in the rich green of Equatorial landscape, its northern half is almost uniformly brown with the desolation of the largest desert in the world. With one side looking on the Atlantic, its cheerless spaces run clear across Africa to the Nile valley and stretch half-way into the next continent. In these melancholy distances "a man," as Kipling wrote with forced cheerfulness, "may carry his next drink with him till he reaches Cape Blanco on the west (where he may signal for one from a passing Union Castle boat) or the Karachi Club on the east. Say four thousand dry miles to the left hand and three thousand to the right." A limitless horizon frames the unprepossessing vista of hard, brown earth, that changes sometimes to whipped sand or carved, unlikely cliffs; and depressed explorers catalogue the dreary alternations of its surface between stony plains and sandy mountains. Human life is banished to more favoured regions, where Egypt basks along the Nile or Morocco and Algeria lie on the seaward slope of the Atlas, or else moves uncertainly across its face with careful navigation from the safety of one small, green island to the next.

This unpleasing portion of the earth's surface had various owners. The French holding was the most extensive; but the least desirable of its expanses belonged to Italy. While there was something to be said for owning the waste hinterland of fertile regions, Libya was almost wholly desert. Along a thousand miles of coast from the edge of Tunis to the Egyptian frontier the Desert met the sea except where the coast range of Cyrenaica lifted above the dismal levels. Here among the green slopes of a less forbidding landscape settlers had arrived from Greece in ancient times, relying on the guidance of the Delphic oracle; and now their Italian successors, guided by a political divinity no less oracular, relieved the over-population of their native land by farming there. For one stretch, at least, of Libya was capable of something more than pasturing Senoussi camels. Deposited at equal distances along a road across the hills, the square white homesteads were more eloquent of a drawing-board in Rome than of the less regular requirements of agriculture in Africa. But the Italian mood was nothing if not classical; and it was echoed where Cyrene (not without help from injudicious restoration) raised its sculptured columns on the grey mountain-side. A hundred miles away the sun looked down on the blue harbour and white houses of Benghazi. The twin black Cathedral domes surmounting its spare Jesuit outline, just eight years old and resembling nothing so much as a pair of opera-glasses, seemed to offer their rounded silhouette as a discreet concession to offended Moslem feelings. The streets were shady; and outside the town a long road drove across the red earth and green fields towards the elegance of the air base, where the new buildings stood in their little gardens.

But the Desert soon closed in again; and as the brown, interminable vista resumed its endless reign, the brief interlude of green was soon forgotten in its drab monotone. Inland the empty distances ran out towards Chad a thousand miles away; and coastwise the waves broke along a sandy shore, where Cyrenaica faced Tripolitania across the great curve of the gulf. Further east faint tracks ran through the desert glare to unnamed crossroads on the way to Egypt, to the dun emptiness that a few camel-drivers knew as Sidi Rezegh and gaunt buildings beside the desert airfield at El Adem, or else turned seawards to unknown harbours where the swell lifted on brown rocks below a little town named Bardia high on the cliffs or crept round the headland into a long bay in front of the white houses of Tobruk. In the little square a modest campanile looked down on the palms and the white oblong of the piazza, and from its balcony the Municipio surveyed the ill-judged ornament of a few iron lamp-posts from Leghorn. The long, unshaded ribbon of the road ran eastwards over the brown levels, until a Roman eagle looked from its pillar at Capuzzo into Egypt.

This was the edge of Libya, where the high cornice of the desert plateau stands up from the sea with a strange look of the carved bastions flanking the Grand Canyon or the knees of seated gods along the edge of a forbidden land, commanding a long, slow curve of blue sea, white breakers, and brown plain that trails into the distance halfway to Buq Buq and, leftwards, the gracious angle in the coast where Sollum crouches between its brown cliff and the sea. It was plain that if war came to Libya, it would be desert war. For behind its beaches the country was a dusty void. Its defence against the French from Tunis or the British from the Nile must be conducted in the Desert; and if the Italians, whose troops were massing there, launched an attack on Egypt, they must cross the same uncomfortable terrain.

Armies had passed that way before, when Egyptian chariots manœuvred in the Western Desert and a cheerful governor reported to his Pharaoh on the smiting of enemies "as far as the western corner-post of the canopy of heaven." A Persian army, launched into Cyrenaica from Egypt, had once laid siege to Barce and on the long road home enjoyed (according to Herodotus) the full discomforts of a desert retreat; and when Islam rode to the west until Okba breasted the first waves of the Atlantic with indignation that he could ride no further in the Prophet's name, the Desert had seen the Arabs go by in the first flush of their new faith. But its hot distances were untroubled now except where British posts faced the Italians across the endless wall of wire strung along the Egyptian frontier by Marshal Graziani with the kindly thought of ensuring the continued blessings of Italian rule to his nomadic fellow-subjects.

For the British were in Egypt. Their strategy had long been sensitive about its safety. "Situated at the crossing of many roads,— by land and sea,—opening to Europe by the Mediterranean, and to the Indian Ocean by the Red Sea, a moment's thought will show that Egypt holds to the East and West a position like that which the defile of the Danube held to the battle-ground between Austria and France, or the Valtelline passes to the Spanish communications through Germany to the Netherlands in the seventeenth century; in a word, that, upon political control of Egypt might well depend the control of the East by a nation of western Europe. To strike at India itself was not at once possible; but it was possible to seize, in Egypt, one of those intermediate objectives before alluded to, and to wait there until so securely established as to be able to push on further" (MAHAN, *Naval Strategy*). That had been Bonaparte's objective in 1798; and his strategical experiment was ended by a swift, destructive exercise of Britain's sea power at the Battle of the Nile. But the lesson of those anxious weeks, when Nelson searched the Mediterranean for the French fleet, was not forgotten; and Egypt remained a vital area in British strategy.

The problem of its security continued to engage the attention of British statesmen through the Nineteenth Century. In the first instance it presented itself as safeguarding the road to India. There were two ways to the East from British ports. The long sea-route led down the South Atlantic, coasted the whole length of Africa and, entering the Indian Ocean round the Cape of Good Hope, first inspired British interest in South Africa. The second reached the same destination by a shorter passage through the Mediterranean and Red Sea, passing across the intervening Isthmus of Suez by the Overland Route. As this lay through Egypt, the country's fate became an object of concern to British policy. Not that it harboured dark designs of annexation. For, as the most enterprising of Queen Victoria's ministers once wrote, "we do not want Egypt or wish it for ourselves, any more than any rational man with an estate in the north of England and a residence in the south would have wished to possess the inns on the North Road. All he could want would have been that the inns should be well-kept, always accessible, and furnishing him, when he came, with mutton-chops and post-horses." But if Lord Palmerston did not want Egypt, he and his successors were tolerably clear that no one else must have it either; and it became an axiom that no other Power would be permitted to control this invaluable halfway-house to the East.

This caution was redoubled, when French enterprise threatened to improve communications by replacing the Overland Route with a canal from Suez to Port Said. Not that Palmerston believed in the canal. For the wild project might, he hopefully opined, be brought to nothing by high working costs and drifting sand. But if it worked, he viewed with deep misgiving French designs "to detach Egypt from Turkey in order thereby to cut off the easiest Channel of Communication between England and British India . . . to interpose between Syria and Egypt the Physical Barrier of a wide and deep Canal defended by military works, and the political Barrier of a strip of sand extending from the Mediterranean to the Red Sea granted away to, and occupied by, a Company of Foreigners." The canal was duly cut; shipping proceeded without misadventure from one end to the other; but the hateful vision failed to materialise, since Egyptian integrity proved to be unimpaired by French domination or by foreign shareholders. Shortly afterwards, indeed, the British Government itself joined their ranks by acquiring a large block of shares under dramatic circumstances which, heightened by Disraeli's master-touch, appealed to the romantic imagination of his fellow-country-men and helped to make the Suez Canal something of a British superstition.

But there was substance in the popular belief, as the Cape route was quite superseded now and the Canal provided the main link in

European communications with the East. "Strategically," in one appreciation (SQUADRON LEADER E. J. KINGSTON-McCLOUGHRY, *Winged Warfare*, 1937, s.v. *The Mediterranean To-day*), "the key to the Empire is the Mediterranean" for the simple reason that it leads to the Canal. So long as that remained in friendly hands, quick passage was assured for British troops and warships to destinations in the East and Australia. But once it passed under hostile control, the whole system of Imperial communications was out of gear. For the journey to the East would be inordinately lengthened by reverting to the old sea-route round the Cape; and an enemy astride the Canal, with the consequent ability to reach objectives in the East before British reinforcements could arrive, was in a position to bisect the British Empire.

Such preoccupations rendered British opinion pardonably sensitive about the fate of Egypt; and at the threat of its approaching dissolution into bankrupt anarchy (with the resulting danger that some enterprising foreign hand might pick up the pieces) even Mr. Gladstone was induced to turn from other problems nearer home, in which he was more deeply interested, to inaugurate, with evident reluctance and after unsuccessful efforts to persuade the French or the Italians to collaborate, a temporary British occupation. As most things in Egypt went (as Herodotus had noticed) by contraries, the provisional contained unlooked-for elements of permanence; and the temporary expedient of 1882 survived its authors. While British soldiers made themselves at home in Cairo and Alexandria, disorder vanished, solvency returned, and the country was noticeably better governed. Indeed, their accidental presence in the country at the time of an alarming outbreak in the distant regions of the Sudan saved Egypt from invasion by the tide of red savagery in which the Mahdi drowned her southern provinces. A long half-century of partnership ensured the safety of Imperial communications with the East. The Sudan was finally recovered, when the slow nightmare of the Mahdist empire died on the smoke of Kitchener's relentless volleys at Omdurman, although a twelve-foot nullah almost cost Britain a Prime Minister, as Lieutenant Churchill charged with the Lancers across the brown *hammada* beyond Kerreri one September day in 1898.

It was now an axiom of British strategy that the Nile valley must be strongly held. It covered the short-cut to India by Suez, and at the same time the long corridor of the Cape to Cairo route through

Africa passed that way. In the war of 1914 it was firmly held against all comers (who amounted to little more than a bewildered Turkish force that stumbled out of the Desert into sight of the Canal) and formed a base for British operations against the Dardanelles and Palestine; and if Britian ever went to war again, it was plain that Egypt had lost none of its significance. Indeed, its value had increased. For now it guarded something still more vital than the road to India.

War depends on movement; and in recent times movement was coming to depend almost exclusively on oil. No aircraft could leave the ground, no transport or armoured vehicle could move a yard, no oil-burning warship or merchant vessel could leave port without it. Lack of oil could paralyse a nation's air force and army and immobilise a large proportion of its fleet; and since wars are not won by grounded aircraft or stationary tanks, access to oil was now a military problem of the first gravity, which faced Britain in a simple and unpleasant form. Five-sixths of the world's supplies were produced beyond the Atlantic, where sea-traffic was exposed to grave interruption in time of war; and nearly half the balance came from Russia and Rumania, which were likely to be inaccessible. This rendered it essential that Britain should be in a position to draw on supplies of oil from Persia and Iraq; and if this was to be achieved, those regions must be covered against any threat.

The long diagonal of the Tigris and Euphrates from Mosul to the Persian Gulf was now as vital to an air-borne Empire as the Suez Canal had ever been to its sea-borne predecessor; and as the Navy had once pivoted on Malta, the R.A.F. was solidly established in the Middle East with headquarters in Egypt and installations in Iraq. But the defence of Iraq against a European enemy did not begin in Asia, since this remote objective could hardly be attained by the invader in a single bound. If it was to be defended, the intervening territories of Syria and Palestine must be securely held; and the first condition of successful operations in the Levant and its adjacent countries was the control of Egypt. In British hands it formed a base of proved utility; but if it passed into enemy control, it would expose the source of Britain's oil supply to imminent attack. For Baghdad was a bare eight hundred miles from Cairo. Egypt constituted "one of those intermediate objectives" defined by Mahan, where the invader could "wait . . . until so securely established as to be able to push on further" and then pass from the Nile to the Euphrates. The resulting blow to

Britain might well be fatal. Had not Bonaparte informed the Army of Egypt that it was "one of the wings of the Army of England" merely on the strength of taking them half-way to India? But Egypt now lay nearer to a still more vital part. For it was more than half-way on the road to oil.

This circumstance gave to the Nile valley a new importance in British strategy; and if war came to the Mediterranean, the defence of Egypt was its most vital problem. On the naval side a fleet based on Alexandria provided the solution; and on land Egypt was little more than an elongated island in a sea of sand. Up-river "a rifle-shot," in Kipling's estimate, "would cover the widest limits of cultivation, a bow-shot would reach the narrower"; and down-stream, where the strange country opened out towards the sea, the flat, unending green of rich cultivation never rose a foot above its level fields, touched with the melancholy of the great plains and unbroken except by a few palms, a camel, or its brown, crumbling towns. On either hand the Desert ran, dry and forbidding, clear to the nearest frontier. As Palestine was in British hands, the grey wilderness of Sinai could now be left unwatched. But on the west, three hundred miles from Alexandria, the long Egyptian frontier marched with Libya. True, Milner had pronounced that "the vast extent of the Libyan Desert puts an invasion of considerable proportions on that side, unless supported from the sea, out of the question" (*England in Egypt*, 1892). That, however, had been nearly fifty years ago, when Tripoli was held by a few languid Turks and desert warfare had depended for its transport on the unaided energies of camels. Now a more enterprising neighbour was installed on the far side of the Western Desert; and it was possible that with motor transport Italian forces might reach speeds and objectives unattainable by caravans. For oil, which had made Egypt still more vital to Great Britain, also rendered it more vulnerable.

Not that the terrain was inviting, since the Desert marched beside the sea from the last dusty yard of Libya to the green edge of the Nile Delta. Leaving the dry rim of the plateau with its odd look of the Bad Lands of the Far West, the coast road wound steeply down the brown acclivities of the Halfaya Pass and drove across the dreary vistas of a long dun heath, that overlooked the salty whiteness of the coastal dunes by Buq Buq and the blue sea beyond, towards a few brown cubes of buildings named Sidi Barrani. Further on, nearly half-way to Alexandria, a land-locked bay showed jade green with the surf breaking on the bar below the little houses and the stony hinterland of Mersa Matruh.   Sometimes the levels changed, and the sea-wind swept the melancholy spaces of an unnamed plateau ; and as the brown distances unwound, a pair of rails crept towards Alexandria from one point on the ruled infinity of the Desert railroad to the next, where a square station building with two arches and a tiny booking-hall lay like a lonely vessel hull-down on the Desert with a railway signal for its mast, and twenty yards of platform slept in the sunshine of 1940 beneath the name of Alamein.

The Western Desert was a forbidding battlefield.   But that was where Egypt would have to be defended, if the Italians attacked from Libya.   For Egypt, once essential to Imperial strategy for the defence of the Suez Canal, must now be held as a fortress covering Great Britain's oil supplies.   Here was its new significance in the age of the internal combustion engine.   The Canal was not so vital now, since the long barrier of Italy could bar sea-traffic through the Mediterranean. But its defence was not without importance.   For though it was not of much use to England, it was essential to deny it to an enemy who could pour reinforcements through it down the Red Sea and into Italian East Africa.   These, added to the forces already accumulated in Abyssinia and Eritrea, might threaten Kenya ; and it would be highly unpleasant for the Royal Navy, which was quite sufficiently occupied elsewhere, to face increasing hostile naval forces at large in the Indian Ocean.

For every reason it was plain that the Nile valley must be held, though its defence presented awkward problems.   At sea, perhaps, the problem was not unduly formidable, since the Italian fleet, though numerous, was likely to prove manageable.   But their air force was both large and extremely promising, and their troops had recent experience of savage warfare in Abyssinia.   Political geography placed them on two sides of the British on the Nile, since they could move overland from Libya on Egypt and from Eritrea on the Sudan.   The British forces were exiguous ; and the problem of their reinforcement was anything but simple.   With sea-traffic through the Mediterranean practically at an end, troopships from Britain would be reduced to the long sea-passage round the Cape ; and even so their safe arrival at Egyptian ports was in grave jeopardy, if the Italians made full use of their opportunity of isolating Egypt by closing the Red Sea.   For Allied shipping might traverse its vestibule between Aden and British

Somaliland in comparative security. But the gateway of Bab el Mandeb was a bare twenty miles across; and though the narrow aperture was watched by French Jibuti and the British at Perim, Italian aircraft were only a few miles away in Eritrea, and for the next five hundred miles the sea-lane passed up the Red Sea within range of airfields in Italian East Africa.

The threat to Egypt was quite manifest. Italian aircraft could, if used effectively, close the Sicilian Channel and Red Sea to British shipping. There was no other means of moving troops, equipment, and supplies to Egypt; and without reinforcements Egypt could not be held. A judicious exercise of air power by Italy could settle the whole military issue in advance by isolating the Nile valley; and if the Italians made full use of their opportunities, this result could only be averted by the arrival of air reinforcements for the British on the Nile. But how were they to come? So long as France was in the war, aircraft could be flown across French territory and might even get as far as Malta. "The importance of France to our Empire air routes becomes at once apparent. Even a neutral France would deprive us of a vital link in our air communications" (KINGSTON-MCCLOUGHRY, *The Mediterranean To-day*). But when they reached Malta or the edge of Tunis, half the Mediterranean and the whole breadth of Libya would still lie between them and Egypt.

The problem of getting air reinforcements to the Nile had received attention since the visible deterioration of Anglo-Italian relations a few years earlier; and the possibility of flying them across Africa was already envisaged. But the beaches of the Gold Coast were a good two thousand miles from the Nile valley. Aircraft disembarked at Takoradi might, it was thought, follow the coast to Lagos and, heading inland from the palms along the waterfront and the bright steel of the lagoons, cross the green tree-tops of Nigeria, where a forced landing would be final. Beyond the sandy reaches of the Niger they would pass from green Africa to brown. Due east from Kano, with all its houses crowding behind earth-brown battlements, the course sets for the Nile valley—six months' journey for a caravan, three weeks' for automobiles, and a morning's flight for fast aircraft —across the dusty width of Africa from Bornu and Chad to the brown levels of Darfur and, at their journey's end, Khartoum lying trim, compact, and orderly at the meeting of the rivers that flow down into Egypt. But forced landings in the intervening waste were prohibitive.

A sharp turn northward and another thousand miles down-stream would bring them to their destination, where, if they arrived, they could take the air again to fight. That was the route along which British aircraft might travel to the war. But it was still comparatively undeveloped, although Imperial Airways had operated regular air services with a ground organisation sufficient for their needs along that route for the past four years. It proved valuable for immediate military use. But landing grounds and services were rudimentary; the unpleasing habits of the local weather over coastal swamps, rain-forests, and deserts had yet to be fully investigated; and new runways and accommodation were required. The long trail across Africa had been blazed.

These were the precarious conditions under which the British must hold Egypt. For the great south-east angle of the Mediterranean was plainly vital to Allied strategy. French forces had been massed in Syria; British warships lay at Haifa in the shadow of Mount Carmel; and an Allied fleet at Alexandria ensured control of the Levant. The board was ample, and the game was ready to begin. Turkey was out of play; Greece, the Greek islands, and the awkward stepping-stone of Crete were neutral; and as the skies of 1940 looked down on the long outline of the Mediterranean, the white houses, the blue water, the brown spaces of the Desert, and the waiting men beside the silent guns, the war crept slowly nearer.

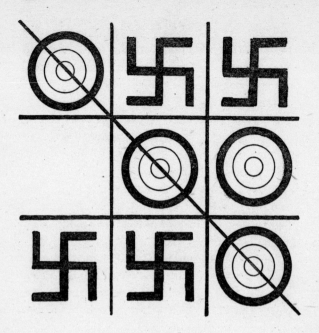

Chapter II

THE GAME

I

IT IS A POPULAR DELUSION, fostered by a large and growing literature of heroic anecdote, that air warfare is a form of personal gallantry rather than a planned form of war. Nothing, in this view, is interposed between the ingenuity of the aircraft designer and the intrepidity of the pilot; and whilst operations on sea and land are generally recognised as being seriously planned, it would almost appear that air operations are sometimes held to consist of throwing brave young men into the air with a bold, haphazard gesture and then hoping for the best. It was natural enough for a nation that had held its breath to watch thin trails of vapour on the English skies of 1940 and had known the profound relief of victory in the air battles over Britain to personify its saviours, to identify them with as many as survived from the "deadly and gallant tournament" (in Raleigh's phrase) which they had witnessed overhead, and to pronounce with their greatest orator that "never in the field of human conflict was so much owed by so many to so few." But their debt, if they only knew it, was also to still fewer, to those who made the plans and trained the pilots. For the fighter pilots whom they glorified were the unfaltering instrument by which sound training and direction applied the principles of war.

There is every excuse for the prevalence of some uncertainty as to the ruling principles relating to air warfare, since its practitioners have been far too busy during the short life of military aeronautics to have much time for theory. After all, land war had a good many centuries behind it before Jomini and Clausewitz enunciated those basic gener-alities which professionals seem to find satisfying; and men had fought at sea for generations before the things they had been doing all the time were plainly stated in the luminous commonplace with which Mahan anatomised sea power. So it is not surprising that air warfare, which emerged from imaginative fiction into operational reality within a single lifetime, is a shade uncharted. Indeed, with technical development proceeding at a rate that outmoded novelties almost before they were in production, it was foolhardy to lay down the law. For precepts applicable to the aircraft of 1918 were plainly meaningless by 1940; and it was anything but simple to state the rules of a game in which the ball was constantly developing a greater speed and higher impact.

2

Military science had received the newcomer with equanimity, since it appeared in the innocent disguise of a balloon. True, an excited Italian Jesuit in 1670 had predicted, with all the fervour of a fellow-countryman of the late General Douhet, total war by airships capable of destroying cities and shipping. But when Montgolfier finally succeeded in exhibiting a sheep, a chicken, and a duck air-borne at Versailles in 1783, this pastoral achievement (followed in the same year by the ascent of the intrepid Pilâtre de Rozier) seemed to promise little more for military purposes than an extension of reconnaissance. The new device was used on a small scale for this restricted purpose in the armies of the First Republic, although on one occasion paper balloons were released over Cairo in order to impress the population, which remained obstinately calm; and a project of subjugating England by an air-borne invasion in balloons, each capable of carrying a thousand men, twenty-five horses, and two field-guns, received short shrift from Napoleon.

Whilst a few eccentrics continued to dilate upon the possibility of releasing unpleasant objects from the sky upon their enemies (Venice was actually bombed by Austrian balloons in 1849), serious development was confined to reconnaissance and artillery observation; and the War Office eventually so far succumbed to the performance of balloons in the American Civil, Franco-German, and Paraguayan wars as to consent to some experiments. These were conducted by that time-honoured repository of military eccentricity, the Royal Engineers; and after the balloons had flown with credit in Bechuanaland and the Sudan, Sir Evelyn Wood was so impressed by their success in a sham fight near Frensham Ponds that a Balloon Section was actually formed in 1890.

These innocent beginnings were maintained by its war service in South Africa, where balloons were used with some effect for reconnaissance; and though the dropping of explosives was actually contemplated in an official publication of 1905, the air was almost exclusively regarded as a place commanding fuller views of what was going on below. This estimate continued to prevail, whilst hardy pioneers experimented with the possibility of aerial navigation in more adventurous machines. The Wright brothers' success in 1903 with power-driven aircraft attracted mild attention; and a parallel experiment in Britain invited the official comment that satisfactory observation was not to be expected from an object moving at the terrifying speed of forty miles an hour. For, as a tolerant historian pronounced, "conservative and humorous minds are always conscious chiefly of the immutable and stable elements in human life, and do not readily pay respect to novelty" (W. RALEIGH, *The War in the Air*, 1922). The development of airships and Blériot's cross-Channel flight in 1909 widened horizons; and in 1911 an Air Battalion was added to the Royal Engineers, of which one company flew aeroplanes. But their functions were confined to the modest duty of reconnaissance, the Army Council commending the new unit in its inaugural regulations as "one of the most valuable means of obtaining information at the disposal of the Commander of an army"; and the same view seemed to prevail abroad, since the sole reference to aviation in a treatise by a leading French military writer (J. COLIN, *Les Transformations de la Guerre*, 1911) which appeared that year was confined to its utility for reconnaissance. Indeed, a Declaration of The Hague Peace Conference (from which the French, German, and Italian Governments prudently withheld their signatures) expressly banned "the discharge of projectiles and explosives from balloons or by other new methods of a similar nature." But in 1911 the Italians, with that good fortune in the use of air power against an enemy without the means to retaliate which grew more noticeable afterwards in Abyssinia, employed aircraft of all types for bombing, observation, and reconnaissance against the Turks in Tripoli.

Experiment proceeded in a hopeful atmosphere with highly unreliable machines, which fully justify the glow of Raleigh's tribute that "the men who explored and took possession of the air in the twentieth century are the inheritors of the men who explored and took possession of America in the sixteenth century." But while the first *Conquistadores* of the air swerved gallantly over (and into) British fields, there was little tendency to enlarge the functions of aviation in war. Even the Admiralty under Mr. Churchill, observing with composure that one intrepid pioneer had managed to take off without misadventure from a ship's deck, included no offensive acts in its enumeration of the duties of its flying officers, which merely comprised reconnaissance, the detection of minefields and submarines, and the direction of ships' gunfire; and the White Paper intimating the conversion of the Air Battalion of the Royal Engineers into the Royal Flying Corps in 1912 was founded on the proved "efficiency of the aeroplane for purposes of military reconnaissance" and a modest claim that "without doubt aeroplanes have now become an important adjunct to the equipment of an army in the field," with the more guarded corollary that "the strategical and tactical uses of the aeroplane as an adjunct to the operations of a fleet cannot yet be forecasted with certainty."

For aircraft were still a mere adjunct, by which a vertical extension of existing forms of war on sea and land might be achieved, although their latent possibilities were actively explored. An enterprising pilot demonstrated that the sudden dropping of 300 lb. (which might have been a bomb) did not effect a total loss of stability in his machine; and this triumph was promptly celebrated by air attacks on dummy submarines. But observation continued to remain their leading duty. On land it was laid down that "their primary duty is searching for information," although there might be other ways in which they would come in handy. Army manœuvres were enlivened by their slightly uncertain presence, one general paying their powers of observation the reluctant compliment that "the aeroplanes completely

spoilt the war" (C. F. SNOWDEN GAMBLE, *The Air Weapon*, 1931).
That, indeed, might come to be their function at a later stage of their
development. But for the present they were officially regarded as an
intermittent form of cavalry without cavalry's ability to operate at
night or in bad weather. Stray bombing from the air was practised
in the Balkan War. But the results were unimpressive, as might have
been expected from projectiles weighing 20 lb. attached somewhat
informally to ropes looped over the pilot's boot and released by
guesswork. British dirigibles were able to make better practice,
although the Field Service Regulations of 1913 still confined their
official duties to reconnaissance.

At sea a more offensive spirit had begun to dawn. For Mr.
Churchill eagerly befriended the Naval Wing of the Royal Flying
Corps (which was subsequently appropriated by the Admiralty as the
Royal Naval Air Service); and it was recognised that aircraft might
have to fight. The defence of vital targets against air attack was added
to their duties; tests were made of their ability to carry machine-
guns and exciting forms of fireworks designed to destroy Zeppelins;
and they even practised launching torpedoes against ships. But a
more immediate duty was involved in the defensive utility of aircraft
in the event of attack from the air. Only a generation earlier, Lord
Salisbury had derided the aggressive spirit of his military advisers,
complaining to a correspondent that "if they were allowed full scope,
they would insist on the importance of garrisoning the moon in
order to protect us from Mars." But what had been a *reductio ad
absurdum* for Queen Victoria's minister was on the point of becoming
an urgent necessity for her grandson's. Perhaps there was no danger
in the settled world of 1914 that any Power would so far forget itself
as to bombard unfortified localities. (It was not long before the
Cabinet gravely consulted the Lord Chancellor as to whether the
installation of an anti-aircraft gun on the Foreign Office roof might
be held to deprive London of its legitimate immunity.) But there
were always dockyards, magazines, power-houses, oil stores, and
airship sheds; and early in 1914 Mr. Churchill told the House of
Commons that "passive defence against aircraft is perfectly hopeless
and endless. You would have to roof in the world to be quite sure."
He preferred to hold, with a sound instinct for air strategy, that "the
only real security upon which sound military principles will rely is
that you should be master of your own air."

Air mastery, as he propounded it, was something to be fought for; and it was not surprising that a few months later, as the skies darkened over Europe, the First Lord warned the Admiralty that "in the present stage of aeronautics, the primary duty of British aircraft is to fight enemy aircraft and thus afford protection against aerial attack. This should be made clear to air officers, Commander-in-Chief, Nore, and Admiral of Patrols, in order that machines may not be needlessly used up in ordinary scouting duties. After the primary requirement is well provided for, whatever aid is possible for coastal watch and extended defence scouting should be organised. But the naval aircraft are to regard the defence against attack from the air as their first and main responsibility" (WINSTON S. CHURCHILL, *The World Crisis*, vol. i., 1923). It was plain that the objectives of air warfare were still fluid. Indeed, its instruments remained a cause of some bewilderment. For one August day in 1914 a round-eyed landing officer at Boulogne despatched the sceptical enquiry: "An unnumbered unit without aeroplanes which calls itself an Aircraft Park has arrived. What are we to do with it?"

3

That was discovered gradually in the course of the next four years. In one sense the war of 1914-18 was a time of retrogression in the art of war. A military deadlock developed early on the Western Front, where operations degenerated into the attack and defence of fortified positions, as practised in the wars of Louis XIV; and those innovations which might have been expected to ensue from recent discoveries were barely noticeable. For the inventions of the Twentieth Century were freely used for military purposes comprehensible to a commander of the Seventeenth. One, perhaps, attained its full results, since the machine-gun was largely responsible for the deadlock on the ground. But the internal-combustion engine applied to motor transport, by which a new mobility might have transformed the face of war, did little more than bring French reinforcements to the Marne in a fleet of Paris taxis and supply the needs of stationary armies on the Western Front with strings of motor-lorries; and its more exciting application to the armoured vehicle, which was to produce entirely new tactics and strategy a generation later, found employment as a mere instrument of siege warfare. In this cautious atmosphere it was not to be expected that so glaring a departure from accepted practice as military aircraft would be permitted to modify proceedings on the ground; and it is possible for one critic to write that "in the main theatre of war they did not alter the course of events by one jot or tittle" (AIR COMMODORE L. E. O. CHARLTON, *War from the Air*, 1935).

But if they did not make much difference, it was already possible to see the ways in which they might one day. At first sight, perhaps, the military value of a weapon is not readily discernible in its performance at a rudimentary stage. Spectators of the first precarious employment of artillery by German gunners in 1331 could hardly be expected to foresee three-day barrages expending fantastic masses of explosive along fronts of fifty miles and delivered by guns in thousands standing almost wheel to wheel. The total weight of bombs dropped by British aircraft in four years of war was no more than 8000 tons, a quantity that their successors could exceed in four nights. Yet if the war of 1914 was no more than a laboratory experiment in air warfare, its outlines were beginning to emerge.

Created for reconnaissance, the Royal Flying Corps reconnoitred to some purpose when they were able to detect German movements groping for an unguarded flank in time to ensure the safe retreat of the British Expeditionary Force from Mons and to bring information which rendered possible the Allied rally on the Marne. But such services were wholly secondary. For they were doing no more than cavalry vedettes could do, if endowed with powers of flight; and, like cavalry, they took carbines and revolvers with them in case they met their rivals in the air. Such encounters were, at the outset, purely accidental. For though air combats had been foreseen in their pre-war Training Manual, it was no part of their duty yet to put out their adversary's eyes by shooting down his aircraft. That came later, when the Royal Flying Corps in search of information found in 1915 that it had got to fight for it.

Air fighting now became the function of an "outer guard" of fighter aircraft that stood between an interfering enemy and their colleagues at their more peaceful avocations of photography and observation over the German lines; and the observer's rifle (to which some enterprising officers preferred a sporting gun loaded with a home-made variety of chain shot involving a good deal of wire) was soon replaced by a machine-gun. Aggressive purposes had been inculcated at an earlier stage in naval pilots. For at the Admiralty, charged with the air defence of London, Mr. Churchill laid it down in September, 1914, that "the great defence against the aerial menace is to attack the enemy's aircraft as near as possible to their point of departure" (*The World Crisis*, vol. i.); and by 1915 he was developing types armed with Lewis guns, as well as others that could carry 500 lb. of bombs. These were intended to operate in the area behind Dunkirk, which had somehow become the Admiralty's province: and Mr. Churchill prescribed that their object "will not be reconnaissance and patrolling, but the attacking with bombs on the largest possible scale of military points on enemy territory. . . . We shall by then have passed the stage of daring exploits, and must acquire the power to strike heavy blows which will produce decisive effects on the enemy's fighting strength" (*The World Crisis*, vol. ii., 1923). Here was evidence of a clear comprehension that aircraft had it in their power to do something more than gather information and make sure that older weapons were pointing in the right direction.

But there were as yet few traces of it in the employment of the Royal Flying Corps on the Western Front, where it continued to perform routine duties in a war that had become one long, depressing routine. For though Lord Kitchener shared Mr. Churchill's broader vision of the use of air power, explaining to two young airmen in front of a big map of Germany early in the war that it would be finished if they could go to Essen fifty at a time, keeping in touch by wireless, and bomb Krupps, their leading occupation was still to ensure by photography, observation, and wireless telegraphy the safe arrival of British shells and infantry at their respective destinations; and this exacting duty was faithfully discharged behind a fighter screen, whose fortunes varied with the alternating progress of British and German aircraft constructors. The Fokker reigned supreme early in 1916. until Allied designers redressed the balance with new types, only to be outclassed again in the next year by German fighters, which were ultimately excelled and subjugated (WING COMMANDER W. SHOLTO DOUGLAS, *s.v.* 'Air Combat,' *Encyclopaedia Britannica,* 1929).

Once more a clearer sense of their potentialities seemed to dawn on the naval airmen. For while military aircraft operated as the dutiful handmaidens of "the vast and paralysed armies that lay help-lessly opposite each other across Europe" (P. GUEDALLA, *Men of War,* 1927, quoted by WING COMMANDER J. C. SLESSOR, *Air Power and Armies,* 1936), a more enterprising policy established a wing of naval bombers not far from Belfort in 1916 for the purpose of interrupting

German steel production in the Saar. Attacks were made on blast furnaces and railway junctions; and these operations seemed to show that air power might render services outside the battlefield by the intrinsic value of its blows at the enemy's war effort as well as by the dislocation of his air force in the battle area in order to provide fighter defence nearer home. The Germans scored two notable successes that year on an ammunition dump and a transport depot. But Sir Douglas Haig was profoundly sceptical as to the results; and the new enterprise received no encouragement in military circles, where the Commander-in-Chief insisted stoutly that "long-distance bombing as a means of defeating the enemy is entirely secondary" to the routine requirements of the armies in the field (H. A. JONES, *The War in the Air*, vol. vi., 1937).

The enemy, less scrupulous or more enterprising, appeared in some strength over London on two fine summer mornings in 1917. Opinion at home was deeply shocked by heavy casualties in the City and the spectacle of hostile aircraft flying in formation, whose progress was apparently uninterrupted by the ineffective powder-puffs of anti-aircraft shells; and the resulting flutter of civilian dovecotes effectively diverted two fighter squadrons from France and relegated the whole problem to the cool hands of General Smuts. That former expert in guerilla warfare against British forces in South Africa was now entrusted by Mr. Lloyd George with the discovery of a solution of the questions involved in home defence and the larger issues of air organisa-tion (now chaotically shared between the Admiralty and War Office) and the higher direction of air operations. These lay at present in the shadow of Sir Douglas Haig; and it was plain that they were unlikely to go very far afield, so long as G.H.Q. retained control. But Smuts' view of air power was more expansive, since he held that "there is absolutely no limit to the scale of its future independent war use." It followed, in his opinion, that its continued subordination was unjustifiable, and the full argument of his Report is highly instructive :

> Essentially the Air Service is as subordinate to military and naval direction and considerations of policy as the artillery is. . . . The time is, however, rapidly approaching when that subordination of the Air Board and the Air Service could no longer be justified. Essentially the position of an Air Service is quite different from that of the artillery arm, to pursue our comparison; artillery could never be used in war except as

a weapon in military or naval or air operations. It is a weapon, an instrument ancillary to a service, but could not be an independent service itself. Air service on the contrary can be used as an independent means of war operations. Nobody that witnessed the attack on London on 11th July can have any doubt on that point. Unlike artillery, an air fleet can conduct extensive operations far from, and independently of, both Army and Navy. As far as can at present be foreseen there is absolutely no limit to the scale of its future independent war use. And the day may not be far off when aerial operations with their devastation of enemy lands and destruction of industrial and populous centres on a vast scale may become the principal operations of war, to which the older forms of military and naval operations may become secondary and subordinate. (*The War in the Air*, Appendices, 1937.)

His conclusion was the creation of an Air Ministry and Air Staff and the amalgamation of the R.F.C. and R.N.A.S. in a new Service, subsequently named the Royal Air Force.

While General Smuts' close argument laid the foundations of the R.A.F. in August, 1917, the military mind retained its doubts. Sir Douglas Haig, deep in the mud of Passchendaele, appeared to question the "advisability, from the point of view of morality and public opinion, of seeking to end the war by 'devastation of enemy lands and destruction of industrial and populous centres on a vast scale.'" Without much faith in its practical results, he uttered a grave warning that "we must be prepared morally and materially to outdo the enemy if we are to hope to attain our ends," while the more alert intelligence of Mr. Churchill at the Ministry of Munitions admitted that "it is improbable that any terrorization of the civil population which could be achieved by air attack would compel the Government of a great nation to surrender" (*The War in the Air*, Appendices, and *The World Crisis*, vol. iv., 1927). He preferred an air offensive of which "the supreme and direct object . . . is to deprive the German armies on the Western Front of their capacity for resistance" by continuous attack upon their bases and communications. Pleading strenuously for a co-ordinated plan engaging all three Services, he advocated a distinctive contribution by the R.A.F., "not merely as an ancillary service to the special operations of the Army or the Navy, but also as an independent arm co-operating in the general plan." This, he thought, might take the form of an all-out attack on German air-bases "and the consequent destruction of his air fighting force." Once air superiority had been attained by this means, Mr. Churchill contemplated a free use of air-borne troops for sabotage behind the lines and low-flying attacks to machine-gun back areas.

But those lively visions of a distant future failed to materialise in 1918. For planning proceeded within the stricter limits of a purely military framework. Strategic bombing, so far as their bomb-loads deserved the term, was regarded as a luxury to be reserved for periods when all tactical requirements with the trench-bound army had been satisfied. A modest striking force, however, was concentrated in the neighbourhood of Nancy under the command of Major-General Trenchard, whose narrow escape from service in the Macedonian Gendarmerie was almost as happy in its consequences as that of General Bonaparte from the Turkish artillery. Their programme was soundly executed; and presently they were promoted to the novel status of the Independent Force, R.A.F. (One sardonic general enquired, "Independent of whom—of God?") For air power was now to be employed on targets of its own selection under the direction of an air command, the Independent Force operating under the direct control of the Air Ministry, untroubled by any allegiance to Sir Douglas Haig or Marshal Foch; and all through the summer of 1918 they faithfully bombed Western Germany with good results on transport, munitions output, and civilian morale. Indeed, their contribution to the eventual collapse of Germany into despair and revolution has never been fully assessed. The symmetrical intelligence of Foch, which concentrated on defeating the German forces immediately in front of him, was not attracted by the notion of releasing man-power for such secondary purposes as the destruction of railway junctions and blast furnaces behind the German line, although he was prepared to countenance such jaunts "in quiet periods." An expanding air force must, he felt, "inevitably be to the detriment of the other arms, and in particular of the infantry still of paramount importance." Mathematically this was indisputable; and there was not much time for flights of fancy in the summer of 1918, which had opened with a German thrust that almost broke the Allied line. Besides, it was unthinkable to Foch that any unit should operate from French territory which was not under his supreme command. But bombing Germany was congenial to M. Clemenceau; and it was finally agreed that Trenchard should command an Inter-Allied Bombing Force of British, French, Italian, and eventually American aircraft, to be constituted for this purpose in due subordination to the supreme command with an appetising list of targets for 1919. But victory was too quick for them; and before the new four-engined Handley-Pages could enliven Berlin with their 250-lb. bombs, the war was over.

Four years of operations in the air above the land fighting had served to indicate some of the possibilities of air warfare; and experience at sea was equally suggestive. For though air power had been mainly used in order to facilitate by observation and patrol existing forms of naval warfare, it was significant that a few ships had been torpedoed by aircraft. The British scored the first success against a Turkish steamer between Constantinople and the Dardanelles; and it was reproduced on more than one occasion by German seaplanes in the North Sea. The bomb was less successful. But it was plain that aircraft might do something more to floating targets than merely indicate their whereabouts to the guns of their own warships. A new weapon was emerging; and its progress was observed with some misgiving by those accustomed to calculate supremacy at sea in terms of battleships. The warning was still faint; but it was audible, and alert intelligences in the United States were actively directed to the problem.

The lessons of the war were, on the whole, suggestive rather than conclusive; and it was substantially true that, in the words of one critic, "however much the course of events in the Great War was diversified by flying, the invention had done nothing towards the creation of a new strategy" (AIR COMMODORE L. E. O. CHARLTON, *War from the Air*). At sea fleets would be accompanied in future by aircraft carriers, by which their range of vision would be extended. But there was no reason to believe that aircraft could turn them from their courses or pursue them to their harbours. Military men admitted the utility of air observation and even air fighting (British aircraft had lent valuable aid to hard-pressed ground troops by bombing and machine-gunning the advancing Germans in March, 1918); and there was unpleasant evidence of their powers of destruction in back areas. But, after all, J. E. B. Stuart and Forrest had raided far behind the Union lines in the American Civil War without creating a new strategy; and need aircraft on such missions be regarded as more than a novel form of cavalry endowed with unusual powers of mobility? Their massacre of retreating Turks, Bulgarians, and Austrians had lengthened the arm of a pursuing army. Destruction from the air was horrifyingly complete; but pursuit was no novelty in war, although the new practitioners were swifter and better armed than mounted men. Their bombing might be viewed conservatively as an extension of artillery. True, it could reach further than the battle area and strike targets deep in hostile territory and unattainable by armies. But there was little recognition that this power might develop its own strategy without regard to the limitations of the land battle. Indeed, at the present stage of its technical evolution it might be reasonable to confine its operations to the battle area. For that still came first in 1918, when the charter of the Inter-Allied Bombing Force expressly laid down that, whilst land operations were in progress, "the requirements of the battlefield must first be satisfied, and as completely as possible," relegating strategic bombing of the interior of Germany almost entirely to intervals of quiet on the Western Front.

4

Air power emerged from the war of 1914-18 with a general recognition of its ability to supply fleets and armies with useful information and a moderate extension of their hitting power. For the professional intelligence is rarely guilty of exaggeration in the case of novelties. Besides, the mind of 1919 was not greatly interested in the course of the next war, since there was ample reason for believing that there would not be one. Even the acute intellect, by which the official history of *The War in the Air* was begun, could write in 1922 that "as observation was the first purpose of aircraft, so it remains the most important," although a wider vision dawns in Raleigh's closing statement that "the forces of the air will be, not a late-found timid auxiliary to the forces of the land or the sea, but their overseer and their director."

But could they do more than direct and oversee the operations of fleets and armies? Would aircraft modify existing forms of war? Had they power to dominate the battlefield or to bar great areas of open sea to battleships? That was the riddle confronting post-war minds, which sought the answer by experiment and deductive reasoning applied with varying degrees of logic to the limited experience of war. Enthusiasts were vastly heartened in 1921 by visible proof that bombs from aircraft could sink ex-German warships, which were available for this experiment off the coast of the United States, since (unlike those awarded to Great Britain) they were still the right way

47

up. A triumphant airman announced that "the first great air and battleship test that the world has ever seen . . . conclusively proved the ability of aircraft to destroy ships of all classes on the surface of the water" (GENERAL W. MITCHELL, *Winged Defense*, 1925); and it was a sobering reflection for an island people that what had been done to warships could be done with equal ease to merchantmen. But though the battleship *Ostfriesland* was indisputably sunk by bombing, it was arguable that the test was hardly a fair reproduction of war conditions, as the vessel was ten years old and could neither move nor reply to the attack. A British expert guardedly inferred that "it is already questionable whether a battleship could survive air attack launched by even a small force of this mobile arm" (MAJOR-GENERAL SIR F. H. SYKES, *Aviation in Peace and War*, 1922); but ample room was left for argument by those who, in Raleigh's phrase, "would all have died to save England, but they held that she was to be saved in the old way, on the sea."

On land aircraft had already proved their usefulness to armies by their powers of observation and destruction on and near the battlefield; and the performance of the Independent Force appeared to show that they were capable of action at some distance from the battle, by which its outcome might be influenced. Could they go further and decide the war? The *Field Service Regulations* prescribed austerely that "the National object in war is to overcome the opponent's will. . . . Since the armed forces are the only instrument of offence or defence, these forces, or such of them as are capable of influencing the decision, must be overcome." That, however, had proved to be a long-drawn and exhausting process engaging millions of men and mountains of munitions along miles of fortified positions; and it was tempting to believe that there was a short cut. If the armed forces of the enemy were his sole defence, it might be possible to aim a blow at the object, which they were defending, by direct air attack upon the national will at home. This would solve the problem without recourse to the interminable stalemate, which was now understood to be the correct pattern of all military operations; and the solution made a wide appeal. One diagnosis of its popularity shrewdly explains that "the new theory of victory through direct air action was only one of the reactions—the war poetry of Siegfried Sassoon was another—from the weariness and disillusion induced by the long war of attrition towards its end" (J. M. SPAIGHT, *Air Power in the Next War*, 1938).

48

Air enthusiasts were gratified by a programme of which the leading feature was the supremacy of bombing; popular imagination, remembering the darkened cities with the warning crack of their maroons, the swish of falling shrapnel on their empty pavements, and the loud detonations, was always apt to dwell on this aspect of the war; and it was alarmingly combined with the new and dreaded possibilities of gas.

This doctrine found eloquent expression in the same year that saw the sinking of the *Ostfriesland* from the air off the Virginia capes, when General Giulio Douhet published *Il dominio dell' aria* in 1921. An enterprising officer with an overwhelming faith in air power, he had commanded the first Air Battalion in the Italian army before the war; his efforts to interest his masters in the products of an engineer named Caproni had a chequered history; and when his country was at war, his convictions so far overcame his sense of discipline as to permit him to speak freely to deputies, and even write a paper for a minister, about the imperfections of the high command. For he was in the grip of an idea; and when ideas about the future struck Italians, their expression was sometimes a shade extreme. It was not long since Marinetti had been impelled to scatter from the Campanile of St. Mark's large numbers of leaflets indicating in emphatic terms the decadence of Venice; and Douhet was, in a sense, a military Futurist. Such candour is apt to be resented; and in Latin countries official resentment takes simpler forms than those by which ill-advised reformers are side-tracked elsewhere. The enthusiast was promptly court-martialled and sentenced to twelve months' imprisonment, an interval of leisure which (like Lenin in Siberia) he turned to useful purpose for the formulation of his views. As the day of his release in 1917 was that on which Italian armies hastily withdrew from Caporetto, opinions derogatory to the high command were less unorthodox; and he was soon raised to the control of the air arm, to dream in vain of mass attacks upon Vienna from the air. When the war ended, he left the army and wrote copiously. His condemnation was subsequently quashed; the impulsive colonel was promoted general; and his views were now formulated with official blessings in his book of 1921. The next year saw the transformation of Italian politics by the Fascist revolution; and Douhet, who had been entrusted to convey the Duce's greetings to d'Annunzio (another air enthusiast), appeared as Commissioner of Aviation in Mussolini's first administration.

For the new era was more favourable to ruthless beliefs of a destructive and mechanical character; and though his doctrine was assailed, the National Fascist Cultural Institute reissued his book in 1927, and a selection of his writings appeared after his death with an endorsement from the pen of Marshal Balbo.

His ideas were simple. For Douhet was a flaming enthusiast, wearing the deceptively practical expression of an implacable logician. Conceiving with most of his contemporaries that land warfare was condemned to the inextricable deadlock of the Western Front, he proposed to use air power in direct attacks upon the enemy at home. If guns had gone to ground in concrete casemates, it seemed far simpler to destroy them in their factories behind the line. A strong belief in gas was allied with a disbelief in the power of civilians to endure bombing, since he was convinced that a daily dose of 300 tons of bombs was bound to end the war. The hostile air force was to be disposed of by a dawn attack upon its aerodromes without the warning of a declaration of war; and in any case he had no faith in the ability of fighter aircraft to avert an air offensive made by a bomber force in greater strength, since *ex hypothesi* the weaker force would never dare to fight. This hypothesis, which led him to a comfortable doctrine of air victory without fighting, was, perhaps, a shade Italian. Indeed, the whole of Douhet's theory of static warfare on ground level and .ctivity overhead seemed more appropriate to Italy than to less fortunately situated countries. For Italian armies could afford to stand on the defensive better than most of their European rivals, since the only land frontier which they were called on to defend consisted of the Alps. His ruthless concentration upon bombing as the supreme purpose of air warfare led him to advocate the virtual extinction of the fighter and the withdrawal of all aircraft from auxiliary duties with fleets and armies, as he reasoned that it was superfluous to divert valuable machines for use in secondary operations. Allowing a few fast, unarmed reconnaissance aircraft, he proposed to stake everything upon a vast Armada of bombers with strong defensive armament, which would command air supremacy and then proceed to the methodical destruction of the enemy below.

One flight of fancy, entitled *The War of 19..* and published in 1930, described the easy triumph of the Germans, who were assumed to have adopted Douhet's system, in a swift air campaign against France and Belgium, who had not. The only sign of grace upon the

Allied side is the wise utterance attributed to a fictitious British critic
bearing the unlikely name of " Sir Lyod " in an unconscious compliment to Lord Lloyd's strong interest in aeronautics.   Whilst the Allies
dissipate their energies in relatively insignificant attacks, the Germans
(Douhet seemed to know the Germans) announce falsely that the
enemy is using gas, use it themselves, eliminate his air force, isolate
his armies by the destruction of their communications, and systematically devastate his towns.   The war was over in two days.

While the prophet passed his declining years in lively controversy
with his critics (Douhet could generally be relied on to give the infidel
as good as he got), his gospel gained adherents.   Fascism claimed his
doctrine for its own, Balbo proclaiming that "for seven years we have
been trying to carry into effect the ideas of that mighty Italian military
writer who, through the vicissitudes of his stormy life, had become
almost a stranger in an Italy not yet regenerated by Fascism."   The
Italian manœuvres of 1931, in which Milan, Florence, Bologna, and
Spezzia were drenched with imaginary gas by massed aircraft, were
an impressive demonstration of his methods, of which a single touch
sufficed to finish Abyssinian resistance in 1936.   Yet Douhet's doctrine,
viewed as an introduction to the subsequent performance of the *Regia
Aeronautica*, was not unlike the first bars of the great march in Verdi's
Aïda—a noble prelude to nothing in particular.   For in air warfare the
Italian pen was emphatically mightier than the Italian sword.

Beyond the Alps his message, as befitted the first candidate for the
vacant seat of an aerial Clausewitz, found interested hearers.   Not that
military minds were incapable of reaching most of his conclusions
without Douhet's assistance.   Germans and Japanese hardly needed to
read technical periodicals in a foreign language in order to recognise
the utility of bombing capitals and grounded aircraft without declaring
war.   After all, non-military minds had led the way.   For H. G. Wells,
who adumbrated something very like a tank in 1903, had displayed
the bombing of the cities to readers of *The War in the Air* ten years
before the Armistice of 1918.   Taken separately, there was nothing
very new in any of Douhet's ideas ; but their formulation as a whole
crystallised a strong contemporary tendency.   Military thought,
numbed by four years of deadlock on the Western Front, acquiesced
in stationary strategy on land, where France was busily constructing
a trench-line *de luxe* along her eastern frontier.   This continuous array
of fortified positions bore the name of M. Maginot and the marks of

Marshal Pétain's fixed belief in the ability of fire-power to resist anything that could be brought against it on the ground. The conception
of stalemate on earth was acceptable to the French high command;
and if this could be supplemented, as Douhet suggested, by checkmate
from the sky, so much the better. A selection of his writings (*La
Guerre de l'Air*, 1932) appeared in French; and these were subsequently
codified in a volume introduced by Marshal Pétain (COLONEL P.
VAUTHIER, *La Doctrine de Guerre du General Douhet*, 1935). The
Marshal, who had announced in 1917 that "aviation dominates war,"
had been thinking about these things as Inspector-General of Air
Defence, a post created for him by Laval on his retirement from
supreme command of the French army. But it took a great deal to
make the cautious old soldier warn his readers against underrating
"as a Utopian or dreamer one who may rank hereafter as the Pre-
cursor"; and this commendation had more than formal significance,
since it was bestowed when the writer was holding office in the Third
Republic as Minister of War. Visibly attracted by the economy of
effort involved in Douhet's programme, the Marshal found himself
in full agreement with the proposal of a supreme command controlling
operations on the ground and in the air, which he had already pressed
with some success upon the sympathetic Laval. As Pétain's programme
was to avert defeat in a stationary attitude before proceeding to victory
by methods that were still undefined, he was more drawn to Douhet
than to de Gaulle, whose new-fangled notions in *Vers l'Armée de
Métier* threatened to break in upon the sacred calm of static warfare
with mobile operations of a most improper character.

While these winds of doctrine swept the Continent, British writers
alarmed their readers with unpleasant gusts of prophecy that left their
towns in ruins. The sharp outlines of Douhet's unprepossessing
edifice emerged with difficulty from the misty atmosphere once
diagnosed by Kinglake as "the true English haze." It was not for
nothing that a British Prime Minister once warned the House of
Commons to "beware of needless innovation, especially when guided
by logic." For the forbidding symmetry of logic, to which Continental minds succumb so easily, is uncongenial to British intellects,
which view systems founded upon theory with the misgivings reserved
by Burke for written constitutions. At first the recognition of air
power as a means of bringing force to bear upon civilians otherwise
than by defeat of their fleets and armies proceeded by stages. For the

moral standards, by which the Nineteenth Century had lived, persisted for some time in the years following the war. Indeed, they were believed to have derived increased validity from the victory of right in 1918; and the distinction between right and wrong had not yet been effaced over large areas of Europe by recognition of the State as a supreme deity. Admitting from the outset that transport and munition works were fair game for aerial attack, the Anglo-Saxon mind on both sides of the Atlantic soon added to the list of targets factories of all types, public utilities, and urban agglomerations, with the uncomfortable proviso that in all probability they were going to be bombed by someone else, because their own side did not do that sort of thing. This chivalrous opinion (reinforced by an increasing faith in anti-aircraft fire) was fortified by the professional reluctance of Service minds to divert valuable hitting power to non-military objectives, as a cavalryman of the old school would have been scandalised by the suggestion that good sabres should be wasted on the enemy's standing crops—or even his school-children. It was almost disrespectful to suppose that other targets might rank with, and even in front of, the armed forces; and at some moments the objectives of air warfare seemed to be in dispute "between views really warlike" (in Kinglake's contrast) "and views which are only 'military.'" Wild-eyed disciples of Douhet prophesied the wrath to come, while less excitable professionals primly replied that anti-aircraft artillery had not yet been heard from, and that his programme, if it was to be effective, called for astronomical numbers of aircraft (LIEUT.-GENERAL N. N. GOLOVINE, *Air Strategy*, 1936). But as the morals of the Continent deteriorated with the advent of totalitarian governments dedicated to a cult of ruthlessness, a British airman in a sober study of realities (WING COMMANDER J. C. SLESSOR, *Air Power and Armies*) recognised the possibility that "armies may become mere holding forces to garrison frontier defences, from the cover of which air forces will attempt to reduce the enemy to impotence and ultimate capitulation by attacks on his essential services and centres of war industry and transportation."

5

Meanwhile the R.A.F. confronted the plain problem of its duties in the post-war world. British solutions are more often founded on the practical requirements of a situation than upon abstract principle, as English law prefers limited decisions of particular cases to codes of universal application. The situation was extremely simple. After four years of war the nation had neither the desire nor the need for extensive armaments; and the R.A.F., which had been the largest air force in the world, controlling more than 20,000 aircraft on 700 aerodromes and consisting in 1918 of 188 squadrons, was reduced in less than eighteen months to a bare 25. The future of air warfare was, so far as Britain was concerned, obscure; and its purposes were in- dicated in a paper prepared with Cabinet approval in 1919 for Mr. Churchill, now Air Minister, by Air Marshal Sir Hugh Trenchard, Chief of the Air Staff (*Permanent Organization of the Royal Air Force*, Cmd. 467, 1919).

There was not much for them to do in 1919. The main thing was to ensure that, when there was, they would be capable of doing it and of expanding for the purpose to wartime proportions once again. What form their operations were to take appeared to some extent in Trenchard's outline.

> The principle to be kept in mind in forming the framework of the Air Service is that in future the main portion of it will consist of an Independent Force, together with Service personnel required in carrying out Aeronautical Research. . . .
> It may be that the main portion, the Independent Air Force, will grow larger and larger, and become more and more the predominating factor in all types of warfare.

The exact nature of its predominance was not further indicated; but it was plain that the decisive operations in the air, which Trenchard contemplated, were to be conducted beyond the range of fleets and armies.

These ample possibilities were latent in a force which was to con- sist for the present of 2 squadrons at home and 18 in the Middle East and India; and their geographical distribution was significant of a new sense of the utility of air power. Whilst home defence made no demands at present on the R.A.F., Asia was far from tranquil in the years following the war, and British aircraft seemed to offer an effective sedative. As Trenchard wrote, "one great advantage of aircraft in the class of warfare approximating to police work is their power of acting at once. Aircraft can visit the scene of incipient unrest within a comparatively few hours of the receipt of news. To organize a military expedition even on a small scale takes time, and delay may result in the trouble spreading. The cost is also much greater, and very many more lives are involved." The quicksilver mobility of air power was earning recognition; and it was decided to locate a strong contingent of the R.A.F. at the crossroads of the Middle East.

> In Egypt it is proposed to station 7 service squadrons. . . . From a wider aspect Egypt is the Clapham Junction of the air between east and west, and is situated within comparatively easy reach of the most probable centres of unrest, and this, added to its natural advantages for aviation, makes it the obvious locality for a small Royal Air Force reserve.

Sunshine and sand became their natural elements; desert aviation soon held few surprises for the R.A.F.; and if they ever had to fight in the Middle East, they would be fighting on familiar ground.

The new weapon was used to some purpose in Somaliland, where long-standing trouble with the Mad Mullah was disposed of at infinitesimal cost in lives and money, and on the North-West Frontier of India. Its services in this region had led Trenchard to express the hope "that before long it may prove possible to regard the Royal Air Force units not as an addition to the military garrison but as a substitute for part of it." The claim was modestly expressed; but if it could be justified, it might be possible to restring a massive and sometimes slightly unmanageable Empire upon the infinitely flexible thread of air power.

The ultimate safeguard of the British Empire had hitherto been constituted in the last resort by the ability of battleships refuelled at a chain of coaling-stations to ensure the movement of its armies to any danger-point. But if this was to be threatened from the air, the R.A.F. might well provide an efficient substitute that would be capable, given aerodromes in the right places, of bringing force to bear wherever it was needed; and in that event it would seem a trifle premature for foreign critics to assume that an eclipse of sea power would necessarily be followed by the collapse of Britain. For this eventuality need not afflict an air-borne Empire; and in the year that saw a battleship bombed from the air and regaled thoughtful readers with Douhet's speculations on the omnipotence of air power, a conference in Cairo under Mr. Churchill, now Colonial Secretary, decided that the R.A.F. should garrison Iraq. No doctrine was enunciated, since Britons abhor a generalisation; and the decision was severely practical, as it would have cost a great deal more to garrison with soldiers. (Similar considerations subsequently actuated the transfer of Aden to R.A.F. custody.) True, air power was to be supplemented by a few armoured cars and land forces under its control; and the complete success of the experiment might leave enthusiastic airmen speculating whether armies should in future remain independent on the ground, as soldiers had once felt their doubts as to whether airmen could be trusted to be independent in the sky. But the plain fact was that air power was now brought into play for the control and defence of vital areas; and its assignment to these duties was far more significant than the proved utility of aircraft in minor forms of savage warfare. For it ensured security abroad by new methods and at a price which Britain was prepared to pay.

Besides, the employment of the R.A.F. for such current purposes more than justified the maintenance of the new Service; and whilst a mood of strict economy in national expenditure prevailed, to say nothing of the sincere and devastating effort to achieve disarmament, the peace-time employment of the R.A.F. in the Middle East went far to maintain the continuity of the air weapon in British hands no less than to familiarise its personnel with a theatre of war that might one day be vital.

The Cairo decision of 1921 was related strictly, like most British decisions, to the business in hand. But it was full of larger implications of a new strategy. The same conference decided to ensure the mobility of British air power in the Middle East by establishing an air route between Cairo and Baghdad, along which the squadrons could be switched almost instantaneously from the Nile valley to R.A.F. stations in Iraq and, by way of the Persian Gulf, to India; and the resolve to safeguard the oil of Iraq and Persia from the air as well as to create a new and rapid road to India was a brilliant innovation, executed in the British fashion with that air of dull routine which deprives most English revolutions of their glamour.

6

The years that followed threw a good deal of light on what aircraft could do, if somewhat less on what belligerents proposed to do with them. Races for the Schneider Trophy established that they would fly faster; and the opening of Empire air routes to the Cape and to

Australia by way of Singapore established that they would fly further. These radiated from Egypt and confirmed the importance of the Middle East in Britain's air strategy. But the military uses of the new weapon were still a matter of conjecture, although it was growing obvious, as the bright skies of 1918 clouded over in the post-war years, that a disillusioned world still had a use for weapons.

The growing menace was reflected in a readjustment of Britain's air power to the new situation; and in 1933, whilst 11 squadrons were still maintained in the Middle East, the main body of the R.A.F. consisted of 42 squadrons at home with the proclaimed and ten-year-old objective of constituting "a Home Defence Air Force of sufficient strength adequately to protect us against attack by the strongest air force within striking distance of this country." This ideal was pursued unhurryingly in the years that followed, as the evidence of Germany's air armaments was forced upon reluctant minds, though official action seemed hardly to keep pace with official promises. The Home Defence Force gradually rose in strength, demonstrating the rare capacity of its original nucleus for almost indefinite expansion; and its potential numbers were increased by measures to expand man-power with the R.A.F. Volunteer Reserve and the Auxiliary Air Force, and to reinforce the aircraft industry by the larger resources of British engineering organised in "shadow factories." It was becoming plain that air warfare was a possibility of the immediate future; and the formation of Bomber, Fighter, and Coastal Commands in 1936 appeared to indicate that it would take more than one form. The public was increasingly preoccupied with its own prospects in an uncomfortable future, of which Douhet's converts conjured up alarming visions, confirmed upon the screen by H. G. Wells' *Shape of Things to Come*. There was a growing feeling that, if war broke loose, air power would bomb Western civilisation to rags; and the ease with which the Japanese were performing this office in the East did nothing to diminish a conviction that London might shortly go the way of Shanghai. The fortunes of Madrid and Barcelona in the Spanish civil war deepened this impression, although it was observed that neither place succumbed to bombing. This, however, was widely attributed to the small scale of the attacks; and the first triumphs of German aggression at Vienna, Prague, and Munich were achieved in the silence of successful blackmail and without the test of war by virtue of a general belief that bombing was irresistible.

Acceptance of this view was less unquestioning among professionals. For though the doctrinaires believed implicitly in the futility of an aerial defensive and one judicious writer was convinced by the lessons of the last war that "a prolonged defensive attitude must in the long run have seriously adverse effects on the morale of the defending airmen" (WING COMMANDER J. C. SLESSOR, *Air Power and Armies*), the R.A.F. had not renounced the defensive weapon of fighter aircraft. Its strength at home consisted in 1938 of 68 bomber and 30 fighter squadrons in addition to those provided for reconnaissance and army co-operation (naval duties had now been transferred to the Admiralty with the Fleet Air Arm), and Fighter Command was in charge of Air Marshal Sir Hugh Dowding, who had already taken steps as Air Member for Supply and Research to arm his squadrons with the eight-gun fighter and made a further contribution in the elaborate defensive organisation of the Command. British thought had evidently not succumbed to the facile view that air warfare was to consist entirely of one-way traffic by massed bombers. Indeed, it had notably preserved its balance in such works ("SQUADRON-LEADER," *Basic Principles of Air Warfare*, 1927; SLESSOR, *Air Power and Armies*, 1936; and AIR VICE-MARSHAL E. L. GOSSAGE, *The Royal Air Force*, 1937) as brought the reader in contact with a mind rather than with an obsession or a grievance, as was unhappily the case in a high proportion of aeronautical publications. The objectives were coolly assessed with a clear appreciation that they could not be reached before air superiority had been attained; and it was recognised that this must be fought for in the sky before ground targets, however tempting, could be reached.

One lesson had been soberly observed, when a period of tension with Italy witnessed the withdrawal of large naval units from Malta to Alexandria in view of the unhallowed proximity of shore-based Italian aircraft. But it was less easy to point the moral of air operations in the Spanish civil war, where German and Italian methods were tried out in the "laboratory of modern battle" (F. O. MIKSCHE, *Blitzkrieg*, 1941). True, air power had been used extensively—first as a substitute for sea power to cover General Franco's initial invasion of his country from Morocco in face of superior naval forces, and later as an active participant in the ground fighting. But was it clear that this *rôle* would have been practicable if the enemy had been adequately provided with anti-aircraft guns? What lessons could be drawn from the successful bombing of relatively undefended towns and harbours? Would it always be possible to destroy aircraft on the ground with equal ease? Did it follow from the absence of parachutists or air-borne troops that this interesting innovation, of which the Russians had lately given an impressive display, was without a future? Whilst experts laboured in a field that has since become a paradise of wisdom after the event, and struggled to discern an outline of the future in the vague and fragmentary indications of the present, a larger public dwelt uneasily upon the fate of Guernica and wondered how soon it would have the same experience.

For the outlines of air warfare were beginning to emerge. It was plain that air power could be used with effect both in the battle on land or sea and at a distance from it. A strong numerical preponderance seemed likely to give the Germans a free choice of where to use it; and their record of inhumanity with submarines and poison gas in the last war, combined with the advertised ruthlessness of their rulers, appeared to render it extremely probable that they would pull out all the stops at once in the diapason of air warfare. Their British adversaries were more attuned to the unpretentious common sense of Mahan's judgment that "naval strategy, like naval tactics, when boiled down, is simply the proper use of means to attain ends" (*Naval Strategy*); and in the air the only drawback, as the summer of 1939 drew slowly on, was that Britain's ends were likely to be much restricted by the inadequacy of Britain's means.

7

When the London sirens moaned immediately after a disconsolate Prime Minister's announcement that the country was at war, events appeared to be conforming with alarming promptitude to the prophets' gloomiest predictions. But nothing happened. Indeed, in Western Europe nothing happened for a considerable time. True, Poland was disposed of in a few weeks, and on lines that would have warmed Douhet's heart. For the invasion was preceded by a dawn attack on Polish aerodromes, by which a high proportion of their air force was eliminated before it could get off the ground; and German aircraft exploited their resulting air superiority in operations over the battlefield and against civilian targets. But in the west there was no sign of "the intense struggle in the air which it is felt will inevitably be the opening act in any future war between European nations" foreseen by every expert of standing. The British Expeditionary Force was shipped to Cherbourg and ports further west without interruption from the air; and its concentration in an area between Le Mans and a town with the depressing name of Laval was undisturbed, although (in the words of Lord Gort's despatch) "the Staff met for the first time the problem arising from the wide dispersion imposed by the necessity to guard against air attack." Presently they moved, quite unmolested, into position on the Belgian frontier; and the war was ready to begin.

But nothing happened. As Nelson wrote of the blockade in 1804, "this is an odd war. Not a battle." After three weeks of intense activity in Poland the guns were silent in the east; and, what was stranger, they were almost as silent in the west, where neither side showed any tendency to venture far beyond the security of its frontier defences. Was this the classic deadlock which had been predicted for land warfare? If so, the situation dear to students of Douhet had materialised, and the next stage would be a vigorous offensive in the air. But as the silence deepened, an expectant world of neutrals began to show signs of impatience. This was not what they had been led to expect of a World War. The skies of Europe were not dark with vast Armadas of contending aircraft or red with burning cities. A few detonations in the east of Scotland were a poor substitute for Armageddon; night-flying over Central Europe with mildly incendiary leaflets, which attained a highly gratifying circulation, might be sound training for R.A.F. pilots; troop concentrations and munition works in Germany were photographed with unabated zest; and the air offensive against the German navy was somewhat impeded by an order to refrain from bombing any vessel lying alongside or near German territory. For land targets were taboo; and in this epoch of unnatural restraint the misadventure of a British bomber, which embarrassed everyone by inadvertently knocking out a German anti-aircraft gun on shore, was very properly suppressed as an indelicate proceeding.

While great European armies hung poised in the frozen strategy of 1939, air power showed no tendency to cut the knot. In France the Air Component discharged its modest duties with the British army, and the Advanced Air Striking Force prepared to bomb targets in Germany from French aerodromes as soon as General Gamelin felt equal to the risk. Their situation on the Continent gave them a geo-graphical advantage, since they were nearer to Germany than any German bomber to Great Britain. But for the present it did not seem altogether wise to provoke the Germans, who might be in a position to command air superiority in the sky over France and would almost certainly exploit it with sustained brutality on anything that lay below. The fate of Warsaw was not encouraging to those who thought of civilisation in terms of Paris; and the British could hardly plunge on a gamble of which the forfeits would be paid by their allies. So long as this cautionary mood prevailed, the inexpressive face of war in 1939 and the first months of 1940 bore a strong resemblance to 1918 without the fighting. For a continuous front ran (as French military thought had predicted) from the North Sea to the Swiss frontier; and the Advanced Air Striking Force stood ready to perform the duties once discharged by Trenchard's Independent Air Force.

But relief came from an unexpected quarter, when the Germans made their descent on Norway in the spring. Air power in German hands had already shown a tendency to trespass on the sea by mine-laying from aircraft and machine-gunning anything afloat in the North Sea from fishing-boats to lightships. But the invasion of a country separated from the nearest point of German territory by at least three hundred miles of sea without securing their communications by a naval victory defied all canons of maritime warfare. This distance was substantially reduced by the simultaneous seizure of Denmark. But it remained true that the invading forces were dependent upon sea communications and that the British navy was preponderant at sea. Indeed, this apparent lapse was authoritatively pointed out by Mr. Churchill, now First Lord of the Admiralty, who informed the House of Commons that "in my view, which is shared by my skilled advisers, Herr Hitler has committed a grave strategic error in spreading the war so far to the north and in forcing the Scandinavian people, or peoples, out of their attitude of neutrality. . . . It is the considered view of the Admiralty that we have greatly gained by what has occurred in Scandinavia and in northern waters in a strategic and military sense. For myself, I consider that Hitler's action in invading Scandinavia is as great a strategic and political error as that which was committed by Napoleon in 1807, when he invaded Spain."

This judgment, as applied to politics, was sound, as a naked outrage upon harmless neutrals was bound to weigh against the Germans;

and its application to the military situation was no less unexceptionable, provided that nothing in the interval had modified the principles prevailing at the time of the Peninsular War. For if the world consisted merely of land and water, it was plain that an overseas expedition lay at the mercy of an opponent with command of the sea, who was free to cut its communications and to overwhelm it at leisure with superior land forces. Neglect of this elementary truth by no less a practitioner than General Bonaparte, enforced by Nelson's broadsides at the Battle of the Nile, had reduced the Army of Egypt to an ignominious evacuation; and it might be felt that what had been true in August, 1798, gave grounds for hope in April, 1940. If so, a British fleet might shortly be expected to control the Skagerrak and to isolate the Germans in Norway, where a British army securely transported across the North Sea would in due course demolish them.

But that was not the way things happened. For the world of 1940 did not consist merely of land and water. A third element could now be used for military purposes. The intervention of air power denied the heirs of Nelson a new Battle of the Nile in the approaches to the Baltic and deprived the British army of a Peninsular War in Scandinavia; and they were swiftly disillusioned by events, as these inviting possibilities evaporated. It was soon found impracticable for surface vessels to exercise command of the narrow seas separating the invading German forces in Norway from their home bases, since these waters could now be dominated by shore-based aircraft; and Mr. Churchill confessed regretfully that "the immense enemy air strength which can be brought to bear upon our patrolling craft had made this method far too costly to be adopted . . . the losses which would be inflicted upon that patrol would, undoubtedly, very soon constitute a naval disaster." By all the rules no German traffic should have passed between The Skaw and Oslo Fiord without permission from the waiting guns of British warships. But the rules of war at sea were somehow changed. For surface craft could not maintain themselves in areas exposed to hostile bombers beyond the range of their own protective fighter aircraft; and the lesson of their relative impotence was to be felt in narrow seas from the Sicilian Channel to Singapore.

Events on land were equally instructive, as the invasion of Norway was based upon a systematic use of air power. When the terrain upon which a British army was to fight for Norway's freedom was surveyed, it was found that every aerodrome had passed into German hands. This meant that the defending forces were exposed to a continuous attack, which they had no means of answering except by the intermittent efforts of long-range bombers operating from Great Britain across four hundred miles of sea. An airfield was heroically improvised for a few British fighters on a frozen lake. But air warfare on this scale was virtually unilateral; and military operations between adversaries of whom only one had access to the air were, as the Abyssinians had found, unrewarding. The campaign in Norway was decided by this simple fact, since the British force could hardly operate successfully on land, if they were continuously bombed, machine-gunned, and observed from the air; and nothing could avert their ultimate defeat, when the ports through which their guns and reinforcements must arrive were methodically reduced by German bombing to heaps of burning splinters. Aircraft could not be effectively resisted without aircraft; and as the Air Minister confessed, "we had no fighter force to cope with the German bombers." Not that Britain was devoid of fighters. But the only way in which they could be brought to bear upon the battle in Norway was from Norwegian aerodromes; and if none were available, there was no more to be done.

For aerodromes are the first requisite of any exercise of air power. There is nothing quite so immobile as a grounded aircraft. Until it can refuel, it is militarily non-existent; and unless this takes place within range of its objective, it is as harmless as a gnat. A strong fighter force in Scotland could not hope to intervene in Norway, which was out of range. The Germans were in occupation of all Norwegian landing grounds; and their prompt action had ensured them a one-sided war on land. This seemed to point to something in the nature of a new direction for military operations, since the possession of aerodromes was now recognisable as a fact of primary importance. German enterprise in securing a chain of airfields in advance had put them in a position to sweep the British out of Norway and to violate all canons of the art of war by maintaining isolated ground forces at points far ahead of their advance, which could be (and were) supplied and reinforced from the air. These results had followed from their initial seizure of the country's aerodromes; and if such advantages accrued from this proceeding, it was evidently time for some revision of the doctrine that the enemy's armed forces constitute the main, if not the sole, objective of all military operations. Soldiers had been taught for at least a century to pursue this simple end and to eschew the chess-board manœuvres with which an earlier age had practised the geometry of war in the Eighteenth Century, when campaigns were elegantly waged for strategic points rather than for vulgar conflicts. But even Napoleon, the high-priest of modern warfare, had admitted that "war is an affair of positions"; and now positions, in the form of aerodromes, were evidently of supreme importance. For the control of these positions had settled the campaign in Norway; and it seemed to follow that war might once again be dominated by territorial objectives and that land operations might resolve themselves into a war for aerodromes.

The Norwegian experience of the Allies had been instructive, if unprofitable. Air power had emerged as an effective instrument for securing command of the sea in narrow waters; and a land campaign had been decided by the control of landing grounds. These results called for reflection on the part of maritime Powers, who were at some disadvantage in the air. But their reflections on the events of April were not prolonged, as May was even more eventful.

8

The campaign of Holland, Belgium, and France, in which two countries were completely overrun and a third successfully invaded, was a strange example of the way in which the Germans managed to achieve surprise by doing precisely what they had already done twice before. As in Poland, Dutch and Belgian cities were bombed at dawn without the usual formalities; and as in Norway, aerodromes appeared to be the first objective of the German thrust. But since more resistance was anticipated, there was a more extensive use of air-borne troops; and by a happy variant large quantities of parachutists were liberally sprinkled on the scene, some of them in costumes calculated to mislead.

These preliminary operations were followed by the main attack, in which air and armoured forces co-operated closely. Swift penetrations by tanks advancing on a narrow front were preceded and maintained by bombing from the air; and the combination punched a hole in the French line at the decisive point not far from Sedan. German ingenuity appeared to have devised a solution for the problem

of providing a swift mechanised advance with artillery support. In
the absence of opposition this combined attack by land and air was
admirably calculated to produce results on the Continent. Employed
against the Poles after the destruction of their air force on the ground,
it had already proved irresistible; and there were grounds for thinking
that it would prove equally destructive to the French. Their military
thought, which rarely ventured far beyond 1918, was not attuned to
mobile warfare; and in this fixation there was little room for a free
use of the air weapon. Less than a year before his hearers had learnt
from General Weygand, who was believed to be Foch's heir, that
"obviously a large and powerful air force will give a tremendous
advantage to those countries which possess one, and will be a serious
hindrance to those which do not. But the infantry remains '*la reine
des batailles*,' since territory must be held, and the winner is he who
succeeds in holding it." The only question, if this defensive programme was to be carried out successfully, was how far French infantry
would be equal to holding its ground under fire. There was little
doubt of its ability to do so in prepared positions, if they were assaulted
in the old way by waves of bayonets following an artillery barrage.
But now the test came in comparatively open country, where air power
in the absence of air opposition had full scope. In the outcome troops
unequipped with modern weapons and untrained for modern battle
disintegrated swiftly under a novel form of attack. General Mittelhauser suggested subsequently that "the technical surprise in this form
of aviation was decisive," though M. Daladier inopportunely pointed
out that when the Germans showed a dive-bomber at the Air Exhibi-
tion of 1938, nobody in Paris had been much impressed (P. TISSIER,
The Riom Trial, 1942). But the real element of surprise in dive-
bombing was moral. Most soldiers might have been prepared for
being shelled, and even bombed, in the ordinary manner; but the
screaming impact of dive-bombers on the troops below was an unpleasant novelty. French units of indifferent quality were quite
unequal to the strain.

This was decisive; and the resulting gap in the Allied line was
never closed. For the subsequent discovery that well-armed and
seasoned troops had relatively little to fear from dive-bombing came
too late. The mechanised offensive and its bold prolongation to the
Channel coast routed the Allies, who were quite unable to contend
with the weight of the German armour or with the pace of the attack.

Their own use of air power in the brief campaign had been more orthodox, Allied aircraft operating against heavy odds in and behind the battle. The French ban on bombing targets in Germany was maintained until the Low Countries had been invaded; but when it was raised, the weight of the Allied bomber effort in the time available at this stage of the war was hardly calculated to arrest the swift movement of German armies. Immense gallantry was displayed in attacks upon heavily defended bridges on the enemy's lines of communication. But it was beyond the power of Allied aircraft to check, or even to delay, the rapid onset of disaster on the ground.

It was plain that the Germans owed their easy victory to a combination of air power with armour on the ground, which no European army at the present stage of their equipment and experience was able to withstand. Their use of air power on land after the initial operations against towns and aerodromes was in direct contrast with that favoured by those doctrinaires, who held with Douhet that it should be exercised in complete independence of operations on the ground. For the system operated by the *Luftwaffe* in 1940 was one of army co-operation in the fullest sense. German military means were calculated to secure the swift attainment of German ends; and they had designed an instrument to win a Continental war. Given the historic national prestige of the German army, it was not to be expected that an airman's view would dominate the *Wehrmacht*. A greater freedom might prevail at sea, where the German fleet was relatively inconsiderable. But on land the army reigned supreme, and air operations were inevitably subordinated to the triumphs of the heirs of Moltke and Ludendorff. This secondary *rôle* was plainly stated by Field-Marshal Kesselring, commanding *Luftflotte* 2 in France and subsequently in the Mediterranean :

> In the present campaigns the *Luftwaffe* could not have fulfilled its task in a war of movement, if in the training and development of its service it had not kept an eye on that one aim—to become a part of the *Wehrmacht*; if it had not striven to think within the *Wehrmacht* framework and to take unconditionally its place in the struggle of the *Wehrmacht*. (F. O. MIKSCHE, *Is Bombing Decisive?* 1943, quoting *Essener Nationalzeitung*, May 21, 1941.)

This programme of complete subordination to the army was faithfully executed by the *Luftwaffe*, an instrument designed with rare ability for army co-operation in a European war. Its purposes were plainly indicated by the character of its equipment, which comprised bombers specially designed for operating in conjunction with ground forces and a large quantity of transport aircraft. Its success in this field was undeniable. But if the changing face of war confronted it with situations which its designers had not contemplated, the *Luftwaffe* might prove less victorious in face of adversaries with a larger view of air power.

But there was no inherent reason why it should not be equal to its next assignment. One portion of the Allied armies, which comprised the British Expeditionary Force and a large French contingent, had backed helplessly against the coast of Flanders. With their backs to the sea and their faces to a grim semicircle of converging Germans they confronted the alternatives of annihilation or surrender, with an outside chance of evacuation from the beaches of Dunkirk. All day long for one burning midsummer week observers saw "what seemed to be vast black shadows on the pale sands . . . enormous formations of men, standing, waiting. . . . They did not seem to change; they did not seem to sit, nor to lie down; they stood, with the patience of their race, waiting their turn" (J. MASEFIELD, *The Nine Days' Wonder*, 1941). Here was a predestined target for destruction from the air—350,000 men immobilised round one blazing port and the strangest miscellany of shipping that the Narrow Seas had seen since the little ships of England came streaming out to battle with the Armada. In the last war a few tons of bombs on Turks huddled in the gorge of Beisan had reduced them to "a dispersed horde of trembling individuals, hiding for their lives in every fold of the vast hills. . . . The R.A.F. lost four killed. The Turks lost a corps." The same doom had overtaken the Bulgarians in the defile of the Struma; and the annihilation of the retreating Austrians after Vittorio Veneto evoked the comment from one soldier that "subsequent examination of the road almost forced the observer to the conclusion that this form of warfare should be forbidden in the future."

These were the classical achievements of bombing in 1918; and there was every reason to expect that the large formations and massive bomb-loads of 1940 would multiply them tenfold. But for the first time since the outbreak of war results fell short of German expectations. For the *Luftwaffe* was cheated of its prey, and Dunkirk ranked as a deliverance which the people of England were dissuaded with some difficulty from regarding as a victory. In the air, indeed, it was a victory of high significance, since the *Luftwaffe* operating from aerodromes close at hand in France and Belgium was defeated by British fighters flying from home bases across at least fifty miles of sea. The watchers on the beaches saw them wheel towards ten, twenty, thirty, forty, fifty German aircraft, spoiling the symmetry of their attack and dismissing numbers of them into the smoke of their own fires in the burning town below. As the days went slowly by, the menace of destruction lifted. Fearlessness overhead was answered by unconquerable gallantry beneath; and the dark masses in the dunes filed down to the water's edge and waded out towards the waiting ships.

A historian had written of his country in another conflict that "as it took to the sea in the sixteenth century to defeat the Spanish tyranny, so it took to the air in the twentieth century to defeat the insolence of the Germans." The victory (for it was nothing less in the air fighting) was unmistakable. Before the week was over, German bombers jettisoned their bombs and ran from British fighters, and their own fighter screen had lost a good deal of its appetite for combat. The price was high, since the R.A.F. fought at a disadvantage, far from home and with the sea behind them. Their time over the battle area was strictly limited by the long homeward journey and shadowed by the risks of a forced landing in the sea. But the retreat was covered by the indomitable rearguard in the sky, which destroyed at least 603 German aircraft for the loss of 130 of their own and 120 British pilots,

> unseen by those you helped to save
> You rode the air above that foreign dune
> And died like the unutterably brave
> That so your friends might see the English June.
>
> .   .   .   .   .
>
> You, from the Heaven, saw, in English chalk
> White, about Dover, some familiar track
> That feet of yours would never again walk,
> Since you were killed and never coming back,
> Yet knew, that your young life, as price paid over,
> Let thousands live to tread that track to Dover.

On the day after operations were concluded at Dunkirk Mr. Churchill detected "a victory inside this deliverance, which should be noted. It was gained by the Air Force. . . . This was a great trial of strength between the British and German Air Forces. . . . Very large formations of German aeroplanes—and we know that they are a very brave race—have turned on several occasions from the attack of one-quarter of their number of the Royal Air Force, and have dispersed in different directions. Twelve aeroplanes have been hunted by two. One aeroplane was driven into the water and cast away, by the mere charge of a British aeroplane which had no more ammunition. All of our types—the Hurricane, the Spitfire, and the new Defiant—and all our pilots have been vindicated as superior to what they have at present to face. When we consider how much greater would be our advantage in defending the air above this island against an overseas attack, I must say that I find in these facts a sure basis upon which practical and reassuring thoughts may rest. . . ."

The achievement of Fighter Command over Dunkirk showed plainly that Britain held a strong defensive weapon. The pre-war belief that there could be no such thing as an aerial defensive was shattered; and as defensive strategy had taken the form of a vigorous and sustained counter-offensive, there was no trace of "the immediately unfavourable reaction on the fighting value of an air force resulting from a defensive attitude," which one expert had anticipated as the consequence of a more passive method. Indeed, the march of science had substantially increased the powers of defence since Douhet's time with radiolocation, which drastically modified the whole outline of air warfare. This, perhaps, was just as well, if England was to be the next objective of the *Luftwaffe*. Its present task in the first days of June was to complete the military demolition of the French, a mission well within its powers. But it remained to be seen whether this perfect instrument for army co-operation would be equal to the task of eliminating Britain's air power before the German army got there; and if experience at Dunkirk was any criterion, the prospect was uncertain. For the German military mind had forged a weapon that was more capable of winning battles on the ground than in the air.

9

The possibilities and limitations of air warfare were growing plain, as the war entered on a new theatre in the Mediterranean. On land the Germans had perfected the co-operation of aircraft with ground forces; but it was possible that at a later stage something higher might be devised in the co-operation of an entire air force with an army.

The *Luftwaffe* had demolished all rival Continental air forces; but its first encounter with the R.A.F. appeared to indicate that some missions lay beyond the range of German methods. It was evident from Norway that the control of narrow seas was profoundly modified by the proximity of shore-based aircraft. Nelson's freedom of manœuvre from Toulon to Alexandria and back again was now a fragrant memory for sailors. Such mobility was now reserved for aircraft. But the air affair was no less susceptible to the Nelson touch. For air combat had a Nelsonian simplicity. "The business of an English Commander-in-Chief being first to bring an Enemy's Fleet to Battle, on the most advantageous terms to himself, (I mean that of laying his Ships close on board the Enemy, as expeditiously as possible;) and secondly, to continue them there, without separating, until the business is decided . . . no Captain can do very wrong if he places his Ship alongside that of an Enemy." There, stated in 1805, was the whole duty of a fighter pilot launched to the attack, since aircraft, while they might be the instrument of offensive or defensive strategy, were denied defensive tactics by the simple circumstance that they could not stand still in the air. Nor was counsel from the same master lacking upon bombing policy. For it was laid down by the *R.A.F. War Manual* that "the bomb is the primary weapon of air power; the bomber is the means of conveying it to its target; an air striking force composed of bombers is the chief means by which a nation wields its air power." Nelson added the corollary: "It is, as Mr. Pitt knows, annihilation that the country wants, and not merely a splendid victory of twenty-three to thirty-six. Numbers only can annihilate."

Air warfare, no less than war on sea and land, had its principles; and it was no less plain that air forces required to be wisely planned and rightly operated before they could commit their young men to the sky and earn the gratitude of nations, of the many for the few.

Chapter III

THE PLAYERS

WHEN AIR WARFARE CAME TO THE MEDITERRANEAN in the second week of June, 1940, the combatants consisted of the R.A.F. and the French *Armée de l'Air* on one side and the Italian *Regia Aeronautica* on the other. But it was highly doubtful if the catastrophic course of operations in the west would leave the Allies free to use more than a fraction of their air forces in the new theatre. The French were desperately engaged under increasing German pressure on a sagging line across the country from the Eastern frontier to the English Channel; and their situation was aggravated by the prospect of an Italian attack in the region of the Alps. They still maintained a considerable army in North Africa with 198 aircraft; and a strong French force with 96 aircraft had been concentrated in Syria and the Lebanon for operations in the Eastern Mediterranean. The remainder of the Allied forces in this area consisted of the R.A.F., Middle East Command, whose ample boundaries embraced Egypt, the Sudan, Palestine, Trans-Jordan, Iraq, Aden, Somaliland, and East Africa. Its duties were officially defined as the defence of Egypt and the Suez Canal and the maintenance of communications through the Red Sea in combination with the French; and the force allocated to this purpose in the main Egyptian theatre of operations consisted of some 64 fighters and 94 bombers, supplemented in East Africa and the Sudan by a further

85 bombers and some fighters from Rhodesia and the Union of South Africa. As the R.A.F. had been created more than twenty years before by the cool intelligence of Smuts, it was fitting that reinforcements from the young South African Air Force should be assembling in Kenya close to the southern borders of Italian territory in Abyssinia. The latest types of aircraft had inevitably been reserved for operations in the west against the Germans, as the requirements of the Middle East Command had not hitherto been particularly urgent; and its commander, Air Chief Marshal Sir Arthur Longmore, described a proportion of his bombers as "obsolescent," an epithet applicable in one opinion to his fighter force as well (AIR CHIEF MARSHAL SIR A. TEDDER, *The Middle East, Flying and Popular Aviation*, September, 1942). But it was not without importance that there were British squadrons in the Middle East whose aircraft and pilots were thoroughly acclimatised. For this area had been the home ground of the R.A.F. since the last war.

These Allied forces were now confronted by the *Regia Aeronautica*, when Mussolini threw 2600 first-line aircraft into the scale. Italian air performances in the last war had been derisory. But since 1922 Fascist Italy had been at pains to create a modern air force, fortified by Douhet's teaching, Balbo's long-distance flights of large formations, and a fine record in the races for the Schneider Trophy. Its pilots had obtained valuable combat experience in the Spanish civil war; Abyssinia had tested its organisation, if not its fighting quality; and the products of Italian engineering were viewed with respect in spite of its undue fidelity to old types of aircraft by reason of their superior manœuvrability, since Italian pilots tended to associate spectacular aerobatics with good airmanship. British estimates before the war assessed their technical equipment as equal to our own and superior in some respects to that of Germany and France, although it was anticipated that higher numbers of Italian aircraft might become unserviceable owing to defects in maintenance. But since air warfare is less dependent on machines than on the men who fly them, it was felt that the R.A.F. was likely to excel the Italians in tactical efficiency. Their pilots were expected to be more temperamental than our own; and though they might perform with credit in air combat, it was doubtful how they would be able to sustain reverses.

These, however, were not in contemplation, when Italy was nerved to risk entering a war that, to all appearances, was practically over.

While two-thirds of their air force was retained on the mainland of Europe, strong contingents in Sardinia and Sicily cast a long shadow on the narrow waters of the Mediterranean. In North Africa, where French aircraft of all types and ages numbered less than 200 on one flank of Libya and the R.A.F. in Egypt on the other was not quite so numerous, a strong Italian force of 200 modern fighters and 200 modern bombers appeared to put the issue beyond question; and the odds were still more favourable in East Africa, where the British were outnumbered by two to one. With substantial air forces based in Libya, Eritrea, and Abyssinia there was some reason to suppose that, even if the war went on, Italian calculations would be justified by victory. An instinct for the winning side had always guided their diplomacy; and when Mussolini, yielding to a well-developed taste for backing military certainties, made his choice in June, 1940, it might appear unchivalrous. But chivalry had never been their *forte*; and the cool dictates of *sacro egoismo*, hallowed by several generations of Italian policy, already showed handsome profits in the form of Libya, the Dodecanese, Albania, and Abyssinia. There was plainly nothing to be feared from France in Europe; and if the grave disparity in air power, by which the Allies were confronted in the Mediterranean, was a decisive element in modern war, Italian strategy need hardly shrink from facing them in Africa.

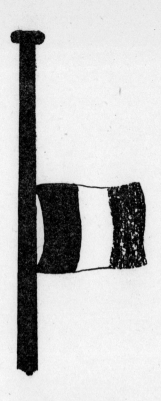

Chapter IV

THE WAR THAT WAS NEVER FOUGHT

AT MIDNIGHT ON JUNE 10, 1940, Italy went to war against the Allies; and for fourteen days the Italians were opposed by the combined forces of France and Britain. The event was not unforeseen, as Italian protestations of devotion to the Axis had been distinctly audible, and their preparations for hostilities had been conducted with all the secrecy of an operatic soliloquy with full orchestral accompaniment. For months Allied commanders had surveyed the problem, indulging in what one member of their staffs termed "crystal-gazing." There had been joint talks in Palestine and Syria; British officers had gone to French headquarters in Tunis and Algeria and even as far west as Casablanca; and since the air route across Africa might be threatened from Italian territory, inter-Allied conversations had taken place so far afield as Chad. At first the French appeared to favour action in the Levant by the forces under the command of

General Weygand at Beyrout. Minds ran on Cyprus and French aerodromes in Syria as stepping-stones to Rhodes and the Italian islands off the coast of Turkey; and the weakness of French military thought for going on with the last war where it had stopped in 1918 turned eager eyes to Salonika and the Balkans, if the war showed any tendency to spread towards the east.

But the cold facts of 1940 were scarcely encouraging to large designs on the part of the Allies; and they were reduced to vague gestures calculated to deter Italy from abandoning neutrality by the movement of single battalions to strengthen the garrisons of Gibraltar or Aden and of single bomber squadrons to defend Egypt or the Sudan from the massive concentrations of Italian aircraft in Libya and East Africa. Allied plans were now severely practical, though not unpromising. For it was plainly reasonable to expect the French fleet to neutralise a large part of the Italian navy and to maintain command of the Mediterranean west of Sicily, while the British fleet at Alexandria controlled its eastern waters. There was some reason to suppose that, in face of an Italian challenge, Allied sea power was equal to keeping open traffic through the Mediterranean to and from the Suez Canal; Malta could still be reinforced by sea or air from French territory not far away; and the French tenure of Jibuti safe-guarded the gates of the Red Sea. On land it was still practicable for the French to invade Libya from the west, although considerable numbers of troops and aircraft had already been withdrawn to France. Tripoli lay within bombing range of French aerodromes in Tunisia. Indeed, two-thirds of the Italian mainland could be bombed from French North Africa; and large numbers of Italian aircraft were retained in Italy for the defence of their home bases, ports, and cities. But the invasion of Tripolitania by French forces concentrated in the Mareth Line was obviously feasible; and it was plain that this move was anticipated by the Italians no less than by the Allies, since Graziani's forces had been grouped to meet it in the west of Libya. Their situation was not wholly enviable, as the British might be capable of launching an attack on Libya from Egypt in the east. It would not be easy for the Italians to maintain a defensive on two fronts with 2000 miles of desert in between; and their air force, although more powerful than its opponents, was likely to be embarrassed by the necessity of "looking two ways."

These agreeable possibilities were open to the Allies when the war

Allied Air Forces Range
June 10, 1940.

Allied Forces Range,

■ Territory in Italian hands
■ Territory in British hands
☰ Territory in French hands

June 10, 1940

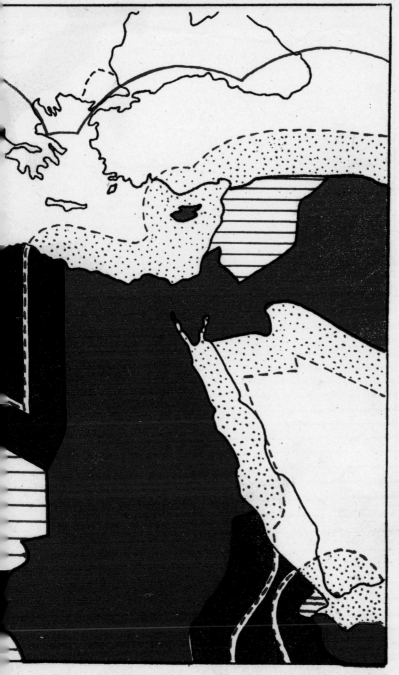

○ Potential Bomber Cover
⊙ Potential Fighter Cover

◯ Potential Bomber Cover

✦ Potential Fighter Cover

against Italy began. But events in Europe were too fast for them. French powers of resistance on the German front were failing visibly; Weygand, recalled from Beyrout to a desperate inheritance of defeat at home, announced that this was the last round; the French Government left Paris for a confused week of argument in Touraine, where the Prime Minister proposed a French armistice to Mr. Churchill and addressed desperate appeals to President Roosevelt; a French military man anticipated brightly that England would shortly have its neck wrung like a chicken; and Marshal Pétain elected firmly for surrender. While this mood prevailed, there was little disposition to use the forces that they could still command against the Italians. For when a British bomber force was swiftly mobilised outside Marseilles for operations against Milan on the first evening of the new war, their take-off was effectively obstructed by French army lorries, although French views were subsequently modified and no impediment was offered later to British raids on Milan and Genoa. The French were reeling, although their instability was not increased by an Italian attack against their Alpine frontier, where six French divisions successfully repelled three times their number.

But the swift impact of disaster on the Continent afforded no reason why operations should not proceed in the Mediterranean and Africa. At sea French cruisers based on Alexandria swept the Aegean, and an Anglo-French fleet shelled the cliffs of Bardia. The air war had opened with a prompt series of attacks on targets in Italian territory from Egypt, the Sudan, and Kenya, and some retaliation by the enemy on Sollum, Mersa Matruh, and Jibuti. The R.A.F. had moved into the Western Desert, and the S.A.A.F. was already challenging the enemy in East Africa. But the French army in Tunisia was never launched to the attack. For within a week Pétain was asking for an armistice. In Morocco General Nogués hesitated; but General Mittelhauser at Beyrout felt no doubts, assuring Wavell of his "unalterable determination to continue the struggle." This was important, as the French Army of the Levant was a substantial force holding territory vital to the defence of Egypt and Iraq; and it was no less satisfactory that Legentilhomme at Jibuti was for holding out as well. In France the Marshal had consented to a cessation of hostilities in all French possessions, colonies, protectorates, and mandated territories, and the demobilisation and disarmament of all French forces. But Hitler's writ did not run in Tunisia, if French warships were prepared to carry on the fight in the intervening waters; and there was no reason why French armies in North Africa or the Levant should pile their arms, unless their local commanders ordered them to do so. Pétain's ecstasy of surrender, which impelled the restoration to the *Luftwaffe* of 400 German airmen shot down by the R.A.F. in France, was infectious. While Darlan hauled down the flag of an undefeated navy, Nogués capitulated in Morocco, Mittelhauser at Beyrout had second thoughts and followed suit, and Legentilhomme was overwhelmed by the *capitulards* at Jibuti. A few brave Frenchmen left for British territory to fight on. But surrender won the day; and the whole face of the war was transformed by the capitulations of June 22 and 24.

The fruits of Pétain's statesmanship were clearly visible on the map. The elimination of almost the whole of the French navy by a single stroke of a dejected old man's pen altered for the worse the entire balance of sea power in the Mediterranean, leaving the British to do the best they could against heavy odds with such naval forces as were now at Alexandria or might become available at Gibraltar. Between these two extremities, 2000 miles apart, they were left without a single friendly port except Valletta; and along the south shore of the Mediterranean 1000 miles of coast had passed overnight into a dubious neutrality, where the vigilance of German and Italian Armistice Commissions would ensure that, if any points were stretched anywhere between Oran and Bizerta, they would be stretched in favour of the Axis. It was more than questionable now whether Britain's sea traffic could pass through the Mediterranean without an operation of war, whose outcome was uncertain; and with the closing of the Mediterranean the main sea route of the Empire had been cut.

It is fair to add that this grave consequence had not a purely naval origin, since in reality air power had gone far to close the Mediterranean. A superb and sustained display of naval gallantry, developed in the attack on Taranto by carrier-borne aircraft of the Fleet Air Arm in November, 1940, and culminating in the victory off Cape Matapan in March, 1941, subsequently redressed the balance of sea power in those waters without reopening the Mediterranean to normal traffic. That was beyond the power of warships, for the simple reason that the sea route to Suez was bound to pass through the Sicilian Channel; and so long as hostile aircraft had power to operate above it from Italian bases, an enemy could obstruct passage through the Mediterranean to

Royal Air Force Range
June 24, 1940.

Royal Air Force Range,

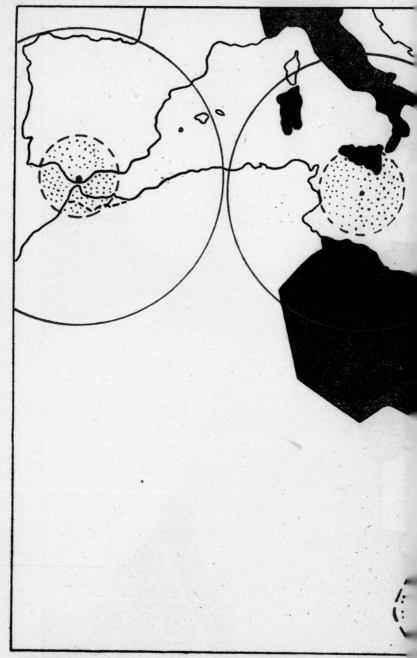

■ Territory in Italian hands
■ Territory in British hands

June 24, 1940

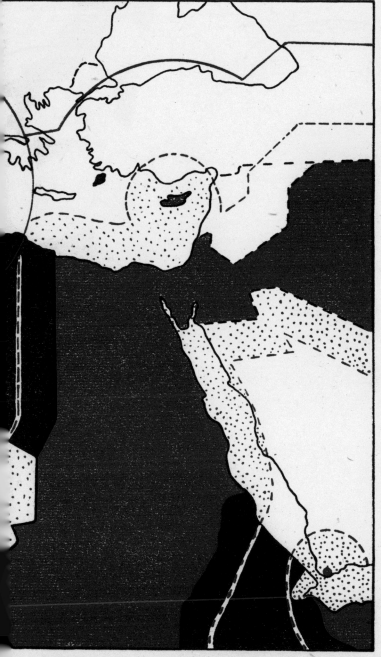

O Potential Bomber Cover

⬤ Potential Fighter Cover

British shipping. War at sea, no less than war on land, was becoming an affair of aerodromes; and though the British held its two extremities at Gibraltar and Port Said and Italian warships showed little tendency to challenge them at sea, the Mediterranean was closed to ordinary traffic by the presence of Axis aircraft on landing grounds in Sicily, Sardinia, and Libya. Reinforcements and supplies for Egypt must now travel round the Cape and through the Red Sea narrows, where they were exposed once more to Italian aircraft based in Eritrea. The sea route to India had been lengthened instantaneously by 4000 miles and that to Singapore by 3000 miles; and these diversions proportionately reduced the ability of British shipping to perform its vital duties. A pre-war appreciation of possibilities in the Mediterranean had estimated that "it is almost inconceivable that Great Britain could find herself without allies, embarrassed in the East, and at war with both France and Italy, or even at war with these two powers alone. . . . If, however, we did find ourselves at war against such a combination, there is no doubt that we should be compelled, temporarily at least, to close the Mediterranean to all British sea and air traffic, to abandon Malta, and to withdraw the fleet" (SQUADRON LEADER E. J. KINGSTON-McCLOUGHRY, *Winged Warfare*); and now something like the inconceivable had happened.

The new situation left Malta dangerously isolated. A too modest estimate of its capacities as an offensive air base capable of striking at the Italian lines of communication between Tripoli and the European mainland appeared to have deprived it of all significance except a certain symbolic value; and it was left to carry on as best it could with ground defences against Italian bombing. The days were distant when Nelson had written, "Malta, my dear Sir, is in my thoughts sleeping or waking." The fleet had been withdrawn some years before; so far as anyone in Malta knew, there were no fighter aircraft; and the island waited for the worst that the Italians could do. It had its first air raid on the day that the war started against Italy, followed by seven more before nightfall and by forty-nine before the month was out. But somebody discovered four Sea Gladiators in their packing-cases awaiting shipment to Alexandria. This windfall was eagerly unpacked and erected; members of the local staff appeared in the unfamiliar *rôle* of fighter pilots; and a few days before the French surrender, this meagre fighter cover under Air Commodore Maynard's command took the air for the defence of Malta. One was shot down at an early stage; but for three long months Faith, Hope, and Charity survived in the blue sky over the grey island to startle Italian visitors to their defenceless target by an unexpected and unpleasant welcome.

On land the situation was no less adverse. There could be no question now of an offensive against Libya by a French army from the west; and Graziani was at liberty to turn his whole weight against Egypt. In the air the R.A.F. was heavily outnumbered on two fronts. For whilst Egypt was exposed to attack from Libya, the Italians in East Africa could threaten the Sudan; and there was nothing to prevent their steady reinforcement from Europe or additions to their strength in East Africa by night flights from landing grounds in Libya. Indeed, it was not easy to see how the Army of the Nile, isolated at the end of the long sea route round the Cape, could survive. Its northern flank had been uncovered by the French defection in Syria; and its protracted lines of communication could be severed by Italian air power in the Red Sea, where the surrender of Jibuti had left a situation of extreme difficulty. Now there was no chance of air reinforcements being flown out from England by easy stages across France and on to Egypt by way of Tunis and Malta, although the threatened island could still be used to break the direct journey of long-distance aircraft *en route* for Egypt; and the possibility that British aircraft might reach the Nile valley by the West African Reinforcement Route was seriously jeopardised. For while the coast was safe in British hands, the air route across Africa was bound to pass through French territory at some point between Nigeria and the Sudan. If the miasma of surrender reached the brown distances of Chad, the route was endangered. But happily brave men were in control; and within a month Chad rallied to de Gaulle under Governor Eboué and Colonel Marchand. (Strange that the name of Marchand, by which Britain had once been challenged on the White Nile in the sad Equatorial landscape of Fashoda, now guaranteed a British life-line.) By the end of August French Equatorial Africa was safely ranged with the Free French; and the way was clear for British aircraft to fly from Takoradi to Khartoum without political impediment. Their ground security was now assured. All that confronted them was 2000 miles of burning sky above an endless waste.

The war in Africa had now assumed the unprepossessing shape of a defence of Egypt, to be conducted at every disadvantage. Instead

Italian Air Force Range
June, 1940.

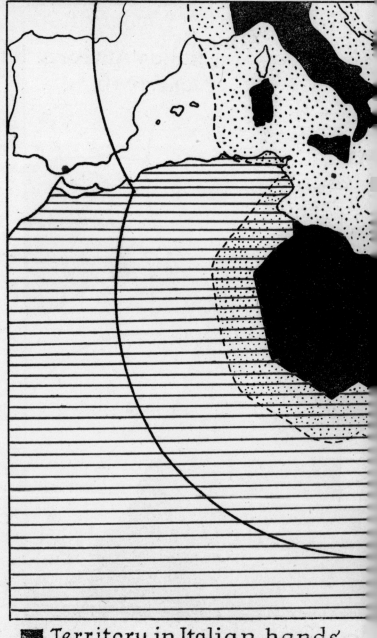

■ Territory in Italian hands
■ Territory in British hands
☰ Territory in French hands

June, 1940

O Potential Bomber Cover
⊙ Potential Fighter Cover

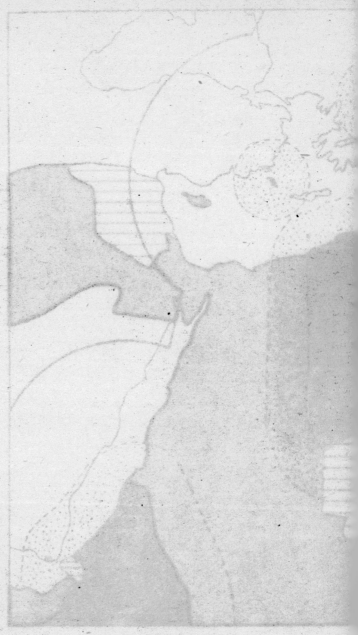

of engaging a portion of the Italian forces in the east of Libya, while their main occupation was provided by a French invasion from Tunisia, Wavell was confronted with 415,000 men opposing 55,000 under his command on all fronts. In the Western Desert he faced 215,000 Italians with a force numbering 36,000; and the odds were even less favourable in East Africa, where 19,000 Imperial troops were opposed to 200,000 Italians. The Nile valley was in grave jeopardy at either end; and it was more than doubtful whether reinforcements could be spared from home or, if any were available, whether they would arrive in Egypt. It was a sad transformation, operated by Pétain's surrender and its spiritless extension to intact French forces overseas.

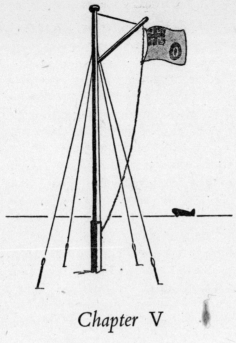

Chapter V

FIRST ROUND

I

WHEN WAR CAME TO THE WESTERN DESERT on June 10, 1940, it came as a complete surprise to those who brought it there. The R.A.F. had just moved up in the form of Air Commodore Collishaw's No. 202 Group, with headquarters at Maaten Bagush a few miles short of Mersa Matruh; and a lean Australian Squadron Leader was listening to the wireless somewhere in the unpleasant solitudes of Daba. He had walked straight out of Lawrence's *Seven Pillars*, since "his hard face, arched eyebrows, and predatory nose set off the peculiarly Australian air of reckless willingness and capacity to do something very soon"; and, in due course, he did it. But at the moment he was listening to the wireless; and the programme of their choice came (by a triumph of Axis propaganda) from Rome, because they liked the dance music. Presently the music stopped, and an exceptionally loud voice began to say something. It demanded the attention of all combatants by land, sea, and air, the blackshirts of the Revolution and the Legions, and the men and women of Italy and the Empire, to say nothing of the Kingdom of

Albania; and it could be heard so far away as Daba. But as it spoke Italian, they could not quite make out what it was saying until the Intelligence officer interpreted. The voice in Rome said something about the hour of destiny which, it seemed, was sounding in the sky. Then it grew more definite, announcing that war had been declared on Great Britain and France, whom it characterised with considerable emphasis, if some confusion of thought, as "*democrazie plutocratiche e reazionarie.*" The remainder of its utterance dealt in sweeping terms with recent history, the sanctity of treaties, the speaker's conscience, and the suffocation of his fellow-countrymen in a sea which he proceeded to describe as theirs. "*Nostro mare,*" said the distant voice. This was a shade obscure for listeners at Daba; and his subsequent appeal to prolific, youthful peoples against others, who (it appeared) were without issue and stood on the verge of their decline, was perhaps above their heads. A word of honest reassurance addressed to Greece and Jugoslavia was no concern of theirs. But the speaker's drift was tolerably clear, when he alluded with emotion to his King and to his German ally. Large numbers of Italians could be heard in simultaneous assent; and as the cheers died away in Rome, there was plainly something to be done by the little audience at Daba. Presently a telephone rang at headquarters, and an Australian voice was enquiring if prompt action was in order. The bombers loaded up; and it was not long before the Italian front areas discovered that they were in the war. Their own command had unaccountably omitted to notify them of this grave event; the most elementary precautions had been overlooked, as their aircraft and petrol were not yet dispersed in anticipation of unfriendly visitors; and, less attentive to Rome radio, they received their first intimation of a great moment in Italian history from the R.A.F. Such are the vicissitudes of impulsive, if prolific, nations launched into war against their warier elders.

The Italian opportunity in July and August, 1940, was immense. Their air power had already closed the Mediterranean and was in a position to close the Red Sea. With Egypt thus completely isolated from all sea-borne reinforcements and supplies it should be a simple matter to secure control of the Nile valley, which they threatened at both ends with vastly superior air and ground forces. All Egypt lay within bombing range of Italian aerodromes. But as the summer weeks slipped by, the opportunity was missed. A few bombs fell on Alexandria, Omdurman, and even Haifa; but no air offensive developed on a serious scale. The sky over Egypt and the Sudan was relatively untroubled by Italian aircraft; and there was no effective threat from bombers overhead to transports bringing Indian brigades up the Red Sea to Port Sudan or Australians and New Zealanders to Suez. A slender British fighter force operating from Aden and Perim, supplemented by patrols from Port Sudan, sufficed to keep the sea route open; the Italians made no attempt to use torpedo aircraft against the vulnerable convoys; and in five anxious months there were only two cases of damage to British ships by air attack in the Red Sea.

Italian strategy preferred the slower method of overland invasion by way of the Western Desert; and as Graziani's forces concentrated in the west with extreme deliberation, British patrols fenced adroitly on the long frontier, where Italian posts waited uneasily in the shade of lonely blockhouses behind the wire from Capuzzo to Maddalena, and in the air Collishaw's diminutive command operated with increasing freedom and effect against odds that were mathematically absurd. Their commander's cheerful buccaneering methods were attuned to an epoch in which bold attack was the sole alternative to extinction and surprise was the only method of attack. For it was growing plain, as "Collie's war" developed, that numbers were not the only test in air warfare. "We'll fox 'em" had become the watchword; and operations were conducted on the simple lines of "Hit 'em hard, then hit 'em again. But do not let 'em know where you're going to hit." At this stage of the Desert war the R.A.F. could scarcely hope to do more than to produce an illusion of air superiority by appearing in unexpected strength at unexpected places. Italian pilots in immensely greater numbers might be expected to display their dash and the combat experience which many of them had brought from Spain, if they were permitted to gain ascendancy for a few days; and this possibility was averted by the *guerre de course*, which Collishaw waged over Libya that summer on the Nelsonian principle that "our first defence is close to the enemy's ports."

For air operations, unlike battles on land and sea, are a continuous affair. They go on, like the weather, all the time without the splendid ornament of battle-names. Their battle-honours are measured by months rather than by the breathless hours and minutes which write the names of victories into history; and as the summer passed, the R.A.F. won the first battle. Grave risks were justified by success, as they looked down at the ravine of Bardia and the white houses of Tobruk. Returning pilots were greeted by a cheerful voice at the telephone, conveying their commander's thanks in the welcoming accents of British Columbia. Collishaw's command was small enough for such personal attentions in the days when night bombing was done by antique Bombays designed for other ends and Gladiators were their only fighters. Towards the end of August a single eight-gun Hurricane arrived. Longmore's policy here and on other portions of his front was to use these precious rarities for attacks on the Italian back areas and thus draw off their most effective fighters for defensive duties; and this portent, which Collishaw termed his "battleship," was operated with consummate showmanship. Working several times a day from different landing grounds and supported by profuse references in the Egyptian press to its alarming powers, it formed a great addition to his spirited illusion act.

There were neither the resources nor the scope for a planned air campaign. Like Nelson in 1796, he might have written that "a sea-officer cannot, like a land-officer, form plans; his object is to embrace the happy moment which now and then offers." The happy moment yielded frequently that summer to his instinctive wooing. He knew the ground; for Collishaw had been some years in the Middle East and had enjoyed Balbo's hospitality in the Italian bases which he was now busy bombing. His methods tended to be individual, and the present scale of operations was well within their scope. For the Italians were kept in a constant state of apprehension by continuous attacks upon their bases and patrols; and the foundations of the eventual breakdown of their fighter force in Cyrenaica were laid in those adventurous months, when the unexpected kept happening to the Italians and their greater strength was wearied in innumerable defensive patrols. Their morale was not improved a few days after the war entered its new stage by a misadventure at El Adem, when the anti-aircraft defences of Tobruk scored one of their rare triumphs by killing their own Governor-General. Marshal Balbo had been travelling by air; and British fighters, to whom Italy at first attributed his end, were not to blame. Lovers of sensation with less experience of Italian gunnery preferred to think that Mussolini, who had already relegated a popular competitor to the relative obscurity of Libya, had now completed his effacement; but accident was a far likelier explanation.

86

The game of harassing the slow Italian advance went on (with continuous attention to a floating crane in Tobruk harbour). One August day 15 Italian aircraft were shot down for the loss of 2. This was encouraging. But the military situation on the ground was less favourable, as Wavell fell back from the frontier in September to hold a half-way house to the Nile valley at Mersa Matruh. British aircraft were fully occupied at other points of the immense command; and Collishaw deluded Italian observers with dummies on his landing grounds. But there were still enough real aircraft left to embarrass Graziani's stately progress into Egypt at the rate of eighteen miles a day towards a few square buildings backed by the blue sea and named Sidi Barrani. By the middle of September the invaders were a good fifty miles inside Egypt, which a bold offensive might conceivably have overrun a few weeks earlier. For the great opportunity was passing; and, as Wavell wrote afterwards, "that the Italians failed to take advantage of their opportunities was due firstly to our Air Force, who in spite of inferior numbers everywhere took and kept the initiative."

2

The problem was still grave. At home the *Luftwaffe* descended upon southern England in the series of air engagements known collectively as the Battle of Britain and designed to form the prelude of invasion. This operation followed the familiar pattern with variations adapted for use against an island. The first requisite of successful operations against England by sea or air was the destruction of the British fighter force. As war had already been declared, it was hardly possible to surprise and destroy them on the ground in time of peace by the simple method, which had been used with such excellent results against Poland, Norway, and the Low Countries and was subsequently followed at Pearl Harbour. (There is no need to search Douhet's writings for the explanation, as the Japanese had done precisely the same thing to the Russians at Port Arthur in 1904.) It remained to draw them by attacking vital targets on the ground and then overwhelm them in the air by greater numbers, as they came up to fight. If all went well, the British fighters would be eliminated; and the way would then be clear for German bombers to treat London as they had already treated Warsaw and Rotterdam. After that a sea-borne invasion need not present any undue difficulty, as German air superiority based on France and Belgium would be in a position to command the narrow seas and to hold off British naval forces whilst a landing was effected. The rest, if the campaign of France was any guide, would be a triumphal progress. It was a captivating pro-gramme; and in August the *Luftwaffe* faced its first major operation in the air, the main attack being entrusted to Kesselring's *Luftflotte* 2.

It failed completely. Attacks on British shipping, ports, and aerodromes brought up the British fighters; but the defenders were not overwhelmed by the aerial offensive. Indeed, as combats developed in the English sky that autumn from Essex to the Isle of Wight, they began to wear it down; and it was plain that the defence was mani-pulated with greater skill and better weapons. German losses mounted cruelly; and in the first four weeks the *Luftwaffe* expended at least 562 aircraft for the destruction of 219 British fighters. The Italians, moved by a knightly ardour to be in at the death, asked for the privi-lege of bombing English targets; and when their wish was granted, they made a brief, unsatisfactory appearance, in which they were shot down in helpless droves and a derisive public was entertained by the discovery that a large cheese and some Chianti formed part of their equipment. There was evidently something wrong with Douhet's notion that defensive operations were impracticable in the air; and British fighter pilots showed no tendency to deteriorate under continuous attack. French experience at Verdun had shown that this might happen when defensive strategy confined itself to defensive tactics. Fighters relegated to the passivity of routine patrols above the ground held by their own troops had failed conspicuously in 1916. But this method did not satisfy the British, who preferred to ensure security by Trenchard's system of a brisk offensive against hostile aircraft over their own territory. For attack was the best defence; and offensive patrols were the tactical expression of defensive strategy. This became the method with which Fighter Command ensured the defence of Britain against aerial attack. It was no innovation, since Nelson had prescribed a similar system of defence against invasion a century before: "The moment they touch our coast, be it where it may, they are to be attacked by every man afloat and on shore. Never fear the event." There was little risk that such a system would en-gender a defensive mood; and Britain's fighter pilots echoed the true Nelsonian exhilaration which had cried, as the Danish round-shot sang over H.M.S. *Elephant* at Copenhagen, "It is warm work, and

Air Chief Marshal
SIR ARTHUR LONGMORE, G.C.B., D.S.O.
From a drawing by Sir William Rothenstein

this day may be the last to any of us at a moment; but, mark you, I would not be elsewhere for thousands."

The defence was steady, though British planning had scarcely bargained for the defence of England against a hostile air force with the landing grounds of France and Belgium at its disposal; and as the Germans turned the weight of their attack on London, it grew steadier. For the British fighter force refused to be eliminated; and in one September day it cost the Germans 185 aircraft to destroy 25 of their opponents. This adverse balance, which debited them with the loss of at least 2375 aircraft in the daylight fighting of three months, was too severe to last; and the *Luftwaffe* declined upon a nocturnal siege of London. As the successive stages of the offensive followed one another with mechanical precision, none of them was driven home; and the aerial prelude of invasion had been definitely checked.

It was plain that an air force designed primarily for close support in land operations was hardly fitted for winning a purely air victory. Its formidable bombers were unsuitable, its menacing fighters were inadequate; and its large fleet of transport aircraft could serve no useful purpose. It is conceivable that a less thorough preparation for winning battles on the Continent might have equipped the *Luftwaffe* more adequately to meet the R.A.F. over England. But that was hardly to be expected of a force created, in Kesselring's definition, "to become a part of the *Wehrmacht* . . . to think within the *Wehrmacht* framework and to take unconditionally its place in the struggle of the *Wehrmacht*."

That autumn England felt profound relief; but the war situation in the Mediterranean was anything but reassuring. It had already been considered in the anxious summer weeks before the German threat developed. Egypt had been isolated by the French surrender; and within a month the Chiefs of Staff at home were dealing with the awkward problem of reinforcements for the Middle East. "It was not an easy thing," as Mr. Churchill told the House of Commons later, "in July and August—if we cast our minds back to that date—to send precious tanks of the best quality, and cannon, of which we were then so short, on that long journey around the Cape of Good Hope, in order to enable us at first to defend ourselves, and later to assume the offensive." But Mr. Churchill was not averse from taking risks—"You will not have any means of abridging this war, or indeed, of emerging from it safely, unless risks are run"—though other minds, more fitted to the cautious speculations of commerce, resisted the temerity of these withdrawals of material from home defence in favour of a distant theatre of war. One August day during a brief lull in the air war over Britain (50 German aircraft were shot down, as it resumed on the next day) Wavell was directed to destroy the Italians in the Desert with a view to the defence of Egypt. He might even, it was felt, contemplate a raid as far afield as Sollum; and his enterprise was stimulated by the promise of an armoured division, which might be expected in October. For it had been decided to reinforce the Middle East; and with the German army twenty miles from Dover it was a bold decision. Official horizons were broadening, as there were actually indications that Malta (where the unequal battle in the sky was still sustained) might be found useful one day as an air base for operations against Italy. But it was still summer; and a great deal could happen in Africa before autumn came with its promise of reinforcements.

For the moment they must do their best with what they had. In the air, Longmore's problem was to juggle the small resources of the Middle East Command between the Western Desert, East Africa, the Red Sea, and the Sudan in such a way that the Italians might not secure those advantages to which their vast numerical superiority entitled them. In the Desert the test was still to come. But there was a great deal to be said for an early liquidation of Italian East Africa, which would finally remove the threat to Egypt from the rear and eliminate the dangers to which British navigation through the Red Sea was exposed so long as Eritrea was in Italian hands. It was tempting to suppose that their strength in this region, though vastly superior, could not be still further increased by reinforcement from outside. But it soon became evident that they were flying long-range bombers from landing grounds in the extreme south of Libya across the intervening territory of the Sudan; the presence of a Japanese freighter unloading petrol at Kismayu was disturbing; and Italian ingenuity was equal to flying dismantled fighters inside large transport aircraft non-stop from Benghazi to Asmara. These were termed "marsupials" by their delighted owners, whose acquaintance with the other (and less helpful) *fauna* of Australia was yet to come.

The Italians were palpably in a position to confront their weaker adversary with a powerful offensive; and though their threat to British shipping was ineffective and they had no luck with their attacks on Aden, they soon moved into the Sudan. Diminutive British forces gave a spirited impersonation of defending armies of uncertain strength with aircraft to match. But early in July Kassala was captured from two Sudanese motor machine-gun companies by an impressive force consisting of 8000 troops with 18 tanks and strong air cover; and a large Italian garrison was cautiously installed in the shadow of the queer, bald mountains that loom (in Doughty's phrase) "like dry bones through the thin air," where the last shelf of the Red Sea hills sinks into the brown distances of the Sudan. At the same time this process was repeated further south and nearer to their own frontier at Gallabat; and two Italian forces stood on Sudanese territory, where they were enthusiastically bombed by a few British aircraft. A cautious enterprise of the same order took Italian forces on the southern edge of Abyssinia a few miles into northern Kenya beyond Moyale.

But their major effort in East Africa that summer was the invasion of British Somaliland. This unappetising territory controlled 500 miles of coast commanding the approaches to the Red Sea; and in British hands it was a standing menace to Italian security in southern Abyssinia and to the only railway running from the sea to Addis Ababa. In 1939 its garrison consisted of a local Camel Corps (including two pony troops) and a rifle company from Nyasaland; and as its frontier marched for 750 miles with Abyssinia, authority was moved to approve additional expenditure of £900 on the construction of concrete machine-gun posts at awkward places in the hills. But its defence was not expected to depend on its own efforts, since British Somaliland adjoined Jibuti, where the French maintained some aerodromes and a considerable garrison. The defence of French and British Somaliland had naturally been viewed as a joint affair, which was manifestly hamstrung by the defection of the French. Some British reinforcements had arrived; but it was hardly reasonable to expect that the little miscellany of local troops, Punjabis, King's African Rifles, and Black Watch would hold out for very long against an Italian force numbering 25,000 men. So far as air operations were concerned, the disappearance of the French was a grave factor, since the Jibuti aerodromes could no longer be used and the defenders now relied entirely upon the little force at Aden. This was already fully occupied with the protection of Red Sea shipping and the defence of its own base, to say nothing of a long-distance raid on Addis Ababa; and when the landing grounds in British Somaliland rapidly became untenable, aircraft operating across 200 miles of sea could hardly intervene effectively in ground operations. The invaders were thus able to secure the benefits of local air superiority. But when the gallant rearguard action drew to its inevitable close, the evacuation of Berbera was safely screened from hostile interference from the air.

As the autumn came, a tide of Empire forces flooded slowly into East Africa. Indian brigades were moving into the Sudan, while West Africans and Union troops appeared in Kenya to dissipate the anxious mood in which an evacuation of women and children from Nairobi had been contemplated. In the air there was so much to be done and so few aircraft with which to do it. But Italian bases on the Red Sea coast were sedulously bombed by obsolescent aircraft that faced abominable weather over jagged mountain ranges; the Patriots in Gojjam, preparing the way for their Emperor's return, were heartened by the sound of British bombs on Italian camps in Abyssinia; and when the army made an effort to recover Gallabat, there was a gallant effort to support the operation from the air. Proceedings were prolonged by tank breakdowns. British air losses against considerable odds proved too severe, and it was quite impossible to maintain command of the air over Gallabat. Italian fighter pilots, who had learnt their business in the Spanish civil war, displayed a high degree of skill and enterprise in air fighting; and their British adversaries were outclassed by higher speed and larger numbers. This inequality was immediately reflected on the ground, where Italian bombing was now uncontrolled; and the temporary failure of air power, by which success was denied to the ground forces, was a melancholy parable of the whole problem of modern war.

3

Six months had passed since the Italians brought war to Africa. It was December now; and they had penetrated hostile territory in Egypt, the Sudan, and Kenya. They were in occupation of British Somaliland, and their attack on Malta was developing at its own pace. But now the island was not quite undefended in the air. Three Gladiators had shown what could be done; and the utility of Malta for satisfying British curiosity as to Italian ports and aerodromes and the movements of Italian shipping by flying-boats on reconnaissance, justified an increase in its fighter cover. Longmore spared them a few Hurricanes from Egypt. Further air reinforcements were flown in from carriers or shipped by convoy; and by the end of the year a full squadron of Hurricanes was rendering attacks on Malta less rewarding. Indeed, the island had gone over to the offensive; and its night bombers were already troubling Brindisi and Bari, until they transferred their operations to Italian shipping at Naples and Taranto. It was plain that, if it could be defended, Malta formed an advanced position of high value to British strategy in the Middle East. Nelson had stated it for the enlightenment of an earlier age: "I consider Malta as a most important outwork to India, that it will ever give us a great influence in the Levant, and indeed all the southern parts of Italy. In this view, I hope we shall never give it up." The broad and simple precepts of naval strategy were largely applicable in air warfare; and now the old reluctance to defend the island was vanishing in a new sense of its utility.

But British strategy in the last half of 1940 was still on the defensive. Assailed in overwhelming strength at home and in Africa, it was hardly practicable for British forces to contemplate offensives of their own. Until the Middle East was reinforced, withdrawals in face of greater numbers were inevitable. Somaliland could not be held; the frontiers of the Sudan and Kenya could not be maintained; and in Egypt Wavell had withdrawn nearly half-way to Alexandria. Heavy blows could still be struck at the Italians, when the Fleet Air Arm swooped on Taranto through the dark of a November night and left two battleships ashore and one leaking large quantities of oil at a most uncomfortable angle. But the incapacitation, permanent or temporary, of Italian battleships still left the fundamental problem largely unaffected, since the game of war was played with other counters now. For the hard facts of geography still contracted the Mediterranean between Sicily and Africa into a narrow channel, where hostile aircraft had it in their power to impede the passage of British shipping; and though the Royal Navy ruled beyond dispute the waves on which it rode, the sea route to Egypt was still round the Cape.

Whilst Wavell waited for his reinforcements and Graziani paused in his advance on Egypt, Italian enterprise had started a new war in Europe. For one October night an ultimatum in the German manner was launched at the Greeks, and their territory was invaded without excuse by strong Italian forces based in Albania. The British Government's guarantee called for some action in defence of Greece; and a fighter squadron was immediately withdrawn by Longmore on his own responsibility from the defence of Alexandria and flown to the new scene of operations. His bold initiative confirmed, this was shortly followed by a second fighter squadron and two bomber squadrons; and these withdrawals made grave inroads on British air power in the Western Desert, already heavily outnumbered by the Italians. The new commitment shadowed Wavell's forthcoming operations by diverting troops to Crete from Egypt; and, with one war on his hands already, he now had every prospect of a second.

These diversions delayed a forward move in Egypt. But Graziani was still passive; and as the weeks passed, air reinforcements reached Egypt by the stepping-stone of Malta and the long passage across Africa from the Atlantic coast to the Nile valley. R.A.F., Middle East Command, with its commitments in the Western Desert, Greece, Malta, the Sudan, East Africa, and the Red Sea (to say nothing of the trans-continental Reinforcement Route), was an exacting charge; and Longmore had already applied for a second in command to leave him free for visiting its many fronts. The first appointment was Air Vice-Marshal Boyd. But when his journey from home was interrupted by a forced landing in Sicily, a mishap entailing his captivity, the Air Staff was forced to guess again. This time the lot fell on Air Vice-Marshal Tedder, who was serving at the time as Director-General of Research and Development in the Ministry of Aircraft Production. More fortunate than Boyd, the new Deputy A.O.C.-in-C., Middle East, managed to reach Cairo. That morning Wavell met the correspondents at Headquarters, informing them that at dawn the forces had begun to carry out an engagement against Italian arms in the Western Desert. It was December 9, and the Army of the Nile could move.

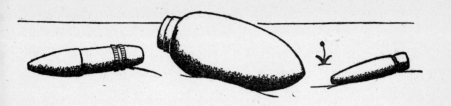

Chapter VI

THE DESERT: ADVANCE

S IX MONTHS TO A DAY after the Italian declaration of war the
blow fell on Graziani. That cautious warrior was on the verge
of an advance along the dusty road to Alexandria when Wavell struck.
There was some temerity in launching his command against 85,000
Italians with 250 tanks and 900 guns; but if Egypt was to be held,
their gradual advance on the Nile valley must be checked. In the air
the same disparity persisted, since the R.A.F. in the Western Desert
was ranged against 250 bombers and 250 fighters with liberty to add
almost indefinitely to their numbers by reinforcement from their
home bases in Italy. Alexandria and the Canal had been stripped of
their defending squadrons; and further reinforcements came from the
Sudan and Aden. This sleight of hand would, it was hoped, enable
them to meet their liabilities in the forthcoming operation. But a
British fighter force of 65 aircraft seemed hardly adequate to deal
with nearly four times their number, even if 35 of them were
Hurricanes.

The first limited design was for an attack on Sidi Barrani and an
advance of 20 miles along the coast to Buq Buq; and the preliminary
contribution of the R.A.F. was heavy bombing of Italian air bases
as far back as Tripoli nearly 1000 miles away. Working from Malta,
which lay in rear of the Italians, and from advanced Desert landing
grounds, they bombed Castel Benito and the Benghazi aerodromes
at Berka and Benina. The destructive force of these long-range
attacks cut deep into the roots of Italian air power in Cyrenaica and
Egypt. Then the range shortened; and night bombers transferred
the weight of the attack to forward aerodromes, where they left large
numbers of Italian aircraft unserviceable and immobilised. The odds
against the R.A.F. were shortened by these operations; and the ground

offensive was ready to begin. On the night before it started, when Wavell's tanks were moving into place, Italian observation was distracted by decoy aircraft in the wrong places and by heavy bomb attacks on their positions, while the Navy shelled shore targets lit by flares dropped from the air.

At dawn on December 9 the offensive opened with a swift advance across the uplands with their oddly Northern look, which form the Sidi Barrani *hinterland*. British bombing was nicely timed to precede attack by infantry and tanks; and though the front was barely 30 miles in length, Italian fighters afforded small protection to their troops. Their fighter force, in spite of its immense numerical superiority, made little headway; and Collishaw's command maintained complete ascendancy. For the long months in which Goliath had been challenged with success by David were bearing fruit. The *Regia Aeronautica* in Egypt had lost its dash. The first week's operations cost them 74 aircraft; and replacements were not easy after the long-range attacks on their rear aerodromes, since a high proportion of their potential reinforcements lay shattered on the ground 400 miles away. This left the R.A.F. at liberty to play its part in the offensive with effect; and Graziani's men were subjected to that combination of air power with armour on the ground, which had won the German victories in France. Their resistance, though determined at some points, was not of long duration; and his explanation to his fellow-countrymen flatteringly attributed this sudden failure to the employment by the enemy of "masses of armoured units, armoured cars, medium and heavy tanks, supported by mobile artillery, and with the effective co-operation of air forces." The latter, "evidently reinforced by new units, continually attacked our troops, back areas, our supply bases and aviation fields at Tobruk and Bardia"; and he recorded ruefully that "owing to fatal adverse atmospheric conditions—first sand-storms, then floods, caused by exceptional rains—our air force could not make all its weight felt in battle." For the rain, it seemed, did not fall on the just and the unjust alike, since plagues in Egypt had strange habits.

In a week the invaders, shedding nearly 40,000 prisoners, were out of Egypt. Their air force was disintegrating; and the British were not far behind. Buq Buq lay behind them now; and as their pursuers swept across the bald brown heath towards the frontier, where Egypt ends and Libya begins, the steep edge of a new country was ruled on the westward sky in front of them. The carved, brown edge of Libya stood up from the dismal levels like a coast, as Doughty had once seen "the coast of the Harra . . . riding high upon the plain." Graziani made an effort to bar the gateway, where the road winds steeply upwards at Sollum; and his air force made a brief return to active life. But they were on the defensive now, and there was no effective air interference with the advancing British troops. Sollum was soon disposed of, and Capuzzo was evacuated in such haste that serviceable aircraft were left on the ground. Now the last mile of Egypt had been cleared; and the Italian collapse enabled Wavell and O'Connor to improvise a further advance.

In the last days of 1940 the enemy showed signs of standing at Bardia. The little coast town, where a street of dainty green and white houses stands on the cliff and a pointed campanile overlooks the small harbour, had been dramatised with some justification as the "Bastion of Fascism." Strongly fortified against attack by land, it was a formidable obstacle. Careful reconnaissance from the air presently disclosed its weaknesses, whilst Italian aerodromes far back in Benghazi were liberally bombed. Particular attention was paid by roving fighters to the road between Bardia and Tobruk, as the fortress was isolated in preparation for a combined attack. The troops moved up across the rolling country behind Bardia; and one night in the first week of 1941 the place was bombed for hours. The bombing went on all through the next day upon a ground-bass of artillery, supplemented by the Inshore Squadron and the deeper note of the Battle Fleet. A little before dawn tanks and great-coated infantry went in to the attack, while bombers dealt with troop concentrations and an Australian fighter squadron flew low to cover the advancing troops. Two days of this rough handling were enough for Bardia, and the place surrendered with another 40,000 prisoners and a fine haul of guns and tanks that would come in useful to the Greeks. For if Britain had few munitions to spare in January, 1941 for a hard-pressed ally, there could be no objection to transferring surplus Italian war material to the new front in Europe.

The contribution of the R.A.F. to the fall of Bardia had been considerable, and the enemy's effort to intervene in the air cost him 17 aircraft. When the ground attack was safely launched, the weight of British bombing was transferred to more distant targets in Libya, where the *Regia Aeronautica* had still to be pinned down and finally destroyed. But this was not so simple with the distance lengthening between their bases and the advancing army. For the R.A.F. had been based 150 miles away in the Western Desert; and as the war moved forward into Libya, they faced an awkward problem. Air warfare on a stationary Western Front in 1914-18 had been relatively free from such complications; and its recent counterpart at home, conducted from fixed bases in Britain, was not troublesome in this respect. But the war in Africa was now developing another pattern. Mobility is the essence of modern warfare, and desert war demands a double dose of mobility. In one sense, the march of science has tended to reduce mobility in war, since mounted men could ride wherever there was solid ground and sailing-ships could run before any breeze. But modern fleets and mechanised divisions are dependent on vast stores of fuel patiently accumulated at fixed points; and air forces are no more than idle masses of machinery in the absence of air bases and supplies. If they were to play their part in Africa, they must acquire a new mobility. The R.A.F., in fine, must learn to be nomadic.

As they grappled with this problem in the first weeks of 1941, a new factor intervened. For the *Luftwaffe* had come to the Mediterranean. The Navy was the first to feel the weight of a new adversary. Hitherto protected convoys had passed through to Malta and Alexandria with no more opposition than was provided by Italian ships and aircraft. But one January morning, as the fleet was covering a convoy westward bound through the Sicilian Channel, an attack was made by German bombers based on Sicily. H.M.S. *Illustrious* reached Malta badly damaged and on fire; and on the next day H.M.S. *Southampton* and *Gloucester* were both bombed with serious results. The convoy reached its destination; but the loss of one cruiser and the incapacitation of an aircraft carrier, a cruiser, and a destroyer was a high price to pay. It was plain that shore-based aircraft, whose command of narrow waters had already influenced events in Norway, could be as troublesome in the Sicilian Channel as in the Skaggerrak; and after the crippled aircraft carrier had limped into Valletta, the immobile target in the Grand Harbour was savagely attacked again by German aircraft. Now Malta learned to know a fresh intensity of air attack; and though its squadrons struck back with effect, a deeper shadow lay across the Mediterranean.

For the moment the German contribution to air warfare in this new theatre seemed to be confined to an attack on British sea communications. A detachment of the *Luftwaffe* was stationed just outside Benghazi at Benina, 200 miles behind the land fighting ; and presently its influence became unpleasantly apparent in an outbreak of mine-laying in the port of Sollum. This effectively denied the harbour to its present owners, who were forced to disembark R.A.F. stores 120 miles further back along the coast at Mersa Matruh and to delay their arrival at their destination by transporting them along a most in-different Desert road. Increased mobility was not assisted by these vicissitudes ; but the advance went on.

The next objective was Tobruk, where a large Italian garrison manned strong defences in the featureless country that lies behind the port. Once more aerial photography explored the army's target ; and the army played a vital part in air warfare by the progressive occupation of Italian aerodromes. For as it covered the brown distances, their forward landing grounds passed into its control ; and the *Regia Aeronautica* was reduced to operating from Gazala and points further west, while Gambut and El Adem were open to the R.A.F. in their advance. Group headquarters had now moved forward to the Egyptian barracks on the headland at Sollum, which had an admirable view and a less admirable exposure to stray Italian bombing ; and their forward units were soon working from Desert runways under the wide skies and biting wind of Gambut. El Adem, which had been the airport of Tobruk and the main Italian air base and repair depot in Cyrenaica, was in British hands ; and exploration of its shattered premises and dusty environs disclosed no less than 40 damaged aircraft. It was plain that R.A.F. attacks had been destructive and that Italian engineering was hardly equal to the exigencies of repair on active service. Indeed, a high proportion of their aircraft casualties should have been reparable, if facilities had been provided ; and there was evidence that the architects of Italian air power had overlooked these details. For engines without air filters, which sang gaily over the grassy aerodromes of Italy, were sadly out of place in the dust-storms of Libya ; a faulty sparking plug impaired one type of bomber ; petrol of low octane value was freely used with bad effects ; and in the absence of spare parts a temporary casualty tended to become per-manently unserviceable.

These defects and the loss of aerodromes adjacent to the fighting gradually eliminated the Italian air force, whilst its strength was dissipated by the constant calls of anxious army commanders for fighter patrols in the sky immediately overhead. Norway had revealed that a campaign could be decided by the control of landing grounds; and now it was beginning to emerge still more plainly that modern warfare might take the form of a war for aerodromes. For Tobruk was scarcely tenable without air cover; and as Wavell's forces edged beyond it to the west, depriving the Italians of every landing ground for the next 80 miles, the fortress waited for its doom.

Once more the familiar process was repeated. While Tobruk was heavily bombarded from sea and air in the last week of January, long-range air action kept the enemy at arm's length in the sky; and the attack proceeded smoothly without interference from above. Aircraft in close support co-operated actively in the assault; and in the almost complete absence of any adversaries (there was only one air engagement on the first day of the attack) British bombers were enabled to play the part of mobile artillery, since the pace of the Australian advance had outrun their heavy guns. The place succumbed on the third day, a melancholy spectacle of broken buildings staring out across the harbour, where the smoking wreck of an Italian cruiser showed what could be done by bombing and the floating crane had ceased to float.

Another herd of prisoners was added to their mounting score; and O'Connor drove deeper into Libya. His further progress was now gravely threatened from behind, where a British offer of troops and armoured forces to the Greeks seemed likely to halt his advance at the point which he had reached. But for the moment Greece was satisfied to face the Italians with her own meagre forces and such aid as could be rendered by the R.A.F.; and Wavell was free to rout them, if he could, in Africa. There were other calls on his command in that continent, where two full-scale offensives were now in progress against Italian East Africa. But there might be time to drive them out of Cyrenaica before worse befell in Europe.

Speed was the essence of his operations; and as the army thrust along the coast to Derna and drove into the Desert further south along the track towards Mechili, the R.A.F. kept pace with the advance. This was not easy so long as German mine-laying from the air rendered the use of any port west of Mersa Matruh highly precarious. Besides, there was an irritating tendency inherent in the bulk and nature of the cargo to load R.A.F. bombs and petrol in the least accessible parts of ships; and it was found almost quicker to transport them overland from the Western Desert. But such deficiencies were

German Air Force Range
February, 1941.

German Air Force Range,

■ Territory in Axis hands

■ Territory in Allied hands

February, 1941

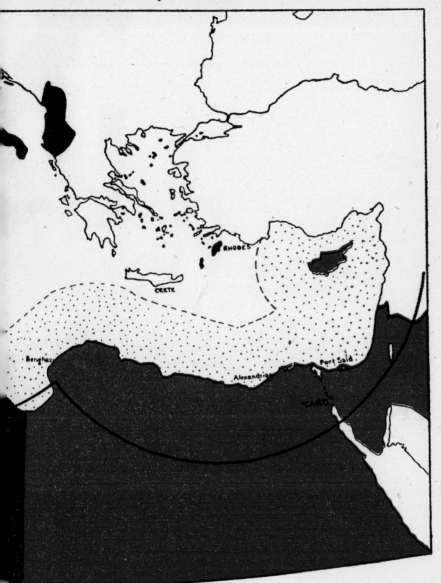

O German Bomber Cover

◉ German Fighter Cover

⦿ R.A.F. Fighter Cover

richly compensated by a haul of priceless stores found on the Italian airfields east of Derna; and these treasures were promptly appropriated to R.A.F. use.

With the whole Desert plateau between Derna and the steep edge of Sollum in their hands, the war for aerodromes was going nicely. Gambut and El Adem were behind them now; they commanded Gazala, Tmimi, and Martuba; and if Derna fell, Italian aircraft would have nowhere to work from nearer than the airfields outside Benghazi. This meant that Alexandria and the Egyptian bases in the Delta were now safely out of bombing range. Besides, the winter rains were likely to affect the Benghazi aerodromes at Berka and Benina, where a richer soil was apt to hold the moisture and might lead to flooding. If so, an adversary advancing from the east and working from the hard, brown runways of Desert landing grounds would plainly be at an advantage, since the defenders of Benghazi would be unable to provide air cover.

Derna fell before a swift attack seven days after Tobruk. Preliminary bombing was hardly requisite, as the place had been a target for some time. Whilst O'Connor's right followed the coastline into the green hill country of the Jebel Akdar, where Italian colonists in uniform white homesteads had farmed a sort of Dartmoor and the grey coast range looks out to sea across the pillared ruins of Cyrene, his left drove due west across the Desert by a brilliant expedient designed to reach the road beyond Benghazi before the retreating Italians could get there. For there was evidence that they were contemplating a withdrawal further to the west; and if Benghazi could be occupied, Egypt would be definitely placed beyond the reach of air attack and Tripoli, the last Italian port in Africa, would be exposed to British bombing. The R.A.F. advance was hardly simplified by the difficulty of stocking forward landing grounds with petrol and supplies; and as they had not yet learnt to be nomadic, transport difficulties were aggravated by the rather ponderous standard of organisation and a shortage of transport aircraft. Besides, long flying hours in severe conditions were telling on their aircraft now. But as the long chain of Italian aerodromes passed by, captured petrol filled some of their deficiencies; and the shattered skeletons of Italian aircraft were consoling evidence of the destruction of their adversary.

The advance went on through the first week of February; and the left hook of the British armour caught the enemy 60 miles beyond

Benghazi at Beda Fomm. The deadly trap owed something to air reconnaissance; and as it closed, the last Italian army in Cyrenaica melted into an untidy carnival of wrecked vehicles and one more endless stream of prisoners trailing across the Desert into captivity. On the next day Benghazi fell to the Australians. The Desert was behind them now; and they had come at last to the green grass and the red earth and the white houses. The blue water of the harbour danced in the winter sunshine; there were trees and arcades in the little streets; and the two cathedral domes looked down on the waterfront. The R.A.F. surveyed the captured airfield at Benina, where they found 87 damaged aircraft near the dainty buildings, which had been the pride of the Italian air force, and dozens more a few miles further on at Berka. The destruction of the *Regia Aeronautica* had been complete. For the full tale of their casualties counted on the long road across Cyrenaica amounted to 1100 wrecks; and Italian military aviation never rallied from the blow.

Apart from technical defects, its vast numbers had succumbed to the pitiless offensive maintained against it from the start by Collishaw's command. A four to one superiority had been completely neutralised by the defensive attitude forced upon them by a smaller adversary. British fighters operated singly, because it was felt that their numerical inferiority would be more glaring in formation. Climbing one by one from their landing grounds, they flew out to sea, gained height, and recrossed the coast at the appointed place to rake anything in sight along the roads. These depredations kept large numbers of Italian fighters busy in a vain effort to intercept the solitary raiders; and such activities, assisted by a lack of repair facilities, progressively reduced the number of serviceable Italian fighters, distracting them at the same time from interfering with the British land forces. Their bombers were indifferent to start with; and with a high proportion of their strength kept on the ground by faulty maintenance, morale was bound to suffer. While the roads behind them lay under constant air attack and every port along the coast between Benghazi and Sollum was exposed to the same danger, their supplies failed to reach them, and a final breakdown was inevitable. Even before it came, the *Luftwaffe* was taking over their duties in attacking British ships and harbours. "*Nostre mare*" had never been conspicuously Italian; and with the *Luftwaffe* established in the Mediterranean it was less so than ever. Presently their German allies began to assume part of their responsibility for air warfare over Africa; and as the R.A.F. was counting its last trophies in the battered hangars of Benina, a more formidable adversary replaced their beaten foe.

More than a hundred miles away the army halted on the last dusty mile of Cyrenaica. February was passing now; and with the growing menace of events in Greece there could be no advance on Tripoli that spring. Besides, there was some doubt about the use of Benghazi as a forward base for the invasion of Tripolitania. In the urge to bring forward their supplies as rapidly as possible supply ships had been sent there before the port's air defence was established; and this light-hearted disregard of the third dimension invited (and received) a sharp and immediate lesson. For if they could take such liberties with safety in face of the Italians, the *Luftwaffe* had no intention of leaving British shipping in peaceful enjoyment of the port or the R.A.F. with un-interrupted use of the Benghazi airfields. While the last outposts stared into the brown distances beyond El Agheila, British strategy had too many distractions in 1941 to take the war further to the west. But in a campaign of nine weeks it had advanced 350 miles and cap-tured 133,295 prisoners with 1300 guns, while the R.A.F. was 800 miles from its depots in the Delta and had earned General O'Connor's tribute :

"Since the war began you have consistently attacked without intermission an enemy air force between five and ten times your strength, dealing him blow after blow, until finally he was driven out of the sky, and out of Libya, leaving hundreds of derelict air-craft on his aerodromes.

"In his recent retreat from Tobruk you gave his ground troops no rest, bombing their concentrations, and carrying out low flying attacks on their M.T. columns.

"In addition to the above you have co-operated to the full in carrying out our many requests for special bombardments, recon-naissances, and protection against enemy air action, and I would like to say how much all this has contributed to our success."

All this had been achieved by No. 202 Group in the first movement of the Desert war; and, incidentally, they had shattered the *Regia Aeronautica.*

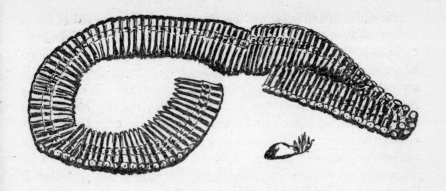

Chapter VII

EAST AFRICA

LIKE CAESAR'S GAUL, the Italian Empire was divided into three parts. Two of these lay in Africa; and the third consisted of a group of islands in the Aegean, from which an air offensive might have had embarrassing effects on British ports and shipping in the Eastern Mediterranean. But after an initial effort against Haifa and the adjacent sea routes no attempt was made by the Italians to exploit the strong position occupied by Rhodes and the Dodecanese; and this part of their possessions relapsed into military insignificance.

The remainder of their Empire was situated on two sides of the Nile valley, flanking Egypt and the Sudan, where two considerable blocks of territory had been brought under Italian rule. In the north, Libya lay along the seashore and reached far into the Desert; and south-east of the Nile valley the vast spaces of Italian East Africa formed an immense triangle based on the Sudan, of which one side looked on the Red Sea through the ports of Eritrea and the other faced the Indian Ocean along the coast of Italian Somaliland. The interior of this vast area had once formed the independent Empire of Ethiopia, now included in Italian territory by the successful aggression of 1936; and since the recent occupation of British Somaliland its coastline ran clear from sea to sea with the exception of a few apologetic Frenchmen at Jibuti. If all went well in Egypt, there were grounds for hoping that Graziani might stretch a hand across the Nile and that Roman Africa would run from Tripoli to Kismayu. Indeed, if Kenya succumbed, it might even run considerably further.

From the British point of view the presence of strong Italian forces in rear of Egypt was a standing menace. The defence of the Nile valley must be gravely prejudiced by a second front 250 miles from Khartoum; and if this source of danger was to be disposed of, it must be dealt with whilst Egypt was still firmly held. For so long as British forces were in control of the Nile valley and the Canal, it was impossible for the Italians to reinforce East Africa except by air. But as their forces in this area consisted of 200,000 men with 400 guns and 200 aircraft, their elimination was a formidable problem for a far less numerous adversary already deeply engaged in the conquest of Cyrenaica and confronted with the growing prospect of a war in Greece.

British strategy in the last weeks of 1940 was nothing if not enterprising; and it strained the limited resources of R.A.F., Middle East Command, almost to breaking-point. Whilst one contingent was busy bombing the Italians in the mountains of Albania and Collishaw's unwearied pilots were harrying them in the Western Desert, air action was called for in East Africa, where three nearly simultaneous attacks were launched in the first weeks of 1941. In the centre, where the high plateaux of Abyssinia shouldered the edge of the Sudan, a ghost walked. Haile Selassie, Emperor of Ethiopia, who had been flown by the R.A.F. from Khartoum to the border, faced towards his capital once more with a large banner and a small column of Sudanese and Abyssinian fighting men, leaving an endless trail of foundered camels and encouraged by such air support as could be spared. In the north, Platt, after flustering his temperamental adversaries with a bewildering profusion of dummy landing grounds complete with property aircraft carefully exposed for observation in the wrong places, a deception reinforced by a heavy traffic of false wireless messages, followed the last Italians out of the Sudan at Kassala and headed across the frontier into Eritrea; and 1100 miles to the south, beyond the mountains and the desert, Cunningham was gathering his forces in northern Kenya for an upward thrust into Italian Somaliland.

These operations were supported by such aircraft as were available in Kenya and the Sudan, whilst a watch was kept from Aden over vital traffic through the Red Sea in the intervals of molesting Italian bases in East Africa. Three bomber squadrons, two of which flew obsolescent, single-engined Wellesleys, one Rhodesian army co-operation squadron, and one fighter squadron from the Union of South Africa were the force now allocated to the Sudan; and their meagre fighter strength was supplemented by diverting a single flight of Gladiators from Egypt. Platt's striking force was constituted by a desperate juggle; and when the 4th Indian Division, fresh from the assault on Sidi Barrani 1000 miles away, arrived in the Sudan, the East African campaign was ready to begin. The Emperor's *hegira* was a constant call on Air Commodore Slatter's limited resources, as Patriot morale in Abyssinia was vastly heightened by the sight and sound of friendly aircraft. Large formations were preferred by eager audiences on the ground; and the transportation of emissaries, money, and supplies by air entailed a formidable series of long-distance flights across a lunar landscape, where forced landings were unthinkable.

But their most serious responsibility was Platt's advance into Eritrea. As this developed, the superiority of their few Hurricanes to anything that the Italians could fly against them was used with brilliant results. Operating at the extreme range of 150 miles from a captured aerodrome just inside Eritrea at Sabderat, they paid two visits in the chilly dawn to the main Italian air bases at Asmara and Gura, where they did extensive damage to aircraft on the ground; and when Barentu fell into British hands, its airfield was used for a repetition of the same process as far afield as Makalle. These long-range attacks by fighters were so discouraging to their opponents that the Italian air force was entirely withdrawn from Eritrea, which they only used henceforward for hasty visits to advanced landing grounds; and their withdrawal, due to the Hurricanes of No. 1 S.A.A.F. Fighter Squadron, had incalculable consequences on the whole campaign, in which air superiority passed irretrievably from the Italians. This was the more surprising, as the *Regia Aeronautica* in East Africa had been together for some time; and their experience had probably endowed them with a higher level of training and *esprit de corps* than that prevailing elsewhere in the Italian service.

Platt's skilful moves developed rapidly into a swift invasion of Italian East Africa from the north-west. The weight of his attack alternated with rare ingenuity between his two advancing columns; and in the first week of February Lorenzini was roughly shepherded out of Agordat, where Arimondi had once outfaced the Mahdists. Now they were falling back on Keren, where an impenetrable mountain barrier stood across the road to Asmara; and the British were not far behind. The pursuit from Agordat was accelerated by the R.A.F., although without those chemical embellishments by which Italian aviation had once simplified pursuit in Abyssinia. For the happy days of 1936, when Badoglio's aircraft harried the routed Abyssinians, were fading now. In that campaign the *Regia Aeronautica* had ruled the skies, indulging freely in what were euphemistically termed "multifarious forms of action from the air" in a long series of excursions rendered most enjoyable by a complete absence of air opposition. One pursuit had seen them make no less than 546 sorties, expending 30,000 rounds of small-arms ammunition and 396 tons of bombs upon a helpless adversary and returning to their bases without loss. But now there were no Italian aircraft at Asmara, Gura, or Makalle, since the Hurricanes had driven them away; and as their reinforcements raced along the road to Keren, they were riding to a battle which the Italians would have to fight without air superiority.

Half-way from Agordat to Asmara the tormented landscape, which an alarmed Italian had once compared to "a stormy sea moved by the wrath of God," rose to a *crescendo* of impassability. Shadowing a valley where the vegetation varied between spiteful thorn and tortured baobab, a line of angry mountains stormed along the sky. Rust-red at the summit and rock-grey on the naked flanks, this was the barrier which Italian strategy resolved to hold against the invaders, a Khyber Pass with a dash of the misshapen mountains behind Rio de Janeiro. From the valley floor a road edged towards it, watched by the gun positions on the heights and winding slowly upwards into the throat of the pass. The British must come that way, unless they left the road to scale the precipices confronting them. That, indeed, was precisely what they did in a desperate succession of attacks in the first half of February, Indians and Highlanders vainly assaulting the unassailable and leaving little more than their own names on the grey pinnacles of Sikh Spur and Rajputana Ridge, except where two battalions still clung to an iron ledge renamed by right of conquest Cameron Ridge. (A livelier mood impelled the British soldier to reserve the name of Happy Valley for a stricken *cul de sac* enclosed between forbidding mountains and completely exposed to Italian gunfire.)

For the moment it almost appeared that Platt's little army had been stopped by the most formidable obstacle in the whole history of mountain warfare, held by at least 23,000 men with 120 guns. Time was passing; and in March, 1941, an urgent call for British troops in Greece took precedence over any possibility of reinforcements for East Africa. If they were going to force Keren, they would have to force it with such strength as they had got; and for an anxious month they held on, while the army trained for a new effort. Their positions in the valley were completely overlooked by the Italians; but British aircraft ensured that this advantage was not exploited by the *Regia Aeronautica*. Working from airfields close behind the line, they bombed the Italians mercilessly on the mountain-tops. Back areas were conscientiously visited; and the detonation of 30,000 shells in a long goods train on the little railway behind Keren was a welcome overture to the attack.

When this was launched in the oppressive heat of a March day, the infantry made for the summits; and the R.A.F. in ancient aircraft were dropping improvised containers full of ammunition and supplies to little parties isolated in impossible positions among the precipices, while they spotted for the British guns and the bombs went down on the Italians in front of their advancing infantry with little margin for mistakes by bomb-aimers. For a week the struggle swayed along the mountain barrier, as detonations rolled round the misshapen peaks and the full heat of African springtime radiated from the naked rocks. When the Italians broke at last (the Duce, with his usual felicity, telegraphing that day to congratulate their commander on his glorious defence), the R.A.F. had earned Platt's tribute to their achievement of air superiority. "By a continuous forward policy they had driven their opponents from the air and destroyed their machines on the ground. The army was indeed grateful for the immunity from hostile air attack thus gained."

This contribution was decisive, since the assault on Keren from the valley floor could never have been launched in face of effective opposition from the air; and while the Hurricanes were in the forefront of the battle, it was made by slow-flying Lysanders, ancient Vincents, and an assorted cellar of vintage aircraft flying over heavily defended areas across a sea of jagged mountains. The pursuit up the winding road towards Asmara was joyfully helped on its way by vigorous air attacks on the retreating enemy; and presently, as Platt telegraphed to Khartoum that he was in the capital of Eritrea and that this was "*not* repeat *not* an April fool," the R.A.F. installed itself among the wooden buildings and verandahs of the Italian aerodrome at Asmara.

It was April now. Events on other fronts were moving; and the eternal juggle, of which British strategy in 1941 seemed largely to consist, withdrew one of Platt's two divisions and a proportion of Slatter's aircraft for operations elsewhere. His next objective was Massawa on the Red Sea coast, full particulars of whose defences had thoughtfully been left in an Italian office at Asmara. The residue of Italian sea power in these waters was effectively disposed of, when five destroyers were located and attacked by the Fleet Air Arm and the R.A.F. Four destroyers and a submarine were eliminated from the air, while naval gunfire accounted for the fifth; and one April day the surrender of Massawa by a discouraged admiral after an unsuccessful attempt to break his sword finally removed the threat to British navigation in the Red Sea due to the presence of Italian forces in Eritrea. For the colony had been entirely cleared, leaving 40,000 prisoners and 300 guns in British hands.

Deep in Abyssinia the Italians were concentrating for a last stand; and as they fell back, their path lay among the ghosts of old defeats. Adowa, where the pince-nez of the ill-fated Baratieri brooded in the shadows, was behind them now; and they had left Makalle, once the scene of a defence whose name stood in the tradition of Italian colonial warfare for the glory typified for other nations by Rorke's Drift or Sidi Brahim and only slightly impaired by an eventual surrender. They were heading now for Amba Alagi, which had witnessed the wreck of Toselli's column forty years before and saw more recently the strategic agony of the Abyssinian armies after Badoglio's victory at Enderta. The brittle edifice of Italian domination in East Africa was collapsing round them. Eritrea had succumbed; British forces under Air Vice-Marshal Reid from Aden returned to Berbera under cover of heavy air attacks on the Italian aerodrome at Diredawa, recovering the lost colony after an absence of eight months; and in the south a graver threat was fast developing.

More than 1000 miles from Addis Ababa, beyond the Kenya border, Cunningham's command had concentrated forces from South, East, and West Africa and Rhodesia in an area exposed to Italian air preponderance. For the *Regia Aeronautica* maintained 88 aircraft within range of the British bases. But no effective use was made of this potential menace; and it evaporated with the arrival of some Hurricanes, which were dispersed along the front and transformed the situation in the air. Apart from these, Air Commodore Sowrey's six squadrons of the S.A.A.F. flew an interesting miscellany of obsolescent British types, diversified by a few German transport aircraft from the Union converted for use as bombers. Their total strength amounted to 94 aircraft; and until they could be assured of air superiority, the land forces moved by night. Directed by a simple policy of "breaking the crust and then motoring straight on regardless of what was happening in rear," they broke the first layer on the Juba. Air interference was discouraged by fighter attacks on Italian airfields at Gobwen and Afmadu; and the destruction of 10 aircraft in the first two days of the advance put the S.A.A.F. well on the road to air superiority. Henceforward the Italians confined their operations in the air to bombing raids on moonlight nights; and Cunningham's command was able to move freely by day.

After an interval of heavy fighting on the Juba the advance into Italian Somaliland proceeded at high speed in the direction of Abyssinia, making full use of the admirable road provided by the Roman conquerors. They had started in the second week of February; and by the end of March they were 200 miles from Addis Ababa at Diredawa, where a fighter attack on the aerodrome and its satellites had accounted for 20 Italian aircraft. The capital was now within bombing range; and one day in the first week of April aircraft, some of which had come from Aden, operated from Jijigga and paid the aerodrome at Addis Ababa a devastating visit. Its fighter cover was disposed of by 2 Hurricanes, 2 Gladiators, and 2 Glenn Martins; and the destruction or damage of 32 Italian aircraft was a rewarding result. On the next day the troops marched in past cheering Ethiopian crowds to find this gratifying evidence of aerial victory distributed in tangled heaps across the aerodrome. Cunningham's astonishing campaign, conducted at a daily average of nearly 40 miles a day, had ended in eight weeks at Addis Ababa; and the contribution of the S.A.A.F. richly deserved his tribute that he "cannot speak too highly of the part played by the Air Forces in this campaign."

The sequel, while the Emperor installed himself once more in his reconquered capital, was scattered

over eleven degrees of a bare brown continent.

Northward from Addis Ababa the Italians toiled up the road to Dessie, which Badoglio's men had traversed in the opposite direction five years before in the "march of the iron will." Their will was less unbending now; but before the month was out, they opposed a stiff resistance to the South Africans in front of Dessie, where aircraft from Aden took a hand and the S.A.A.F. operated in close support, leaving the Hurricanes and heavy bombers to make long-range raids from Addis Ababa. Air combat was infrequent now; but ground targets abounded, and one Italian column in the hills was harried from the air until it abandoned its motor transport, dwindled steadily, and eventually surrendered to the long arm of air power.

Further to the north the Duke of Aosta, Viceroy of East Africa, was waiting with 20,000 men in the shadow of Amba Alagi; and after the surrender he testified to the demoralising effect of machine-gunning by Gladiators and Lysanders. For air action was conducted, in the terms of one account, by "an antiquated air force, pointed with 10 Hurricanes"; and after a vigorous attack one more campaign was closed by a surrender, with the tall Duke striding down a mountain road and the pipes of the Transvaal Scottish wailing out "The Flowers of the Forest."

The rest was a far-flung succession of mopping-up operations conducted by a dwindling force, as British troops and aircraft were drawn away to other theatres. But enough were left to deal with scattered groups in Gojjam and the distant region of the Lakes; and as the summer passed, R.A.F. aircraft were dropping ammunition and supplies to the Punjabis at Wolchefit and maintaining pressure on the last Italian stronghold at Gondar. By that time the last yard of East Africa had ceased to be Italian; the menace of 200,000 men with 200 aircraft in the rear of Egypt was completely liquidated; and of the three parts of the Italian Empire only two were left.

Chapter VIII

GREECE

EVENTS IN GREECE had shadowed British operations elsewhere since October, 1940. For at that stage of the war, with the German air attack on Britain still in progress and British forces in retreat at almost every point of the defensive circle round Egypt from the Western Desert to East Africa and the Sudan, Italian policy took its courage in both hands and went to war with Greece.

The risk was moderate, because the Greeks were not expected to resist; and the gains in territory and prestige seemed likely to outweigh the present yield of the Italian demands on France, with which the Germans showed little tendency to reward their hungry ally for his late arrival at the feast. But his calculations were impaired by that fatal ignorance of history, which is common to dictators. For the knowledge of these potentates rarely extends to any date more distant than their own ascent to power; and when Mussolini counted on a bloodless victory, he was reckoning without the Greeks.

The cheerful gallantry, which had faced greater odds at Marathon and Salamis and in the long vicissitudes of their struggle with the Turks for independence, now disturbed the programme. For the Greeks were not designed to play a passive part in history; and in 1940 they refused to fade into a deferential background, against which Italians might conduct a military promenade through Greece. They proposed to fight; and this decision put the Italians to the disagreeable necessity of undertaking an invasion of Epirus from their bases in Albania across rough country with the winter coming on. But if the

Greeks would not see reason, if the brutal logic of weight and numbers made no appeal to the clear Greek intelligence, there was nothing else for them to do; and though some professionals might hesitate, the Duce approached the problem without undue diffidence. The ground, perhaps, was hardly favourable to a swift offensive of the latest pattern favoured by the German armies in their brilliantly successful operations along the broad highways of the Low Countries and France. But Spain had not been easy; and northern Greece was not so bad as Abyssinia, from which they had emerged successfully. Weight was bound to tell; and if the Greeks insisted upon fighting, it looked as if the fighting could only end one way.

True, Great Britain had guaranteed Greek independence and integrity. But in October, 1940, with Graziani's armies half-way to Alexandria and the *Luftwaffe* attacking London, that hardly seemed to matter very much. For it was highly doubtful how far Britain would be able to support a friend in need on the continent of Europe. A Greek request for assistance in the air on the outbreak of war was met, however, by the immediate despatch of a contingent of the R.A.F. from Egypt; and while Malta turned its night bombers on to those Italian seaports in Apulia and Albania which were serving as invasion bases, Air Commodore D'Albiac's command in Greece soon amounted to two squadrons of medium bombers, supplemented by visiting detachments of heavy bombers from Egypt for work on moonlight nights, with a fighter force consisting of one Gladiator squadron and one mixed Blenheim squadron.

Their contribution could not be any larger, since it was already more than could be conveniently spared from Africa. Besides, it was as much as could be operated from such aerodromes as were available in Greece. For this factor seriously limited the scale and efficacy of air operations in the north. There was not a single all-weather aerodrome in existence on the mainland of Greece; and the possibilities of airfield construction were restricted by an unhappy combination of weather and high politics. The season was uncomfortably late; and by November it was raining hard. Sites in the Larissa plain were flooded (one British fighter squadron was grounded for ten days); and further east the relatively level ground near Salonika, which lay within striking distance of the front, was out of bounds for the depressing reason that the Germans (who had not yet gone to war with Greece) would object to British military preparations in the path of

an eventual advance across the Balkans and might react by making it.
For Greek policy at this stage was reluctant to provoke invasion by
the Germans; and these considerations limited the R.A.F. to two
airfields on the outskirts of Athens and to such landing grounds as
could be found in the hills close behind the front.

The problem was to operate their little force to the best advantage
against odds that were, in its commander's hopeful words, "only
some four or five to one against us"; and it would plainly be most
usefully employed in bombing the Italian bases on the coast. While
the Greek air force, flying an assortment of French and Polish aircraft
with immense gallantry, was in process of elimination in the sky over
the land fighting, British bombers took off from Athens in full view
of any local Germans who might care to look and flew a good 200
miles across the mountains to Valona or Durazzo, where they encountered uniformly noxious weather and strong Italian fighter
opposition with ample warning of their approach. These circumstances rendered operations somewhat costly, since raiders who arrive
just when and where they are expected are apt to pay the price.
But they were more successful than might have been feared; and the
effect upon the Greeks was heartening in the extreme. The first
R.A.F. casualty was accorded an almost royal funeral in Athens;
stranded air crews made triumphal progresses shoulder-high through
cheering villages, where Mussolini's name accompanied by homicidal
pantomime was found to be an effective substitute for eloquence;
and low-flying aircraft dropped food for the advancing Greeks or
Christmas toys for the Greek children at Corfu. The fighters were
kept busy on offensive patrol over the front or escorting bombers,
one Gladiator squadron shooting down 42 of its opponents in 55 days
for the loss of 5 aircraft. But as the year advanced, the weather in the
mountains grew more formidable, and increasing numbers of modern
fighters appeared on the Italian side. It was becoming obvious in the
last days of 1940 that there was not much more to be done until the
weather mended and more airfields were available.

Early in the new year a Greek offensive was launched against
Valona. In the air the R.A.F. was now diverted from strategic
bombing to close support of the land forces with excellent effect on
Greek morale, one anxious general imploring Air Vice-Marshal
D'Albiac to restrain his pilots from the undue risks involved in flying
low over the enemy. The bombers were fully employed; and a high

level of success in air combats was scored by their escorting fighters, which destroyed 93 Italian aircraft, with 26 more "probables," in the first three months of 1941 for the loss of 8 British fighters, of which 6 pilots were safe. They had been strengthened by the arrival of 6 Hurricanes; and this formidable reinforcement disposed of 4 opponents on its first appearance. A week later, on the last day of February, 1941, the Hurricanes with a Gladiator squadron accounted for 27 Italian aircraft without loss in full view of both armies in Albania; and this Homeric conflict earned Longmore's tribute to their brilliant work "in bad weather, over mountainous country and from waterlogged aerodromes."

But the situation was not growing any easier with the halting of the Greek offensive before it reached Valona and the imminent arrival of a British Expeditionary Force in Greece. Beyond the mountains in the north large numbers of German ground staff, wearing civilian clothes to satisfy the exigencies of Balkan neutrality, were constructing airfields in Bulgaria; and there seemed every prospect that D'Albiac's tired squadrons, which now amounted to three of medium bombers and four of fighters, would shortly have the *Luftwaffe* on their hands. Meanwhile, as the March days went by, their tasks were multiplied by the provision of air escorts for incoming convoys and air defence for disembarkation ports. Aerodrome construction was partly suspended in favour of camp building and road repairs for the arriving army; and their limited supply of transport was diverted to the immediate task of disembarkation. It would not be long before they were called upon to provide air support in Thessaly and Macedonia for operations on an Anglo-Greek front in addition to their existing commitments in Albania and Epirus, to say nothing of occasional attacks on Italian aerodromes in the Dodecanese, whose aircraft had been giving trouble by attacking shipping and mining the Suez Canal; and it was not surprising that their commander issued a plain warning that "owing to the small numbers of R.A.F. squadrons that can be made available, the lack of suitable aerodromes in this country and the fact that we will have to fight on two fronts, it will be apparent that the air support which can be provided at any rate for some time to come will be far below that considered necessary for the efficient conduct of war."

Their co-operation with the Navy was more rewarding. It had begun with the fine performances of aircraft of the Fleet Air Arm

operating with torpedoes against shipping at Durazzo and Valona
from a shore aerodrome in a fold of the Epirus mountains with olive
groves on the hillside and a family of bears in occupation of a cave in
the cliff face a little higher up. At noon on March 27 the R.A.F.
reciprocated by sighting three Italian cruisers 120 miles from the
safety of their own coast and steaming steadily away from it; at dusk
the Battle Fleet, accompanied by two flotillas of destroyers and a
cruiser squadron, slipped out of Alexandria. The hunt was on; and
Cunningham steamed westwards through the night. By the next
morning he was 400 miles away; and soon after dawn one of his
aircraft found them in the broad channel not far south of Crete. All
that morning the Italians were attacked by carrier-borne aircraft and
by the Fleet Air Arm working from a shore base in Crete; and later
in the day more aircraft were flown off from H.M.S. *Formidable* to
immobilise the Italian flagship and her companions by torpedo
attacks. Their mobility was already impaired by the R.A.F., which
had located them earlier that afternoon and sent out five waves of
bombers from Greece. They found five Italian cruisers in unpleasant
weather, scored direct hits on two of them and a destroyer, and left
one cruiser seriously damaged. This performance earned the
Admiralty's "great appreciation of the most welcome and invaluable
co-operation of the Royal Air Force with the Mediterranean Fleet,
South and West of Crete. We think the manner in which your
Squadrons found the enemy and bombed them deserves high praise,
and their success no doubt had a great effect on the Italian morale
generally." Late that night the Battle Fleet encountered this disconsolate armada, accounting for three cruisers and two destroyers in
the flaming darkness. It was a remarkable achievement of combined
naval and air operations, in which Cunningham was able to report
that "five ships of the enemy fleet were sunk, burned or destroyed as
per margin" for the loss of a single aircraft.

The Battle of Cape Matapan crippled the Italian fleet's ability to
interfere with British shipping in the Eastern Mediterranean. This
might render a vital service to the Expeditionary Force in Greece,
whose sole communications were the sea route between Alexandria
and the Greek coast; and its safe arrival at its destination without the
loss of a single man, gun, or vehicle was brilliant evidence that there
was nothing to be feared from naval action in these waters. The
victory at sea confirmed it. But that was not to say that their com-

munications could be guaranteed against a graver menace, if these ever came within range of shore-based aircraft. In that event the victory of Matapan would be a brilliant irrelevance. For the control of narrow waters had been seriously modified by the application of air power; and there was nothing to suggest that what had been proved in Norway was untrue in the Mediterranean. When the road to Greece and Crete was exposed to dangers from the air, these could only be averted by victorious air action, which depended in its turn on a sufficiency of aircraft operating from bases within range; and if those requirements could not be satisfied, a naval victory, however heartening, would not suffice to turn the scale.

Indeed, it was noticeable that a naval victory, which had driven the Italians from the sea and would in other days have transformed the situation in the Mediterranean, left it substantially unmodified. For though they had been duly driven from the sea, British shipping still preferred to travel round the Cape to Egypt. Protected convoys fought their way from east or west to Malta. But the Mediterranean remained closed to through traffic; and it was plain that something more formidable than the guns of Italian warships had closed it. While they no longer ventured out of port, an obstacle that the victorious Battle Fleet had not accounted for could still impede British navigation through the Sicilian Channel; and the unpleasant paradox was reinforced by a continuance of Axis traffic on the vital sea route between Italian ports and Tripoli. This was particularly heavy in the early months of 1941, when German aid in troops and armoured vehicles was in course of shipment to Libya. By all the rules of naval warfare a decisive victory at sea should have rendered it impracticable. But they somehow seemed to be inoperative; and though the Prime Minister was able to report that "our submarines and aircraft have taken a steady toll of the transport carrying German troops and vehicles," the victory of Matapan was not reflected in a disappearance of Axis shipping from the narrow waters between Italy and Africa.

It was April now; and the situation darkened rapidly in Greece. When the German blow was due to fall, the R.A.F. mustered a serviceable strength of some 80 aircraft out of a total force of 192 against approximately 800 German and 310 Italian machines. The situation was irreverently summarised by one participant as "all the Wops in the world and half the Jerries versus two men, a boy, and a flying hearse"; and the facts bore him out. For 450 German fighters were opposed by less than one-fifth of their numbers, of which only two squadrons flew modern aircraft; and the disparity in bombers, which was merely four to one, hardly redressed the balance. Besides, the enemy was in a position to renew his strength from home bases, while the unpleasant situation that was fast developing in Libya effectively disposed of any possibility of R.A.F. replacements coming from Egypt. There were plain limits to the gallant policy of "bluffing a full house with a couple of pairs." It had worked brilliantly in Africa and Greece, so long as the opposing hand was played by the Italian air force. But how long could it be maintained in face of the *Luftwaffe*? German methods, German numbers, and the higher quality of German aircraft constituted a more formidable adversary for the small British fighter force, which it might lie beyond the power of a dwindling strength of Gladiators and Blenheims pointed with a handful of Hurricanes to resist.

If their strength was insufficient at the start, it was likely to grow less without much hope of reinforcement; and as the fight proceeded, their difficulties would increase by reason of the conformation of the country over which they had to operate. For Greece lay in the rough shape of a triangle based on the main Balkan range and pointing south. So long as it was intact, the defenders might operate from airfields in the plains of Salonika and Larissa; but if these were penetrated, they would be driven south towards the point of the triangle, and then their aircraft would be reduced to operating from bases in a steadily contracting area exposed to an increasing weight of enemy attack.

This uninviting prospect was faced cheerfully; and in the first phase, as the Germans surged across the frontier on April 6, their advancing columns were heavily attacked. An encounter between 12 Hurricanes and 30 German fighters, of which 5 were shot down without loss to their opponents, was encouraging; and that night the heavy bombers went to Sofia. Then a grey blanket of cloud and fog shrouded the mountains in the north; and for days it was not easy to find their targets. But the squadrons flew indomitably, taking toll of German armour and vehicles. Marching columns in Bulgaria and Jugoslavia felt the weight of their attacks; but Bulgaria was still the road by which the Germans reached the Aegean, and Jugoslav resistance was insufficient to prevent a fatal thrust through Monastir, which broke the Greek defence in two. Their forces in the west fell back with bitter feelings from the ground which they had wrested from the

Italians in the long winter struggle; and as human nature is sometimes too weak for strategy, they were scarcely equal to further effort on these cruel terms. The last two R.A.F. squadrons left in Epirus withdrew from the collapsing front; and their withdrawal was not simplified by the last-minute arrival of stray Jugoslav aircraft escaping from the invader and requiring food and petrol.

On the right three Greek divisions and some 35,000 fighting troops from Wavell's force in Africa with upwards of 100 tanks fell back to face the Germans in a new position further to the south. The R.A.F. worked hard to take the weight off them, and an Australian correspondent wrote on April 13 that "our men have not yet been worried by enemy aircraft." The price was high. That Easter afternoon 6 Blenheims took off from their mountain valley, circled above the olives and the grey cliff where they used to watch the bears, flew into the north-east, and none returned. For the slow bombers were no match for Messerschmitts in daylight, although night raids were still rewarding, as the railway sidings at Sofia and the bridge at Veles became aware.

The weather was improving now; and as the Germans brought their fighters quickly forward to new landing grounds on captured Jugoslav territory they registered their presence by a series of attacks on troops and bases in the Larissa plain. While convoys on the road were raked at short intervals, every Blenheim on one airfield was destroyed and three Hurricanes at another were attacked by German fighters in the act of taking off, the sole survivor managing to shoot down one of his adversaries. At night the bombers still went manfully to German aerodromes. But as the territory under Anglo-Greek control contracted under German pressure on the army, it was impracticable to maintain air bases further forward than the Athens area. This condemned the R.A.F. to operate their dwindling strength from a small number of target areas familiar to the enemy and at ranges rendering effective action almost impossible. Aerodrome defence was barely practicable in the absence of sufficient anti-aircraft guns or radiolocation equipment; there had been neither time nor labour to construct shelter pens for aircraft; and the Greek observer system ceased to function. Their strategical dilemma was tragic. For as their numbers were insufficient to defend them from the Germans, they were bombed on the ground, when they ventured near enough to protect their own troops; and if they moved out of range, they were too far away to furnish air cover.

The end came swiftly. When the Germans came through the clear April sky to Athens, watchers on the ground saw the whole British fighter force go up to meet them. Assembled from three broken squadrons, it numbered 15 Hurricanes in varying degrees of disrepair. But anything that could get off the ground was flown that day; and they went racing up the sky to meet at least 100 (some said 200) German aircraft. The dive-bombers flew low; and a great ring of fighters circled over them, as the Hurricanes swept up to fight. In one long day of fighting, while the hills of Attica looked on and the sea glittered beyond Salamis, where the little ships of Greece had once withstood the great armada of the Persians, the tattered aircraft and their weary pilots charged and charged again into six times their number. Five of them were lost; but they brought down 22, with 8 "probables." The balance had been bravely struck. But that left only 10 of them still capable of flying. The carved benches of the great theatre under the grey shoulder of the Acropolis five miles below them through the bright air had never seen a nobler tragedy than that battle in the clear Athenian sky, which drained the R.A.F. at Athens of one-third of its fighting strength.

Withdrawn to Argos, a few fighters (including some new arrivals from the Desert) still survived to cover the evacuation. But they were attacked on the ground with heavy loss; and a remnant of 6 Hurricanes and 14 Gladiators left for Crete. It was just eighteen days since the Germans had invaded Greece. The bombers had left earlier; and a fighter force was formed in Crete to cover, if it could, the evacuation fleet and its destination. The military situation seemed to promise a Dunkirk in sunlight. But Operation "Demon" was more formidable than Operation "Dynamo." For Suda Bay was three times as far from the Piraeus as the British coast had been from Dunkirk; and when the Germans reached the Argos airfields, it would lie within bombing range. Besides, three battered fighter squadrons were hardly comparable with the full strength of Fighter Command operating from their home bases. But they made the effort, maintaining patrols over the shipping; and, in Air Vice-Marshal D'Albiac's opinion, "it was due largely to their efforts that such a large proportion of the British forces in Greece were evacuated."

The R.A.F. had many problems in the last half of April. Flying-boats dropped into the long bay of Cattaro under the Montenegrin hills to fetch away the young King of Jugoslavia; and another

Sunderland carried the King of Greece to Crete. Returning aircraft took off from Greece with loads fantastically in excess of their capacity; one flying-boat accommodating (if the term was applicable) 81 passengers in place of its civilian load of 30 and 8 more in the lavatory. Their fighters patrolled the crowded sea route, eliciting from one weary evacuee the tribute that "Dunkirk was just a rehearsal for this. They tried to get us three times, but every time a fighter drove them off." Unarmed civil aircraft joined in the work, as the little ships of England had come swarming out to Dunkirk. But this time the evacuation was across 150 miles of sea; and though 1470 men were brought off by air, it was not easy for a serviceable force of 43 fighters to protect the long seaway between the beaches (Athens was unusable) and the coast of Crete. Greek waters were patrolled by Blenheims; and the approach to Crete was guarded by their handful of Hurricanes and Gladiators, while flying-boats were on the watch for a return of the Italian fleet. In five nights (the *Luftwaffe* refrained from night bombing) a total of 25,435 men was lifted from the beaches by unwearied naval gallantry and shipped to Crete under the frayed air cover afforded by 23 fighter Blenheims, 14 Gladiators, and 6 Hurricanes.

The war in Greece was over. In six months of fighting the R.A.F. had destroyed 259 aircraft in combat and on the ground, with 99 more "probables." The price in air combat had been comparatively light, since their own losses did not exceed 72 aircraft; but ground attacks had cost them a further 55, and the retreat had forced them to leave 82 behind. The balance was still in their favour. But when the Germans came, an infinitely weaker adversary was unable to protect his air bases, from which the requisites of defence were largely absent. In these circumstances there was no hope of maintaining that degree of air superiority which had been largely attained against the Italians; and in its absence the land forces were bound to suffer.

It had been a tragic episode. Now they were back in Crete with the Germans creeping steadily towards them. Egypt was still held behind them. But even there it was impossible to echo the well-timed reminiscence of the poet Clough, with which the Prime Minister heartened his countrymen that week. For if the hopeful drift of world politics in April, 1941, was aptly summarised in the poet's cry,

But westward, look, the land is bright,

this sentiment was not reflected in the outlook from the Nile valley.

Chapter IX

THE DESERT: RECOIL

As spring came to the Desert, blurring its arid outline with a sudden haze of green in unexpected places, Wavell's outposts stood at El Agheila staring into Tripolitania. Their swift advance had carried them half-way to Tripoli. But with a large proportion of his troops and aircraft engaged in Greece there was no prospect of advancing further.

British strategy continued its eternal juggle; and the deft transfer of its inadequate resources from one theatre of war to the next corner of the world where they were badly needed resembled nothing so much as the sleight of hand with which bystanders are left in doubt as to the thimble under which the pea reposes. (One participant, who preferred to think in terms of poker, recorded that "the bluff is a trifle thin in places.") The first juggle had withdrawn aircraft and troops from the Desert for the conquest of Italian East Africa. Then, their task brilliantly begun, they were shifted back across the board; and as the game went on, the bluff succeeded. Surprising victories were won at widely separated points by small, but sufficient, forces whose arrival and departure had been admirably timed. At this point developments in Greece imposed a second juggle, transferring a high proportion of their strength to Europe and leaving Africa largely uncovered. The Italians, it might be hoped, were unlikely to be enterprising after their discouraging experience in this theatre and, with any luck, would leave the British in control of Cyrenaica. At any rate, there was no means of reinforcing them; the demands of Greece were palpably more urgent than the safe retention of their Desert conquests; and as the British forces could not be in two places at once, there was plainly no alternative. Meanwhile it was to be hoped that nothing would occur in Africa by which their nakedness would be exposed; but even if it did, their situation would be embarrassing rather than fatal. It seemed unlikely, though, with the Italians thoroughly disorganised by their defeat and Tripoli 400 miles away behind the Desert haze.

This estimate, like Mussolini's when he made the error of reckoning without the Greeks, was defective for the simple reason that it reckoned without the Germans. As their Italian ally seemed incapable of holding his own territory and it would be highly inconvenient to have the British overrunning the whole of Libya and making direct contact with Weygand and the French in Tunis, something must be done to stiffen the Italians. The war on ports and shipping had been taken over by the *Luftwaffe*, whose presence was already noticeable in air attacks upon Benghazi, rendering its harbour quite unusable. This dislocated the supply of bombs and petrol to the R.A.F., since these had now to be disembarked in the greater safety of Tobruk and brought forward over 250 miles of road. The next stage was to take a hand in the land fighting; and the *Afrika Korps* was born of this decision, whilst Rommel got his chance. As Italian reinforcements poured across the straits to Tripoli, the best part of a German division made its way to Africa. For in spite of Italian naval inferiority the sea route was still open, though considerable numbers were flown across in transport aircraft. German dive-bombers were soon operating from the neighbourhood of Tripoli, while their fighters worked from forward landing grounds; and as the spring advanced, it was estimated that their air strength in Africa amounted to 174 aircraft, consisting of 90 Messerschmitts and a bomber force of 84.

The British, who had now withdrawn some 200 aircraft and 58,000 men to Greece, were in no position to win more victories in Libya. Indeed, their modest aspiration was to hold the ground that they had won; and if they were not called upon to fight for it, this might be possible. At Army Headquarters a Military Governor ruled Cyrenaica from the pleasant shade of Barce; and the R.A.F. had been reduced to something less than peace establishment, leaving the air defence of Cyrenaica, if challenged by the German striking force, to four squadrons. For No. 202 Group had withdrawn to Egypt, and its weary air crews were mostly hard at work elsewhere. The supply of aircraft in the Desert was severely limited by the drain to Greece and still more distant destinations; and it was not easy to keep serviceable those they had. This, indeed, was only possible by incorporating parts of damaged aircraft in other invalids whose cases were less advanced, a form of cannibalism which no air force can survive for long. But these desperate expedients were imposed on Middle East Command by a situation in which there was far more to be done than aircraft with which to do it; and there was every indication that there would soon be less. For the reinforcements reaching them from home by way of Malta and West Africa were failing to keep pace with the rate of wastage. A total loss of 184 aircraft in the first three months of 1941 was hardly balanced by the arrival of 166; and a portion of the new arrivals were Tomahawks from America, that were quite unfit to operate until the "teething troubles" to which new types are subject had been overcome.

In Cyrenaica one of their four squadrons worked with the army, while two squadrons of Hurricanes protected Benghazi and Tobruk and some night bombers attended to the busy port of Tripoli, assisted by aircraft from Malta. German air attacks continued on Benghazi; and presently they visited the forward areas and airfields in Cyrenaica, even ranging as far afield as Tobruk. This activity was rather unexpected; and a fighter squadron due to leave Tobruk for Greece was kept in Libya. By this time the German force in Africa was estimated to amount to two divisions, of which one was armoured; there were signs of landing grounds not far behind the border; and heavy traffic was observed along the coast. It was plain that there would shortly be work for the small British force in Cyrenaica to do. They soon became aware of something moving in the Desert to the south of them round their unguarded inland flank and fell back from El Agheila. For a simple pattern was imposed on Desert strategy by the broad fact that, whilst one flank could always rest securely on the sea, the other was bound to be exposed, unless it was prolonged indefinitely into the heart of Africa; and as neither side could face a threat to its communications in a region where life and movement both depended on the regular arrival of water, food, and petrol from behind, it followed that the Desert war became a long succession of outflanking movements to the south, to which the threatened side normally reacted by a withdrawal closer to its base.

The threatened force at El Agheila promptly fell back 70 miles to Agedabia, where they were attacked in the course of a few days by German dive-bombers and armour, accompanied by Italian infantry. While the R.A.F. bombed and machine-gunned the advancing enemy, long-range bombers visited his aerodrome at Misurata. But the weight of their attacks was insufficient to avert the blow; and when Agedabia was overrun, one flight departing hurriedly as tanks appeared along the Desert skyline, their tenure of Benghazi less than 100 miles away was obviously insecure. For if the intervening ground could not be held, the white seaport with its pair of black cathedral domes would have to go; and the adjacent airfield at Benina was evacuated. The first week of April was confused, with the army falling back to the high ground behind Benghazi and things moving at a pace which made it difficult to know at any given moment just where anybody was. Squadrons did their best to provide information and molest the enemy in the intervals of rapid and continuous withdrawals from threatened landing grounds; and when the Deputy Air Officer Commanding-in-Chief, Middle East, flew up from Cairo to see things for himself, he was warned off from landing at Benina just in time to save him from a welcome by the *Luftwaffe*. Boyd was already a prisoner in Italy; and it was just as well that Tedder should not follow him. But his engine failed over the Desert near Mechili; and after a forced landing in the wilderness he was completely lost. He might have stayed there unless chance had eventually brought along a stray Blenheim, whose sergeant-pilot flew him back to Cairo. That imperturbable metropolis, where lights were bright in the Egyptian black-out and taxis were still setting down their cheerful fares along the crowded terrace of Shepheard's Hotel, contrasted oddly with the collapsing front in Cyrenaica. Tedder, who was feeling tired after his rescue from the Desert, subsided with a book. It opened, with a rare sense of fitness, at King Henry's speech before battle; and he read,

> We few, we happy few, we band of brothers;
> For he to-day that sheds his blood with me
> Shall be my brother; be he ne'er so vile
> This day shall gentle his condition:
> And gentlemen in England now a-bed . . .

Six hundred miles away a meagre force was still falling back, as the Germans groped round them to the south.   Their line was somewhere in the hills near Barce now, with aircraft working from Maraua and Derna.   Hurricane patrols were busy, the destruction of 14 hostile aircraft for the loss of 2 in a single day being satisfactory ;   and bombers managed to relieve the pressure on an isolated Indian brigade in the Desert.   But the weight and pace of the attack, coupled with the constant threat of an outflanking movement to the south, hustled them along in the direction of the Egyptian frontier ;   and as they continued to fall back, the rungs of the long ladder slipped through their fingers.   Benghazi was behind them now ;   Barce could not be held ;   and the long road through the green hills of the Jebel Akdar was an endless line of retreating British transport, watched from the roadside by the empty windows of square, white Italian homesteads. The situation was, to say the least, confused ;   and the unhappy mis- adventure of Generals Neame and O'Connor added to the confusion. For an attempt to evade the stream of the retreating traffic by a sweep- ing detour ended in their capture by the tommy-guns of German motor-cyclists not far from the lonely spot where Tedder had been marooned two days earlier.

The retreat went on along the coast, while the Germans seemed to be racing eastward through the Desert on their flank to get across the road to Egypt, as O'Connor's armour had once raced to Beda Fomm to cut off the Italians.   They were steadily outflanked at point after point.   Derna was gone ;   Tobruk was isolated ;   Bardia was untenable ; and Rommel's first encounter with a captured officer consisted of the curt ejaculation, "Sorry, outflanked."   That was his ruling passion.   But as he felt his way further and further round their inland flank towards the steep edge of Libya, where Mussolini's desert ends and Egypt begins, he had omitted to eject them from Tobruk and subsequently paid the price of his omission in a year of bitter fighting.   It was, perhaps, his first major blunder, induced by concentration on his adversary rather than on the terrain or else by the obsession of his sweeping movement through the Desert to the south of them.

With the front receding at this pace it was not easy for aircraft to operate effectively.   Withdrawn at first to the Tobruk area, they found themselves once more among the wreckage of El Adem.   But they were forced to move again, two squadrons closer to Tobruk and the rest beyond the Egyptian frontier.   For though Tobruk still held out, the advancing enemy had reached the high ground overlooking Sollum 75 miles further on; and in three breathless weeks the British had been hustled out of Cyrenaica with the lonely exception of Tobruk. For some time longer a slender fighter force maintained itself there, operating from a besieged fortress and against enormous odds that commanded an uninterrupted view of their take-off from a landing ground that lay within easy range for shelling. One squadron managed to shoot down 19 of its opponents in a fortnight; and when it challenged a two-day series of raids by 100 bombers covered by about 150 fighters and contrived to destroy 12 of its opponents, with 2 "probables," for the loss of 3 Hurricanes, it was a noble effort. But Tobruk became impossible as an air base; and such cover as could be given was now provided by aircraft from Maaten Bagush operating from an advanced landing ground near Sidi Barrani, while the bombers pounded airfields further to the rear.

The R.A.F. was back once more at its old bases in the Western Desert. April was half over now; and the front line ran from the brown cliffs above Halfaya to the sea. Collishaw was in command again and his pilots harried traffic on the long road that ran for 300 miles behind the land fighting. From El Agheila to Benghazi fighter Blenheims attended to wayfarers; long-range Hurricanes took up the tale beyond Benghazi; and Hurricanes in pairs operated in the nearer areas. But Tripoli was out of range now, though the bombers did their best with Benghazi and the enemy's aerodromes; and fighters made his life uneasy on the roads. His thin-skinned vehicles were systematically raked, until he was driven to post isolated tanks, like anchored flak-ships, at five-mile intervals along the road. This seemed to indicate that Rommel and his Italian colleagues had no more active use for them that spring; and after a successful brush that cleared the British from Halfaya Pass and a determined effort at Tobruk in the last week of April, the Desert war came to a halt.

Now they were very nearly back where they had started from five months before; and though they had scored considerable successes in the air during the last hurried phase, the Hurricanes destroying 73 aircraft, with a further 16 "probables," for the loss of 22, their situation in the Western Desert was less comfortable than it had been when they confronted the Italians.

Crete
May, 1941.

Crete

Benghazi

German Fighter Range

May 1941

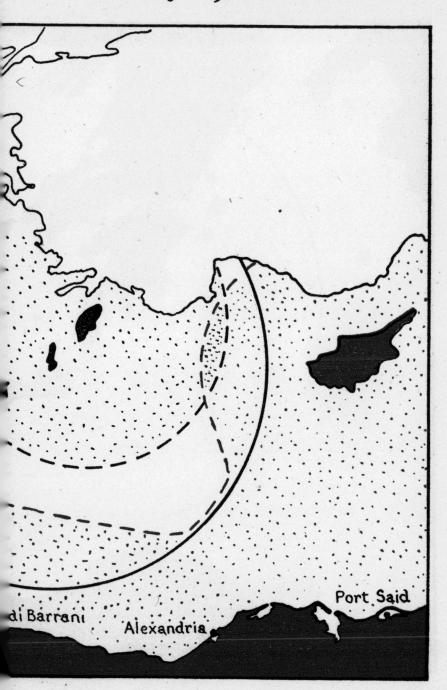

di Barrani   Alexandria   Port Said

R.A.F. Fighter Range ✳
German Dive Bomber Range ○

May 1941

R.A.F. Fighter Range
German Dive Bomber Range

Chapter X

CRETE

O N APRIL 30, as destroyers lay waiting off the coast of Greece
to make a final search of the deserted beaches after dark for the
last survivors of a British army and sixty German tanks were creeping
over the uneven surface of the Desert towards the waiting trenches at
Tobruk, a train left Hildesheim. They took the best part of a week
to get into the Balkans; and the glider pilot noticed that the Danube
was in flood. A parachute battalion, which came from the same
neighbourhood and also belonged to *Fliegerkorps XI*, started from
Germany that week and travelled with an air of mystery. Their
badges were removed; all parachute equipment was kept under lock
and key; no private papers could be carried; paybooks were ex-
changed for identity cards giving no indication of their unit; there
were strict orders against posting letters or buying picture-postcards;
and they were not allowed to sing the parachutist's songs. This
limitation of their repertory was a sad deprivation; and their motor
transport did not look the same with their heraldic panther painted out.
Even the medical arrangements were furtive, since particulars of their
inoculations were only imparted to the doctor of a glider unit with
unusual precautions. The stealthy travellers were all in Greece before
May 15. The gliders, of which they had about 75, had been rigged
in the neighbourhood of Salonika and flown south to Tanagra, where
they were visited by General Student (his soldierly handshake heartened
the glider pilot) and told that they were bound for Crete. The parachutists had assembled in Bulgaria and travelled overland; and
Operation "Merkur" was ready to begin.

The plan was simple. Crete lay within 120 miles of three German aerodromes, of which two had been created and one enlarged in the past few weeks. For the German mind had grasped the significance of rapid aerodrome construction in modern war. Their victory in Greece was largely due to the performances of German engineers in this field and their consequent ability to operate an overwhelming fighter force from new landing grounds. Before they had disposed of the last British elements on the mainland, they were already busy looking for fresh sites of airfields, from which the war could be carried further south. One was found at Mulaoi in the Peloponnese; four transport aircraft brought down the construction engineers; and the aerodrome was in use within a week. Another was located on the island of Melos, where an Allied garrison was still holding out. But the survey party started work before the fighting ended; local labour and British prisoners were employed; and in three days they had a landing ground. Scarpanto in the Dodecanese lay still closer to the nearest point of Crete; and the Italian landing ground was rapidly improved. This gave the Germans a ring of aerodromes from which single-engined fighters and dive-bombers could operate against the island, whilst at least ten all-weather aerodromes on the mainland were available for larger aircraft.

Such facilities enabled them to formulate a simple plan. The problem of attacking islands from the air was no novelty to the *Luftwaffe*, which had already attempted something of the kind against Britain; and, as in that case, the first phase of Operation "Merkur" was to consist of the elimination of the British fighter force. (It might be easier to deal with less than 40 aircraft than it had been to challenge the full strength of Fighter Command.) When this had been achieved, the *Luftwaffe* proposed to isolate the island by a series of attacks on shipping. Their attacks upon its ground defences would be followed by invasion by air and sea. This was, perhaps, the unwritten chapter of the Battle of Britain, of which the page was never turned because the narrative was rudely interrupted by the eight guns of Dowding's fighters. But Crete, where there were only 6 Hurricanes, might be a simpler matter.

The force allotted to the attack on Crete consisted of 180 fighters, covering 330 bombers, with at least 600 aircraft available for towing gliders, dropping parachutists, or the transport of air-borne troops. There were approximately 10,000 parachutists, 5000 air-borne troops, and 750 glider troops, in addition to 7000 men who were expected to arrive by sea. The time-table provided for a descent of glider troops and parachutists to capture aerodromes and ports. These were to be followed by landings at the captured points effected by some 12,000 men of a Mountain Division arriving in aircraft and ships; and it was felt that an invading force of 22,750 men should suffice to deal comfortably with the defenders, whose strength was at first estimated by the Germans as 5000 troops. The original intention had been to use the veterans of the air-borne invasion of Holland, who made their appearance in the Balkans that spring. But the hills of Crete appeared to call for mountain troops. Besides, there would soon be work for troops accustomed to a less uneven terrain in the plains of Russia. An order confidently intimated that "*Fliegerkorps XI* supported by *Fliegerkorps VIII* will capture the island of Crete"; and as their preparations were concluded with a careful study of the target maps and photographs and the issue of a German-English phrase sheet including the singularly handy sentence, "If yu lei yu uill bi schott," all arrangements for a most enjoyable occasion seemed to be complete.

The island, which had been in British occupation since November, was defended by a force (including non-combatants) of less than 28,000 men, of whom under a quarter were fresh troops, in addition to 11 Greek battalions. Staffs and units were improvised of weary men rescued from the Greek retreat; and equipment was in short supply. Their artillery consisted of 4 howitzers and 18 anti-aircraft guns; their armour amounted to 22 tanks of all classes; they were lamentably short of motor transport; and trenches were dug with steel helmets in default of spades. If they were attacked by air, the R.A.F. in Crete could muster 12 fighter Blenheims, 12 Gladiators, and 6 Hurricanes, together with 6 aircraft of the Fleet Air Arm. This meagre force, without spares or maintenance facilities, would be condemned to operate from two unfinished aerodromes at Heraklion and Maleme and a landing ground at Retimo (work on other aerodromes was abandoned in face of the danger of air-borne invasion); and the loss of Cyrenaica had left them dangerously isolated. For so long as Cyrenaica was held, they were within 200 miles of British aerodromes in the neighbourhood of Derna, and there was some hope that fighters from that quarter might be able to afford them some additional protection. But when the line receded into Egypt and the

R.A.F. returned to its old bases in the Western Desert, the fate of Crete was sealed. For now they were at least 300 miles from the nearest fighter squadron on the mainland of Africa, a range at which no Hurricane could operate. This, perhaps, rather than an invasion of Egypt, at which he made no serious attempt, had been the main objective of Rommel's race to the Egyptian frontier. For German strategy appeared to recognise that modern warfare had become a war for aerodromes. The campaign in Norway had been decided by control of aerodromes; rapid aerodrome construction had brought victory in Greece; and the result in Crete became a foregone conclusion as soon as German short-range fighters and dive-bombers were in a position to operate from aerodromes within 120 miles of Crete against an infinitely weaker adversary, whose main fighter force was 350 miles away.

This left the island to its own diminishing resources apart from such support as night bombers from Egypt and even Beaufighters from Malta could afford by hammering the German airfields in Greece, where they struck heavily at rows of transport aircraft. The attack had opened, as in Britain, with operations against shipping followed by attacks on aerodromes. These were opposed by the little fighter force in Crete, which had now been reinforced by the few Hurricanes that could be spared from Egypt. But as the total contribution to their strength from this quarter only numbered 10 during the whole course of operations, it was hardly calculated to modify the situation in the air, which continued to be dominated by the German masses. Indeed, their intervention, as they skimmed across the summer seas, hampered by long-range petrol tanks, to join a battle against a fighter force nearly 200 strong, was an act of hopeless gallantry recalling nothing so much as an aerial Charge of the Light Brigade. As the German bombers flew over with strong fighter escort or their fighters came in low to attack, the odds against the R.A.F. were anything between 7 and 10 to 1. But Group Captain Beamish put up a handful of weary men and worn-out aircraft that had served their time in six months of hard fighting further north in Greece. The tired ground staff without equipment managed somehow to get their decrepit charges in the air; and in six days of combat over Crete the little band of fighters shot down 23 of their opponents, with 9 "probables," damaging a further 41. But their own numbers shrank steadily. The Blenheims, which were quite unable to contend with

German fighters, had been sent back to Egypt; and by May 19 only 3 Gladiators and 4 Hurricanes remained. There was no more that they could do. The remnant was withdrawn to Egypt at first light that morning; ground staffs stayed behind in case it should prove possible to operate aircraft from Cretan aerodromes again; and the last stand of the fighters over Crete had ended.

The fighter force had been eliminated; and the sequel demonstrated that islands within range of shore-based aircraft cannot be defended once they lose their fighters. Sea power, it seemed, was not enough, since it could not be exercised in narrow waters without air superiority; and the subsequent events caused some concern at home. This, however, was unnecessary, as Britain had already proved that islands which retain control of their own sky are not invaded. Crete merely reinforced the lesson by an unpleasant demonstration that, when they lose it, invasion follows.

Operation "Merkur" was now free to pass into its next phase. An aerial offensive had stripped the island of its air defences; and its sea communications had been virtually cut by attacks on shipping. For out of 27,000 tons of stores despatched to Crete by sea they had landed a bare 10 per cent., leaving 3400 tons at the bottom of the sea and 21,000 tons turned back to Egypt by the aerial blockade of Crete. On the morning after the last British fighters left (it was May 20) heavy bombing drove the troops to cover. Soon afterwards observers on the ground noticed German aircraft circling noiselessly over the north-west of the island and landing in all directions. As there was no sound of engines, although the bombing still went on, they concluded that these must be gliders. They appeared with a strong escort of fighters and dive-bombers over the aerodrome at Maleme and two adjacent points; and their object was to land sufficient men to paralyse the few British anti-aircraft guns and to cover the next wave of the invasion. At one point, where their air cover failed to appear and the British guns were not where they expected them, they had no success; and watchers on the ground were gratified to see some gliders prematurely unhooked over the sea, whilst others were shot down, a number crashed on landing, and the rest were rounded up. It was plain that the use of gliders was a precarious experiment. But a fair measure of success was scored in the neighbourhood of Suda Bay and the aerodrome at Maleme; and the way was clear for the next stage of the air-borne invasion.

Fifteen minutes later the bombing died away, and in the silence the sky was full of transport aircraft flying singly in all directions and disgorging a steady rain of parachutists. Most of the parachutes were green and white; but some were edged with red, and others of a larger pattern were attached to bulky objects. It was raining men and large bright metal cylinders; and soon air-borne troops as well emerged from transport aircraft, which crash-landed on the beaches near the threatened aerodrome. The parachutists after some initial success encountered more opposition than they had bargained for; and when some more were dropped that afternoon with similar pre-liminaries in the neighbourhood of the aerodrome at Heraklion and the landing ground at Retimo, the defenders seemed to have the situation well in hand, as (by one account) "the great black troop-carriers with their yellow noses came lumbering in. Many were hit by A.A. fire and crashed in flames, throwing off sparks of helplessly blazing parachutists as they came down. Others were driven out of line, ran into parachutists descending from other machines and made off festooned with the casualties of a fearful kind of air road-accident." By nightfall something like 750 glider troops and 7000 parachutists had been dropped in Crete without unduly serious effects except at Maleme, where the aerodrome was in some danger.

The German plan was obviously to secure a landing ground for air-borne forces and a port at which troops and equipment could be disembarked; and all through the next day they increased their pressure on Maleme with further waves of parachutists and troop-carriers. That night a German convoy sailed for Crete with rein-forcements of troops, guns, motor-cycles, automobiles, and light tanks. This was the sea-borne wing of the invasion. But it was never seen in Crete, because the Navy found one section of it in the night and the rest on the next day. Sea power, it seemed, could still bar the sea route to Crete, although it was beyond its power to open it to an effective stream of British reinforcements; and with the enemy in almost undisputed mastery of the air route this service might delay, but could never hope to alter, the result. Indeed, the price of naval operations conducted within range of shore-based German aircraft and beyond the reach of air cover from Egyptian aerodromes might almost seem excessive. For the ships could see the bombers wheeling over Melos, as they circled on returning to their base for more bombs and climbed away again with a fresh load; and the Prime Minister reported the loss of 2 cruisers and 4 destroyers and damage to 2 battle-ships.

In Crete the situation darkened, as the German bridgehead on the aerodrome at Maleme was steadily enlarged. An attempt to recapture the lost ground was defeated by bombing and machine-gunning from German aircraft; and efforts by the R.A.F. to intervene from Egypt were largely unsuccessful. One attempt to move 12 Hurricanes to Heraklion ended in the arrival of 3 serviceable aircraft, though some bombers attacked enemy positions in the island that afternoon and German transport aircraft on the ground were attacked from the air on the same evening. There was a succession of night raids on Maleme by a few heavy bombers, and some fighters managed to keep up the attack by day. But the scale of their offensive was quite insufficient to prevent the spreading of the German stain in Crete; and as the days went by, the situation on the ground steadily deteriorated. The area controlled by British troops contracted slowly, until by May 28 there was no alternative to evacuation. The air-borne invasion, which had landed about 35,000 men in Crete, had succeeded in eight days.

The final stage confronted the survivors with a withdrawal across 440 miles of sea to Alexandria. The prospect was not cheerful, as the British fighter force had been kept busy covering an aircraft carrier that had been bombed in an attack on Scarpanto as well as other warships in Egyptian waters. But it passed off better than might have been expected. For the scale of German air attacks on the evacuation area was noticeably lighter now; and there were signs that *Fliegerkorps VIII* was in course of transfer to a new scene of operations further north. German, no less than British, strategy consisted of a juggle, although it had far more to juggle with; and once Crete had been secured, the *Luftwaffe* was moving off towards the Russian frontier. In four days and nights of evacuation 14,580 men were brought out of Crete by naval gallantry and under fighter cover provided by aircraft operating at a distance of 250 miles from their bases in the Western Desert; and it was noticeable that, with one exception due to inaccurate information, no ships were lost where fighter cover was available. It was all over by June 1.

It was just a month since the troop train left Hildesheim; and Operation "Merkur" had demonstrated vividly the possibilities and limitations of air-borne invasion, of which the capture of an aero-drome was plainly the first requisite. It also taught a number of instructive lessons on the practice of aerodrome defence and the elementary truth that an island, once denuded of its fighter force (for which there is no naval substitute), loses at the same time its insular immunity from invasion.

Chapter XI

IRAQ

EIGHT HUNDRED MILES DUE EAST OF CAIRO, beyond the stony hills of Palestine and the old, bald desert of Arabia, a broad river flowed past a dingy city. It was the first week of April, 1941; and crowds were surging past the scrofulous arcades and through the dreary streets of unimpressive shop-fronts, as the mosques looked down from their bright towers on Baghdad. For Rashid Ali, who lived in a pleasant house just up the river, had seized power in Iraq. His purposes belied the roses and sweet peas in his front garden, which faced the broad sheen of the Tigris with a slightly unexpected air of Surbiton, since the *coup d'état* was highly welcome to the German Embassy; and some light was cast upon his motives by the revealing circumstance that four Iraqi generals, who participated in the new regime, were popularly known as "The Golden Square." While the lawful Regent and his friends were romantically flown to safety by the R.A.F., these gentry constituted an unpleasant threat to British peace of mind in an area vital to British strategy.

For it had long been recognised that access to the oil of Persia and Iraq was a primary necessity in time of war. Fleets, aircraft, and armoured vehicles, to say nothing of the entire apparatus of military transport, were all dependent on this fuel; and with five-sixths of the world's oil located on the further side of the Atlantic and nearly half the rest far out of British reach on neutral territory in Russia and Rumania, the sources of supply in Persia and Iraq became an object of increased anxiety. Any threat to the tranquillity of Iraq would endanger output in the northern oil-fields, interrupt the flow of oil along the pipe-line leading to the waiting tankers off the coast of Palestine at Haifa, and might ultimately silence the roar of aircraft engines and the grind of tanks and lorries in the Western Desert. Besides, a hostile government in Iraq might render it extremely difficult for British forces to protect the Persian oil-field 350 miles further east, if this were ever threatened; and risks could not be taken in a region upon whose security so much depended. For the road to India by air lay through Iraq and down the Persian Gulf. Maritime communications had once linked the Empire, and in that epoch a strong British superstition safeguarded the Suez Canal with elaborate precautions. Concern for its security had actuated British policy in the Middle East for two generations and brought British forces into Egypt. When the next stage of development was reached and vital traffic became air-borne, it was plain that similar precautions were called for in Iraq.

After the detachment of Iraq from Turkey in 1918 these took the form of a British mandate, followed subsequently to the recognition of Iraq's independence by the maintenance of R.A.F. stations on Iraqi territory. For a time the security of the country depended on the R.A.F. and its local land forces, known successively as the Iraq Levies and the Air Defence Force. The R.A.F. had learnt to view the burning sky and baking sand of Iraq with varying degrees of affection; and though this interesting experiment in the control of wide territories from the air was largely terminated by the creation of an Iraqi army under its own government, they were still maintained at vital points.

Sixty miles across the desert from Baghdad, where the great sweep of the Euphrates leans towards a lake convenient for Empire flying-boats *en route* to India, innumerable iron roofs, a tall water tower, some hangars, and an aerodrome announced the presence of the R.A.F. Inside an eight-mile circuit of impressive iron fence the station buildings stood along tree-lined roads that bore familiar

English names. There was a good deal of grass, a golf-course, and a polo-ground; and though the brown Iraqi desert ran for miles beyond the fence, where hyenas howled at night and the heat danced by day, a cheerful show of stocks, sweet peas, and roses recalled the innocence of cottage gardens two thousand miles away. Built for comfortable residence in a trying climate rather than for defence, the station at Habbaniya made no concessions to the unpleasant thought that any-one might ever go so far as to attack it. For the site was completely overlooked by a desert plateau, which commanded the aerodrome and the defenceless grey roofs of Habbaniya at short range.

This residential spot was now the home of R.A.F. (No. 4) Flying Training School, where a small body of instructors, including some Greeks, disposed of less than 80 aircraft. By no means all of these were capable of operating under war conditions, since at least one-third were quite unsuitable and all were marked by educational rather than by fighting qualities. In any case, there were not more than 35 pilots, of whom the majority were instructors who had done no more than circuits and landings for some time, whilst a few of the pilots had not flown very much in recent years and one or two, having flown too much, had been sent to Habbaniya for a rest.

Their prospect of a rest began to fade in the first week in April, as Rashid Ali made his *coup*. The moment was uncomfortable for the British forces in the Middle East, since Greece and Cyrenaica were both lost that month; and with two losing battles on their hands in Europe and Africa it hardly seemed the time to inaugurate a third campaign in Asia. But if Iraq was in danger, something must be done. Some infantry was hurriedly flown in from India; and a brigade ready to embark for Singapore and waiting by its transports at an Indian port was suddenly diverted to the Persian Gulf. Rashid Ali received the news of their arrival at Basra without enthusiasm; and when he made difficulties about allowing them to stay there, the situation in Baghdad began to look extremely grave. The diplomatic problem was sufficiently exacting for the British Embassy without the added complication of a large number of women and children in close proximity to the roaring streets of an excited Eastern city; and presently it was decided to remove this ill-timed reminiscence of Cawnpore. One hot afternoon a long procession of cars, omnibuses, and R.A.F. trucks left Baghdad and headed for the desert. The roaring city was behind them now. But when they reached Falluja, they were held up by Iraqi soldiers armed with tommy-guns, until a tactful Flight Lieutenant persuaded a policeman on point duty at the bridge to let them pass; and soon they were inside the iron fence at Habbaniya with about 1000 R.A.F. personnel, 1200 Iraqi Levies, and 350 men of The King's Own Royal Regiment, who had arrived by air from India. The weather was exceptionally hot; and it was far from reassuring to observe that the Iraqi army seemed to be following them up the road.

These uninvited guests, who numbered anywhere between 5000 and 8000 men, had a liberal supply of artillery, machine-guns, light tanks, and armoured cars; and their officers had told them that they were going on an exercise. But should anything more serious be contemplated, it looked very much as if they could have Habbaniya for the asking. For the threatened place had no means of replying to artillery bombardment except two vintage howitzers, a fragrant memory of the last war, appropriately relegated to decorative duties on the lawn outside the Aircraft Depot. These veterans were stripped, cleaned, and overhauled. But there were no anti-aircraft guns; and if an enemy attacked the place there seemed to be no means of stopping him except the Flying Training School.

This fact dawned on those zealous educators at an early stage, although the Iraqi air force could muster about 50 first-line aircraft (including American bombers and some fast Italian fighters) superior to anything at Habbaniya. Inside the camp the polo-ground and golf-course, whose bunkers had been sacrificed, were amalgamated to form a relatively safe dispersal area. All aircraft were fitted with unaccustomed bomb-racks; tests appeared to show that an Audax, capable officially of carrying eight 20-lb. bombs, could take the air in safety with a load of two 250-lb. bombs; a few time-expired Gladiators from the Western Desert were hastily rejuvenated; and the pupils were regaled with an unexpected and intensive course in rear-gunnery and bomb-aiming. These labours promised an effective force of some 64 aircraft; but as they would be short of pilots, the balance was made up by pupils and anyone who cared to come along.

The day after the arrival of the refugees from Baghdad a practice alarm brought everyone into the defences before dawn. The large civil population of the camp, which accommodated a good deal of labour with its families, was quietly informed of the position. They responded without undue dismay and with a prompt regard for

previous instruction in air-raid precautions. The remainder of the day
was fully occupied in making up lost time on training; and as Iraqi
troops had been reported in the neighbourhood and the mail for
Baghdad was turned back on the desert road, there seemed every
prospect that they would shortly have a chance of demonstrating their
proficiency.

In the first light of the next morning (it was May 1) they could
see troops on the plateau overlooking Habbaniya. Men were digging
trenches, installing machine-guns, and making themselves quite at
home; motor transport was in movement; armoured cars commanded the aerodrome at a range of 500 yards; pom-poms had been
mounted in convenient positions to fire at aircraft coming in to land;
and their commander intimated courteously that, as the camp had
been surrounded, all flying was to cease and any aircraft ignoring these
instructions would be fired on. This elicited the firm reply that air
training would continue and that immediate reprisals would follow
any act of war committed against British aircraft. Preparations were
accelerated; aircraft were bombed up; and an experimental flight
over the Iraqi positions drew no fire. This was, perhaps, as well, since
the entire body of R.A.F. personnel required to start and service
aircraft, if active operations should ensue, was hard at work digging
trenches and manning machine-guns elsewhere. A further note
invited the unwelcome visitors to withdraw from the plateau,
intimating that their failure would constitute an act of war. That
evening a meeting at Headquarters decided that, if they were still
there at dawn, they should be attacked by every aircraft that could
get off the ground. For the camp could not be left exposed to the
Iraqi guns, and this menace must be dissipated at all costs.

It was thought afterwards that Rashid Ali had precipitated his
attack a trifle prematurely in advance of the arrival of German aid.
True, some German aircraft were expected, if Marshal Pétain and his
ministers facilitated their arrival by the use of French aerodromes in
Syria; the German Embassy in Baghdad was prodigal of good advice;
and Field-Marshal von Blomberg's son was detailed to take part
in operations. But there was a good deal to be said for launching
the affair at a season when the rivers of Iraq were all in flood, impeding
the movement of relieving forces from the south except by air or
across such bridges as they might contrive to improvise. May was
the season of high flood; and it was now May 1. It was not easy to

see how Habbaniya could be relieved. If it fell, the whole position in Iraq was gravely compromised; and as the sun went down that night, about 2500 men with 64 aircraft, 18 armoured cars, 2 ancient howitzers, and a few trench mortars and machine-guns, some corrugated roofs, and an iron fence stood between the British Empire and defeat.

The night passed quietly. Just after three o'clock in the morning the dark hangars were alive with men, as aircraft taxied out to take off in the half-light and everyone (the sick parade had vanished) came down to see them off. Presently the miscellaneous armada of Habbaniya was air-borne; and soon the greying sky was full of aircraft of all shapes and sizes (and no very recent date) flying at all levels and in all directions and waiting to start bombing punctually at five o'clock. It was most alarming for their occupants to have assorted aircraft "approach unseen and flash past causing pilots nearly to die of heart failure. Camouflaged and uncamouflaged Audaxes went past at every angle, and Wellingtons" (some heavy bombers had flown through the night to join them) "would sail overhead leaving the trainers bucketing about in their slipstream." The first bombs went down on the dark range of the escarpment at five o'clock; and it was not long before the Iraqi guns retaliated with fierce anti-aircraft fire and a bombardment of the camp. With aircraft flying at about 1000 feet holes soon began to appear in wings, and bullets came up through cockpits. One Oxford was shot down in flames, losing an instructor and two pupils; but all the rest were landed somehow in spite of wounds and damage, an Audax returning with 52 bullet-holes. The Wellingtons, operating in daylight for the first time in their history, put in some admirable work, although they suffered badly; and when one of them force-landed under fire on the aerodrome, the crew sprinted for the trenches, whilst a persevering tractor did its best to salvage the aircraft. But salvage work is not facilitated by heavy shell-fire; and though the tractor was escorted by an armoured car on either side and its driver managed to attach a rope to the damaged bomber, a direct hit by a shell set the Wellington on fire and did some damage to the tractor, leaving the driver to escape uninjured in an armoured car, and shortly afterwards the Wellington blew up. Operations continued under heavy fire all day; and aircraft working from the main aerodrome, which lay within half a mile of the Iraqi guns, had (in the words of one qualified observer) "no time to linger." Starting up behind the hangars, they took off by opening their throttles inside the iron fence, dashing through the gate, racing across the aerodrome quite irrespective of the wind, and making a steep climbing turn to miss the plateau; and when they returned, a steep turn between hangars served to elude pom-pom fire, followed (if they were lucky) by a landing, a sharp turn inside the gate, and a quick run to safety round the corner of a hangar at twenty miles an hour. For flying conditions at Habbaniya were *sui generis*.

At noon Iraqi aircraft made an ineffective effort to attack the camp, followed by intermittent bombing. But though the bombers were too fast for anything on hand to catch them, and conditions in Headquarters Mess were not improved by a sudden stream of bullets through the ceiling (which sent the occupants to ground under the furniture and left a pair of storks on the roof overhead completely unconcerned), it seemed unlikely that Habbaniya would succumb to air action. Their real danger came from shelling. For the station, a great defenceless city of grey, corrugated-iron roofs, lay naked in the sights of the Iraqi guns on the plateau. No gunner ever had a more helpless-looking target, as it spread beneath a sullen sky at the comfortable range of 1000 yards and without a gun to answer back. The tall water tower and the power station were particularly prominent; and if they were hit, it was all over with Habbaniya.

Iraqi gunnery, however, proved unequal to the test, although it gave the camp a most unpleasant day. One officer on telephoning for an ambulance and encountering some scepticism on the part of the authorities, who asked if he was really being shelled, considerately held his telephone receiver just outside the door. All official doubts were dispelled by the ensuing sound-waves; and the sceptic, ejaculating "Good God!" despatched an ambulance forthwith. But though the station churches sustained some damage owing to the powerful attraction invariably exercised by places of worship upon indifferent gunners, the water tower was never hit. The bombardment, which might so easily have been conclusive, seemed to lack direction. No German hand was there to guide; and it was thought that some lucky bomb from one of Habbaniya's aircraft had either liquidated the Iraqi command or sent it back to seek repose at some more restful distance.

The weary day dragged to a close; and when it ended, the Flying Training School still held Habbaniya. But now only 42 of their aircraft were serviceable; and the enemy were still established on the long shoulder of the desert overlooking them. Their fate was exercising the distant minds presiding over troop movements, who had quite enough to think about just then without the addition of trouble in Iraq. For British forces had been driven out of Greece and Libya within the last few days. But it might be possible to send some reinforcements. Some R.A.F. armoured cars were rushed straight from the Western Desert to Trans-Jordan across Egypt, Sinai, and Palestine, covering 1000 miles in 48 hours, taking an hour's rest, and then fighting a successful action against heavy odds at a vital point on the pipe-line. There was a brigade at Basra; and a force was on its way from Palestine. But Basra was 300 miles away by air, and the only way from Palestine lay across 500 miles of desert. Relief from either quarter must take time to reach them; and on a cautious, perhaps too cautious, calculation it looked unpleasantly as if the relief of Habbaniya was a forlorn hope, which must depend for its uncertain chances of success on how long they could hold out.

The days that followed were an indistinguishable nightmare. Work began half an hour before dawn and went on until after dark; flying was continuous; and the women and children were evacuated by air, the transport aircraft taking off for Basra under cover of dive-bombing by versatile Audaxes. They took to night flying, a disagreeable pastime where no flare-path could be used and a blind take-off was followed by a landing in the light of the aircraft's own landing lamp, hurriedly switched on when the altimeter registered a height of 50 feet and promptly switched off again on touching down. Their numbers dwindled, as the toll of wounded pilots rose; and conditions were too difficult for pupils to be used. The wastage of aircraft was formidable, only 4 out of 27 Oxfords remaining serviceable after three days of fighting, although in diagnosing their condition no account was taken of any damage except to vital parts. But a few Blenheims reached them; and the pilots were surprised to find that landings at Habbaniya now involved a fast and complicated game of hide-and-seek round station buildings. Ranging further afield, the little force attacked Iraqi aerodromes, destroying numbers of aircraft on the ground; supplies intended for the troops on the plateau were sedulously bombed on the way from Baghdad; and by May 5 the besiegers were beginning to taste all the pleasures of a siege themselves. For their food, water, and ammunition could only reach them by the desert road, which was commanded by roving aircraft from Habbaniya; and on the fifth morning of the siege Habbaniya awoke to find that the plateau was empty.

The tables had been neatly turned, an impressive demonstration of what can be done by an educational establishment when really roused; and now Habbaniya went over to the offensive. For the rebels were still across the road to Baghdad, where the Embassy maintained an uncomfortable existence with a total armament (located in the Chancery) consisting of some rifles and a few tear-gas bombs for the protection of 350 British subjects. It would be some time before relief could come; snipers on adjacent house-tops made things unpleasant; and as British aircraft came over regularly to drop conciliatory leaflets, an ungrateful public made a habit of shooting at anything in the sky over Baghdad. On May 6 an attack in the direction of the city was launched from Habbaniya. The enemy was strongly posted near a village picturesquely known as "Teeth of the Wolf" (but its name, Sinn El Dibban, sounded better to the troops as Sidi Barrani); and now the Flying Training School put out its powers in the form of a combined operation by infantry, armoured cars, and aircraft. The ground force was constituted, apart from three companies of The King's Own, by Iraqi Levies, who had served with the R.A.F. since the stormy days after the last war. Few communities have shown more courage than the Assyrians, when their Patriarch declared war upon the Turks in 1915 from the heart of the Turkish Empire; and their gallantry was duly rewarded by a long alternation of massacre and migrations, until the Levies were embodied. Transferred to the R.A.F., the Assyrians served them faithfully, trim, dark, and soldierly in their slouch-hats, Christians and Moslems marching beside Yezidis of more dubious theology; and now their chance had come.

The fight was stiff at Sinn El Dibban. But the pair of ancient howitzers recovered their lost youth; and the enemy's morale was gravely shaken by the arrival of 4·5-inch shells, which left them with an uneasy feeling that heavy guns had been miraculously flown up from Basra. When the rebels endeavoured to move up reinforcements in Baghdad motor omnibuses, they were caught by aircraft on the road. Habbaniya sent out everything that could fly; and for two interminable hours they bombed a long column of jammed vehicles. One pilot reported a solid sheet of flame for 250 yards along the road, to the accompaniment of exploding limbers; and Rashid

Ali's rebellion never recovered from that dreadful holocaust on the Falluja road.

The next problem was to clear the way to Baghdad; and with the broad Euphrates running strongly at full flood success depended upon bridging operations. Their artillery and armoured vehicles had been substantially increased by captures from the enemy; and in the air it was now growing possible for pupils to replace their tired instructors. (Proficiency in real operations was rewarded by the remission of further training.) But if there was bridging to be done, it was not altogether easy to see who or what would do it. Dinghies from the R.A.F. Sailing Club on the lake reappeared as pontoons; and a quantity surveyor was seen toiling on the ropes beside Command Accounts, while civilian workmen hurriedly attired in R.A.F. uniform worked as coolies in a temperature of 115° in the shade with the Equipment Officer, two assistants of the Financial Adviser, and three engineers from the Air Ministry. Perhaps it was not quite the way that military bridges were constructed before spellbound audiences at the Royal Tournament. But their work held; and when a general said afterwards that the campaign had been won on two wire ropes, the sole correction offered by a conscientious C.R.E. was to amend the text by substituting one wire rope and a manila cable.

But though the ground position was improving with the loyal efforts of the Levies and a steady flow of reinforcements by air from Basra, there was one more battle to be fought over Habbaniya. Just a week after the Flying Training School had saved itself by its incredible exertions, perspiring men were working on the new flying ferry, and a pilot on patrol over the Baghdad aerodrome saw a Messerschmitt 110 coming in to land. Few sights were more unwelcome, as there was nothing to be said for meeting fast German fighters in old training aircraft; and if the *Luftwaffe* was coming to Iraq, it might have things its own way. But the malcontents in Baghdad hardly made the best of this formidable aid, as it was their cheerful habit to shoot at all aircraft, and this time they scored an unusual success. For when it landed, it was found to contain Field-Marshal von Blomberg's son, who was to take charge of operations in Iraq; but he was in no state to do so, as he was dead. An intervention by the *Luftwaffe* a few days earlier might well have been decisive, and one bomb on the water tower would have finished Habbaniya. But their attention had been concentrated on the exciting preliminaries of Operation "Merkur" in the aerodromes surrounding Crete. For the Germans, too, had more than one thing on their hands in May, 1941; and when they had time to think of Iraq and to move some aircraft down, the loss of Blomberg seemed to dislocate the affair. They came by way of Syria, where Marshal Pétain and Admiral Darlan had been most obliging about refuelling facilities at French aerodromes; and now they were based on Mosul. But although the prospect was alarming, Habbaniya made the best of it. Two Hurricanes, an unexpected windfall from Egypt, went off to deal with Mosul; and though some Heinkels appeared over Habbaniya in full view of the blue lake and the great curves of the river and the grey station roofs, they failed to do much harm. The relieving force from Palestine was drawing near at last; and though it was attacked by Messerschmitts on the last lap of its race with time, their intervention failed to check it. The desert column reached Habbaniya on May 18; and the combined forces advanced on Baghdad, where a mood of penitence was now requesting British aircraft to refrain from attacking non-military targets.

Hostile forces barred the way near the bend of the river at Falluja, where the same lack of enterprise that had omitted to destroy the water tower at Habbaniya now failed to blow up a five-span bridge across the broad Euphrates. The place was carried by stiff fighting and a brilliant use of air-borne troops in an outflanking movement; and while German aircraft with their customary chivalry "took great pains to shoot up the British General Hospital" at Habbaniya, the road across the brown desert towards Baghdad was open. The crowded Embassy could hear the slow approach of British bombs and gunfire, as ears in Lucknow had once strained to catch the marching lilt of Colin Campbell's pipes; and before the month was out, Rashid Ali and his friends were off, leaving his flower garden by the river to worthier successors, who would appreciate his roses. The party (most appropriately, as it seemed to readers of the *Arabian Nights* and amateurs of Christmas pantomime) numbered about forty.

On May 29 peace returned to Habbaniya, where the Levy band was marching in the evening light along the shady station roads with their familiar English names; and soon Baghdad was asking for an armistice. A telegram informed the Air Ministry that a flag of truce had followed closely on a full-scale air attack on the barracks and aerodrome with screaming bombs of local manufacture, adding cheerfully, "The money is in the bag." This diagnosis was confirmed on the next day, when the Regent was escorted in triumph to his capital; and a further telegram reported that Baghdad airport was in use by the R.A.F. The day ended in congratulations at the palace in the presence of a large diplomatic company, only slightly marred by the absence of the Japanese minister.

It was June 1; and in one hectic month a Flying Training School had made 1600 sorties, dropped 100 tons of bombs, and fired 250,000 rounds. Powerfully aided by the Levies and by reinforcements of troops and aircraft (to say nothing of their two decrepit howitzers, which shortly afterwards withdrew to honourable retirement on the lawn outside Headquarters), they had saved Iraq and the whole position in the Middle East. Indeed, they had saved something more. For three weeks later the Germans went to war with Russia; and they had saved the road through Persia, which was now vital for the transit of Allied aid to the U.S.S.R. If that was to be safeguarded, Iraq must be in sure hands; and by a strange conjunction of events Habbaniya had helped to save the Kremlin.

The significance of their achievement was not missed by one qualified observer. For one evening, while the fight was still in progress, a Messerschmitt had landed in Renfrewshire; and when Rudolf Hess announced the terms on which his Führer was prepared to stop the war, the sole requirement outside Europe (apart from something about the German colonies) was that the British should evacuate Iraq.

Chapter XII

SYRIA

MAY WAS HALF OVER, when events in Iraq disturbed the peace of other lands beyond its border. The strain was passing at Habbaniya; and the desert column was a few days off. One Wednesday (it was May 14) a local diarist recorded "a quiet and uneventful day." True, the first German aircraft had been noticed on the day before; but as they had not yet made their presence felt, events at Habbaniya fell below recent standards of excitement. But less than 300 miles away, where the pipe-line ruled across a rust-red desert crosses the Trans-Jordan border near a point bearing the simple and euphonious title of H. 4, something else was happening that afternoon. A pilot on reconnaissance returning from patrol reported the unusual spectacle of some big German transport aircraft coming in to land at a French aerodrome in Syria. He had stayed long enough to notice that there were only two lorries with tins of petrol to refuel them before they could take off again for Iraq; and as the *Luftwaffe* had no business at Palmyra and seemed likely to be detained there for some time, two extremely junior R.A.F. officers sought authority to point out the error of its ways. This, they felt, could best be done by the one fighter at H. 4 with incendiary ammunition. Their proposal was promptly submitted to the general by a youthful Flying Officer, who remarked hopefully that if he could get off right away, while the enemy aircraft were refuelling, he thought that he could write the whole lot off on the ground.

"Are you two young gentlemen aware," enquired the general with propriety, "that we are not at war with Syria?"

"Yes, sir," the Flying Officer replied, "I know, sir; but I think it would be a bloody good idea if we were."

This contribution to high policy was fairly well received, the general observing that although he refused to be forced into acts of aggression just before lunch, the thorny problem might be referred at once to their respective Headquarters. Pending a reply the youthful pair returned to supervise the rearming and refuelling of their precious fighter; and when the answer came to hand by two o'clock that afternoon, they were gratified to learn that reinforcements in the welcome form of two fighters and three bombers were already on their way and that, when these had arrived, the impulsive Flying Officer was authorised to "commence his act of aggression." Two hours later the little force took off for Syria to find the Germans still in unlawful occupation of the landing ground at Palmyra. They dropped their bombs; and then the one fighter of H. 4 with two supporting Tomahawks went down to put the trespassers out of action.

It was plain from this prompt vindication of the niceties of international law that the possibility of hostilities in French mandated territory occasioned small surprise. Indeed, there had been symptoms of a German thrust in this direction so early as April, when it was hoped that the French garrison might even venture to resist; and Wavell had been warned. For a German wedge driven into Western Asia from the shores of the Levant to the Tigris above Mosul might have grave consequences. Enemy control of this region would effectively encircle Turkey, caught between the new masters of the Balkans and a hostile force in Syria, which might bar the road to British aid from Palestine. Besides, access to Syrian aerodromes, which General Dentz at Beyrout and his Vichy masters seemed willing to concede, afforded an invaluable chain of stepping-stones,

by which German aircraft could proceed from the Greek islands to
Iraq. This reinforcement of the hostile forces round Baghdad must
be averted; and while Mr. Eden warned Marshal Pétain and Admiral
Darlan of the consequences of their laxity, British bombs went down
on the aerodromes outside the wide and towered city of Damascus,
where the quiet merchants sit before their little doors along "the
street called Straight," and at Rayak in the broad, green corridor that
runs between the bare flanks of Lebanon a few miles from the broken
majesty of Baalbek.

These operations in the third week of May and a failure of the
German time-table to synchronise with events outside Baghdad
helped to avert the threat to Iraq. But so long as Syria lay open to
the German forces, the threat to Palestine remained and the Turks
might be cut off from any chance of Allied aid. Vichy's eccentric
notions of neutrality had not sufficed to keep this vital area out of
play; and it was plainly necessary to take some further steps in order
to control it. The war in this region, at least, had unmistakably
become a war for aerodromes; and British strategy, for once, struck
first. Early in June Anglo-French forces converged on Syria. The
main thrust was up the coast towards Beyrout along a seaboard where
the terraced hills and olive groves look out to sea and useful aid might
be expected from the fleet. In the air a single bomber squadron and
about three squadrons of assorted fighters were matched against 92
French aircraft. Both sides received some reinforcements in the
course of operations, the French increasing to a strength of 159 with
a valuable accession of specially selected and experienced fighter
pilots. But the Germans showed no tendency towards open intervention in the conflict which they had precipitated between former
allies.

The ground offensive was preceded by an air attack on the French
bases as far afield as Aleppo. Oil supplies between the folded hills of
Beyrout and the great sweep of the bay were conscientiously attacked;
and local watchers were a shade surprised to notice that this steady
onslaught of the R.A.F. on a strictly military objective was followed
by attacks in swift succession on the Municipality, the Christian
Brothers' school, the most respected mosque in the vicinity, and other
targets admirably calculated to arouse local indignation against the
invaders. But some light was shed upon the mystery by the discovery
of an unexploded German bomb in an adjacent field, as well as a few

splinters of a German bomb not far from the American University; and one judicious neutral, who observed the war from Beyrout, was led to the conclusion that the 29 air raids which they endured included some for which the R.A.F. was not responsible, a view supported by the fact that the Fleet Air Arm and the R.A.F. record a modest total of 16 attacks. Apart from this ingenious contribution the *Luftwaffe* abstained from any active share in operations, withdrawing their aircraft and specialists from local aerodromes and, as in Iraq, leaving their allies to fight a losing battle. For the German aptitude for cutting losses extended with still greater equanimity to other people's.

The offensive opened with aircraft operating in close support of the land forces and containing the French warships working from Beyrout. A strong proportion of the British fighter force concentrated on providing air cover for the Navy, which constituted the left flank of the advancing army and was well within the range of shore-based aircraft; and the Fleet Air Arm scored a notable success by sinking a French transport bringing reinforcements to the defenders. Indeed, British aircraft were conspicuously successful in searching the sea-lanes and attacking shipping bound for Beyrout. This achievement afforded an unpleasant proof that the French in Syria must now rely upon their own resources, while the Allied forces could be freely drawn from Egypt and Iraq. While the advance crept northwards up the long, low Tyrian shore, the R.A.F. with a daily force of some 80 aircraft flew out to sea to bar the way to any sea-borne reinforcements. The orange groves of Tyre were soon behind them; and that week they passed the small white houses that had once been Sidon. Far to the east, beyond the Andine vistas of grey rock and white snows of Lebanon, Punjabis and Rajputs were fighting bravely in the hills outside Damascus, and the desert column from Iraq groped its way towards the lonely arches of Palmyra. Before June was out, bombs were falling on General Dentz's headquarters at Beyrout, accommodated in the Residence. This dainty edifice, whose arched verandahs had once housed a Casino for Turks in search of recreation, now lost one corner in its violent encounter with a sterner customer, although its view of the race-course and the great shoulder of the mountain-side beyond was still unimpaired. The general was voluble in indignation at this violation of his privacy and moved to a hotel with a sea view. But when the R.A.F. pursued him to his new address, General Dentz left town and spent his final evening in the hills.

For once the R.A.F. was relatively free to bring its weight to bear upon an adversary without undue preoccupations on the subject of supply or of operations elsewhere. New types of aircraft—Beaufighters, Tomahawks, and Marylands—were beginning to appear; and for the moment, apart from Syria (and not counting the dying embers of Italian resistance in Abyssinia), they had only one war on their hands. Squadrons could be switched from the Western Desert with the certainty of prompt return at need; and as the winds of war veered a little in their favour, they seemed to have outgrown the desperate expedients of recent months. Their weight was freely used on shipping (Beaufighters from Cyprus taking a hand), railways, and motor transport, and in attacks on grounded aircraft. The latter method was particularly fruitful, a series of 140 sorties destroying 36 French aircraft and damaging 107 more. In an aerial offensive of five weeks the R.A.F. destroyed or damaged four-fifths of the opposing air force at a total cost of some 12 aircraft. The French had fought tenaciously; and their discouraged troops were streaming northward from the still, blue bay, where the tall cypresses look down on the red roofs of Beyrout. But there was little more that they could do; and on July 12 an armistice ended the unhappy business, leaving General Dentz to inform his officers in a final speech that he would be back among them in November. Until then, however, and (as it proved) for some time longer, the Lebanon and Syria were free from Germans, and a cleaner tricolour than Vichy's waved above the Residence at Beyrout.

Chapter XIII

PERSIA

ONE FURTHER ASIATIC COMPLICATION stood between
Middle East Command that summer and a single-minded
pursuit of victory in Africa. Beyond Iraq the great quadrilateral of
Persia housed a vital source of oil and contained the sole overland
route by which munitions from the West could reach Russia. It was
already plain that if the armies of the U.S.S.R. were to hold the
German rush, British and American supplies were badly needed and
the Persian reinforcement route must be kept open; and so long as
Persia remained a field for enemy activities, its operation was highly
uncertain. An Anglo-Russian ultimatum was followed by joint
military action. While the Russians moved in from the north, British
forces landed at the head of the Persian Gulf and operated overland
from Iraq. It was all over in one hot August week.

The R.A.F. participated from their bases in Iraq. Four squadrons
at Shaiba and three more at Habbaniya shared the duty of supporting
the land and naval forces and dropping leaflets (and occasionally
bombs) for the removal of Persian misconceptions. The local air
force, which mustered about 100 pilots, showed little tendency to
intervene after a destructive attack on their aerodrome at Ahwaz;

and an air-borne landing of Baluchis in the oil-field safeguarded a vital objective. Fighter patrols protected the great refinery at Abadan, while bombers attacked gun positions on the Paitak Pass; and so far as fighting was concerned, this was their leading contribution. For in the absence of squadrons trained in close co-operation with advancing troops they were judiciously confined to attacks on recognisable objectives. Whilst operations were in progress, bombers from Habbaniya regaled the populations of Persian cities from Kermanshah to Ispahan with informing literature; and a final bombing of Ahwaz was followed by its capture and an armistice. August went out upon an interlude of politics that ended in an abdication, a new Shah, and a treaty which ensured the safety of Russia's reinforcement route no less than the defence of India from any menace in the west.

The swift campaign had closed an awkward gap; and the security of Persia was the fruit of victory in Iraq. As the Prime Minister reported, "the Allied front now runs in an immense crescent from Spitzbergen in the Arctic Ocean to Tobruk in the Western Desert . . . we have joined hands with our Russian Allies, and stand in the line to bar the further eastward progress of the enemy."

Chapter XIV

THE DESERT: THRUST

W AR HAD STOOD STILL IN THE DESERT since the late
spring days of 1941, when Rommel's first offensive from
the west sent them scrambling back to their starting-point in Egypt;
and two armies lay watching one another through the dusty glare
along the line of the frontier. The first need of British strategy was
now to concentrate on the defence of the Nile valley. But divergent
calls on the small forces in the Middle East had followed one another
with increasing urgency; and in one anxious April week, which saw
a tired British army leaving Greece and Rashid Ali crouching in
Baghdad for his spring on Habbaniya, they mounted to a shrill
crescendo. It was an exacting time, in which the R.A.F. had somehow
contrived to make a limited supply of aircraft face in all directions.
For Longmore's tenure of the Middle East Command was a protracted
and successful juggle, in which quickness of hand deceived Italian
eyes and his squadrons operated with astonishing success against
fantastic odds. The first phase of the war in Africa had seen them
sweep an immeasurably stronger enemy out of the sky over three
vast provinces in Libya, Eritrea, and Abyssinia; Malta had been held;
and when war came to Greece, they had done all that was possible.
If their resources were insufficient to deny Greece and Cyrenaica to
the *Luftwaffe's* simultaneous attacks, they were not to blame. Deft
handling had enabled them to live through the lean years. But
Longmore's happy gift for "bluffing a full house with a couple of

pairs" resisted the temptation to denude the skies of Egypt by expending a dwindling fighter force upon the wasted gallantry of hopeless rearguard actions, as Dowding had once conserved the strength of Fighter Command against demands from France in order to retain sufficient aircraft for the eventual defence of Britain. For the main position in the Middle East was still intact. Egypt and East Africa were firmly held; there was nothing further to be feared from the Italian air force; and on June 1, 1941, as Longmore handed over his command to Tedder, who had been in charge since the early part of May, much had been gained and nothing vital had been lost.

But the situation inherited that summer by his successor called for steady nerves. Cyrenaica and Greece had gone; Crete was going; Iraq was threatened; and it was growing plain that something must be done to safeguard Syria. At sea the Mediterranean west of a line from Cyprus to Daba lay within range of German aircraft, and it was doubtful if the Navy could move freely without fighter escort 50 miles from Alexandria; and on land the crowded cities and vital depots of the Delta had now come within bombing range of a more formidable enemy than the Italians. That was the unpleasing picture which confronted Tedder, as his duel with the *Luftwaffe* began.

In the Desert, as spring turned to summer, dusty men at large in the brown distances along the edge of Egypt began to learn what Doughty meant by "that giddy heat upon the crown of the head; the ears tingle with a flickering shrillness, a subtle crepitation it seems, in the glassiness of this sun-stricken nature; the hot sandblink is in the eyes, and there is little refreshment to find in the tent's shelter; the worsted booths leak to this fiery rain of sunny light." The Desert army was re-forming on a line running inland from the shattered masonry that overlooks the sea at Sidi Barrani, confronted across 50 unshaded miles by an enemy established on the carved, brown edge of Libya beyond Sollum. Axis forces looked down into Egypt from the cliffs of Halfaya and the stony desert plateau round Capuzzo. There were some grounds for thinking that their advance on Egypt had been arrested by R.A.F. attacks on their communications, since it was not easy for Rommel to accumulate supplies for his next move with British aircraft busy on the long road behind him and their bombs going down on quays and shipping at Benghazi. A German letter-writer had enquired indignantly, "Where is the German Air Force? Maria, it is worse here than in France. There I was in the front line, but here I must stay behind and take the identity discs of the dead. For the first time in my life I lost consciousness, whether from hunger or the sight of the horrible wounds I don't know. Whoever gets out of this hell can thank the Lord." Their main objective was his petrol; and a welcome interlude of inactivity by hostile aircraft seemed to indicate success.

The enemy had cleared all Cyrenaica except where Tobruk, a lonely island of resistance deep in Axis territory, was still held against them; and an effort to relieve it with R.A.F. support broke down on an encounter not far from Capuzzo with more hostile tanks than had been expected. At midsummer a more elaborate attempt, adorned with the name of Operation "Battleaxe," proceeded smoothly in its early stages until a military situation of some intricacy developed in the dusty *hinterland*. The R.A.F. had been required to provide the advancing land forces with an impenetrable "umbrella" against air attack. It was not altogether clear that hostile wasps were any likelier to be deterred from depredations on the military tea-table by a display of vigour in its immediate vicinity than by the methodical destruction of their nests in attacks on hostile aerodromes. But there was always a strong preference for the reassuring sight of friendly aircraft over-head; and exercises of air power out of sight, though often infinitely more effective, tended to be out of mind for the troops below. Besides, it was not easy to determine at what height the required "umbrella" should be unfurled, as the dreaded downpour might either take the form of high-level bombing or of low-flying attacks. But the R.A.F. complied with the requirements. The fighter force was duly concentrated on this defensive *rôle* to the detriment of more rewarding operations; and in the outcome German aircraft hardly intervened. It was not improbable that they were running short of petrol; but as sufficient fuel was still available to leave their land forces with a high degree of mobility, it would appear that Rommel, if he had to choose, preferred to move his tanks and motor transport. On the ground he gave an excellent display of his abilities as a divisional tactician. As the *imbroglio* developed, Wavell was flown up to see things for himself in the brown spaces south of Halfaya; and whilst aircraft bombed the enemy's advancing columns (their intervention was thought to have extricated an Indian division from an awkward situation), Operation "Battleaxe" ended where it had begun. That night Axis forces got as far into Egyptian territory as Buq Buq. But in the morning they were gone, leaving the empty Desert dancing in the midsummer heat.

There was so much to be done in Egypt before they could perfect a weapon for the reconquest of the Desert. If the R.A.F. was to become a Desert force capable of highly mobile operations in the wilderness, the squadrons must learn to be nomadic. For organisation on a "station" basis was far too unwieldy for swift movement. Mobility meant more motor transport for the carriage of their bombs and petrol, since aircraft could only operate within the radius of their supplies, and these could only move at the pace of their vehicles. This limitation restricted the range and swiftness of air power; and the comparative immobility of squadrons in the Desert had hitherto been remedied by friendly contributions from the army's transport, eked out by welcome captures from the enemy. But mobility was far too vital an ingredient of victory in air warfare to be left on this precarious footing; and it was plain that they must make more permanent provision.

If mobility was an essential element of air power, the maintenance of aircraft faced them with a need of equal urgency. Repair and Salvage Units multiplied; a Base Salvage Depot was created for the transportation of crashed aircraft from the front for reconstruction at base depots; and control was simplified by the appointment of a Chief Maintenance and Supply Officer. These unromantic measures formed the staple of Tedder's activities in Cairo, where Air Vice-Marshal Drummond was now his Deputy A.O.C.-in-C., Middle East; and as the summer months went by, their strength in serviceable aircraft gradually multiplied itself by three. For the lean years were passing now. Tomahawks came in increasing numbers from America to reinforce their fighter strength; Bostons and Marylands appeared among the bombers, to say nothing of more familiar types from home.

That summer the conclusion of the Abyssinian campaign released South African land and air forces for operations further north. One S.A.A.F. squadron had already served in the defence of Alexandria; some of their bombers fought over Crete; and they played an active part in Operation "Battleaxe." After midsummer they moved up in force to taste the joys of Desert flying on a lighter diet and a lighter soil, which soon revealed the ills that aircraft are heirs to in the absence of air filters. But their standard was maintained on the new scene of operations; and when Smuts met them in the Desert, he found some-

Royal Air Force and
Axis Air Forces Range
June-November, 1941.

Royal Air Force and Axis Air Forces Range,

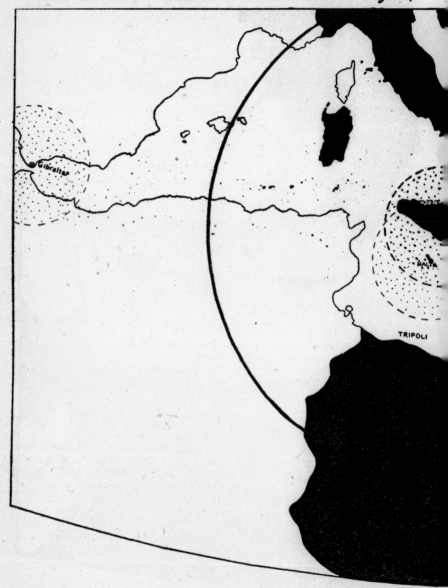

○ German Bomber Cover

◉ German Fighter Cover

◉ R.A.F. Fighter Cover

June -November 1941

Territory in Axis hands ▪

Territory in Allied hands ▪

Territory in Axis hands

Territory in Allied hands

thing encouraging to say to Tedder about "the Air, the architect of victory." Was he not the patron of the R.A.F. ?

Victory, perhaps, was not far off that summer, as Auchinleck took over the command from Wavell. Week after week the squadrons attended with unfailing punctuality to their duties of bombing hostile shipping at Benghazi and escorting friendly shipping to Tobruk. For if there was sometimes a close season for fighting on the ground, there was none overhead. Air-warfare went on all the time; and bomber crews made the 900-mile run from the Delta to Benghazi, halting to refuel in the Desert, with a suburban milkman's regularity. Tobruk was a more formidable problem. It was beyond their power to give fighter cover to the lonely garrison of that forbidding spot, where the defenders listened helplessly to hostile bombers warming up their engines on the airfield at El Adem for the short run that would bring them overhead in a few minutes. But if it was impossible to exercise air power in their defence for lack of aerodromes within fighter range of Tobruk, it played a vital part in their supply. For their life depended on a slender line of coastwise shipping, maintained with unexampled fortitude in waters far in front of the British line. Leaving the little port of Mersa Matruh, it stole along the coast towards Tobruk; and it had now become the business of the R.A.F. to protect shipping against air attack all the way from Sidi Barrani to Bardia, leaving the remainder of the passage to be covered after dark. But even this restricted area could only be patrolled by fighters in constant danger of attack by German aircraft operating from their Desert bases in overwhelming strength; and they depended upon forward landing grounds precariously held by light forces in advance of the main British army. Small wonder that this contribution to the defence of Tobruk, made with long flying hours over the blue sea in face of heavy odds, was highly valued. For every ship that made the battered harbour, where a broken town of empty windows stared blindly from the long, grey headland, owed its safe arrival to the R.A.F.

Life in the back areas was not wholly uneventful either, since Lower Egypt was now within range of German bombers from Crete and Cyrenaica; and a successful attack on one R.A.F. depot in the Delta emphasised the undesirability of retaining too many precious eggs in a single basket. But German bombing policy failed, on the whole, to make the most of its advantages. For while British bombers

struck with effect at enemy supply lines from their forward bases in
the Western Desert and with a growing sense of the offensive value
of Malta (as Messina and Palermo learned to know), there was little
corresponding effort by the *Luftwaffe*. Indeed, a high proportion of
their bomber force was diverted to escort duties with sea-borne
convoys; and some random bombing of Alexandria and the Canal
was no substitute for a methodical attack on British bases. With
Crete and Libya in his control, the enemy had temporarily won the
war for aerodromes; but he failed to use his victory. As the summer
passed, events in Russia diverted large numbers of German aircraft
from the Mediterranean; and with this drain on enemy reserves it
was not easy for him to replace unserviceable aircraft in Africa. Later
in the year, however, steps were taken to redress the balance; and
Field-Marshal Kesselring's *Luftflotte* 2 was transferred from the Russian
front to headquarters in Rome, controlling the local *Fliegerkorps* X
and bringing *Fliegerkorps II* to Sicily. Kesselring in Rome was
matched against Tedder in Cairo; and the test could not be far off.

In the Desert Collishaw had been succeeded after five years in
the Middle East by Air Vice-Marshal Coningham, a New Zealander
of immense energy and rare powers of leadership, in whose sound
belief the war of machines depended ultimately upon men. That
was in August; and a few weeks later Rommel made a move, feeling
his way round their inland flank with a strong force of tanks. But
this time his passion for outflanking movements was unsatisfied, as
they were caught refuelling deep in the Desert by two S.A.A.F.
bomber squadrons. Few targets are more inviting than 120 immobile
tanks with their attendant transport; and after an uncomfortable day
of bombing they returned to their own side of the frontier. The
British were almost ready now to move, with General Cunningham,
who had been responsible for a brilliant campaign in Abyssinia,
commanding the Eighth Army in a bewildering profusion of his
namesakes, since his sailor brother was in command at sea and the
new A.H.Q., Western Desert, was in charge of Coningham. His
fighter squadrons were a formidable array of modern aircraft with
Hurricanes predominating and a wing of Tomahawks. There were
no Gladiators in the Desert now; and the old days of gallant make-
believe were over. When the moment came for an advance, they
proposed to preface operations on the ground by interrupting and
destroying enemy supplies. In the next phase a series of attacks on

hostile fighters in the air and on the ground was calculated to deprive the enemy of his power to interfere with land operations, since his bombers could not operate without their fighter cover; and once this duty was discharged, the R.A.F. would be free to work with its own advancing land forces. The main purpose of the offensive, which was to be known as Operation "Crusader," was to destroy the Axis armour and thus open the path for an advance further to the west; and when the time came, the Tobruk garrison would join in the advance. The move was nicely timed to anticipate an expected enemy attempt to eliminate that troublesome *enclave* in Axis territory.

In the opening phase Benghazi and the chain of bases—Derna, Gambut, Bardia, and Gazala—between the enemy's back areas and his front line were sedulously bombed from Egypt, whilst aircraft from Malta struck at Naples and Palermo, where his shipping started from, and struck once more at Tripoli, where it arrived. There were some novelties, as 4000-lb. bombs were used on Naples, although an experiment with two Flying Fortresses from Egypt was less successful. Meanwhile the fighters maintained a high degree of activity in order to obstruct the enemy from watching British preparations for the offensive. A week before it opened the air attack was switched from the enemy's supplies to his air forces; and bombs went down on aerodromes and petrol dumps at Berka, Benina, Barce, Derna, Gambut, Gazala, Martuba, and Tmimi, doing a good deal of damage to repair shops, hangars, runways, and aircraft on the ground. As the hour of the offensive came nearer, there was an increased demand for aerial reconnaissance; and Boston bombers made their first appearance in the Desert in this harmless *rôle*. A spirited attempt to drop parachutists for the purpose of sabotaging aerodromes in the neighbourhood of Tmimi and Gazala under cover of a heavy night attack with bombs and flares failed owing to bad weather, though one party of survivors managed to get back to their own lines.

That night the weather was conspicuously vile; and as the rain drummed on the Desert in the intermittent glare of a catastrophic thunderstorm, the British armour moved up to the wire unobserved.

There was a silver lining, though. For when November 18 dawned, some of the enemy's aerodromes were waterlogged, leaving the R.A.F. fewer adversaries to fight in the sky and more aircraft to damage on the ground. As they swept overhead, the watchers on the Desert

floor enjoyed the novel spectacle of a sky full of friendly aircraft—
"Whole shoals of fighters went careering by, glinting like little silver
splinters in the sun. Bombers cruised steadily overhead with their
fighter escorts fooling all round them." There had been nothing
like this for them to see in Greece. In those days it had been almost
second nature to dive for cover when anything flew over them. But
now the tables had been turned; and as the troops moved forward,
British fighters had some trouble in finding anything to fight. There
were a few combats over Martuba; they shot down some transport
aircraft not far from Barce and destroyed four petrol tankers on the
road; and S.A.A.F. bombers even left their mark on the main landing
ground at Gazala without meeting opposition. Air warfare was still
comparatively uneventful on the next day, as the tanks ploughed
forward through the brown immensities towards Sidi Rezegh.

This time direct assault upon the fortified positions between
Capuzzo and the sea was to wait until the advance had gone beyond
them. It was not to open with frontal attacks on Sollum and the
brown cliff-face of Halfaya, pitted and pock-marked with their
machine-gun nests. For Cunningham's attack, by-passing the heavily
defended area between Sollum and Bardia, thrust straight across the
wilderness towards Tobruk with the strange freedom conferred on
military movements by armoured vehicles at large in the dry spaces
of Africa. As the Prime Minister reported, "the conditions are in
many respects like those of sea war"; and he told the House of
Commons later of "a widespread and confused battle of extremely
high-class combatants, mounted upon mechanised transport and
fighting in barren lands with the utmost vigour and determination."
By the second day of the offensive they had reached the neighbourhood of Sidi Rezegh, and on the third the forces in Tobruk were
ordered to break out in their direction. As the tank battle proceeded
in the stony scrub, there had been a slight increase of air fighting.
Hurricanes were used with bombs; fighters were assiduous in their
attention to the enemy; and by November 21 it was possible for a
cautious expert to affirm that complete air superiority had been
attained. Indeed, one rapturous staff officer, remembering an evil
past, announced that it was "like France, only the other way
round."

But the resemblance failed to last, and two days later the advance
was checked on all its fronts. At this stage the enterprising Rommel

poured a miscellany of armour, guns, and motor transport through the British lines. Shooting its way through back areas, it even reached the Egyptian frontier and penetrated to a region of highly vulnerable dumps and airfields. (Cavalry had done such things in the American Civil War, when Forrest and J. E. B. Stuart led Confederate troopers on long raids far behind the Union lines.) As this menace curled like a whip-lash round the British rear, air action seemed the best and quickest means of dealing with it. Attacked by Hurricane bombers on the second day of its career, it was bombed again with heavier projectiles, which scored with serious effect on its vulnerable tail of motor transport. An armoured raid without a friendly aircraft over-head has no answer to hostile bombers; and the ground troops whom they encountered showed no tendency to disintegrate. This was far less enjoyable than the armoured gallop across France to Abbeville and the sea in 1940; and the raiders were hunted by a pack of Blen-heims (including some Free French). The Fleet Air Arm took a hand, until they turned for home, pursued by bombers, worried on the flanks by armoured cars, and headed thoughtfully into the waiting arms of British tanks not far from Gambut. Their effort had been unsuccessful in inflicting any major damage or in diverting the British land forces in the Desert south-east of Tobruk from their objective. But in its swiftness and a certain tendency to disregard the factor of air power it was typical of Rommel's methods.

It was December now; and as the tank battle proceeded in the dusty wilderness, Ritchie had succeeded Cunningham. An improve-ment in co-operation between ground and air forces became notice-able; and the R.A.F. continued to play their part in the land battle. Their activities had left the Germans practically blinded in the air; they were attending conscientiously to the unarmoured tail of transport and supply that lay behind the German tanks; and General Freyberg informed them that "your fellows have been simply magnificent, and my men are full of admiration and gratitude." For they had earned New Zealand's thanks by prompt action on an armoured column that was threatening his command. While the fighting swayed in the approaches to Tobruk, the long arm of air power reached out, and Tedder shifted the attacks of home-based bombers in Great Britain from railway yards in Naples to the docks. At the same time Malta was desired to "keep its eye on the Libyan ball." For the game of air warfare was played on a gigantic board. But their main concern was still the land battle, where Boston bombers now appeared for the first time and the new Beaufighters showed their paces in attacks on motor transport. For the Prime Minister had ruled a few weeks earlier that, on Auchinleck's intimation "that a land battle is in prospect, the Air Officer Commanding-in-Chief will give him all possible aid irrespective of other targets, however attractive. The Army Commander-in-Chief will specify to the Air Officer Commanding-in-Chief the targets and tasks which he requires to be performed, both in the preparatory attack on the rearward installations of the enemy and for air action during the progress of the battle"; and it was comforting to have one soldier's appreciation for "the magnificent co-operation of the R.A.F.," which had supplied a "constant stream of valuable information," while their fighters provided "almost complete protection" and the bombers disorganised the enemy, "often in answer to calls from my troops." This tribute foresaw that they were "on the way to a new standard of inter-Service co-operation," which was one day to form the main achievement of the Eighth Army and the R.A.F. in Africa.

Early in December the enemy began to weaken under his long pounding in the Desert. With Rommel in retreat the road to Tobruk opened, and they headed west towards Benghazi. But that week, as victory began to dawn in Africa, skies clouded further east; and bombs went down one Sunday morning on Pearl Harbour. The menace of Japan was already drawing off valuable squadrons for the defence of Burma and Malaya; and now it threatened to dry up the springs of American aircraft supply. For British strategy with its world-wide commitments and severely limited resources could rarely afford the luxury of concentration on a single object. If Singapore could not be left uncovered, Middle East Command must look after itself; and at the moment it seemed capable of doing so. For it had attained air superiority in the Desert and played its part in the defence of Tobruk; Malta was striking hard at the enemy's supply lines; and their rear had been safeguarded by the contribution of air power to successful operations in Syria, Iraq, and Persia.

Now they were on the track of a retreating army headed for Benghazi. Tobruk was safe behind them; and a British army was west-bound across Cyrenaica once more. It was just eight months since they had passed that way with Rommel at their heels. That had been in April; and now December saw them in pursuit of their elusive foe over the familiar course. There was a notion that he would stand to face them at Gazala; and they moved against his line through the pale darkness of a sand-storm with faces whipped by the driving sand and the dry scent of the Desert in their nostrils. But he was gone, leaving an Italian rearguard; and the hunt careered at large across the earth-brown desolation in long parallels of dust-clouds, as their motor transport went racing to the west. Pursuit was anything but simple for the R.A.F. The fighters had been working at the limit of their range in order to reach the vicinity of Tobruk, and medium bombers were still operating from the Delta. Now the fighters were moved forward to the great airfield at El Adem under the gaunt wrecks of Italian buildings, with light bomber squadrons a few miles behind them on the bare plateau of Gambut. This advance was far from easy with vast quantities of petrol to be moved by road. But they managed to dump 10,000 gallons at Gazala, while the landing grounds were still under shell-fire; and for two hazardous days R.A.F. working parties plied their trade in advance of the front line. For mobility was the main sinew of air victory; and as the last of the retreating enemy left Mechili, the advance R.A.F. party reached the landing ground and had 15,000 gallons of fuel there by the next day, with the result that one day later four squadrons were operating from the landing ground and four more were refuelling for operations further forward. It was plain that air power depended upon ground staffs; and this was plainer still, when a working party, consigned to a site deep in the Desert far ahead of the army and warned that a landing ground would be required by noon, cleared runways measuring 1000 yards by 11.30, as the first squadron landed, and had four squadrons suitably accommodated on the next day, with more coming in for fuel and a force of bombers standing by. Desert life, it seemed, had taught the R.A.F. to be nomadic.

As the pursuit swept across Cyrenaica, they dealt with the retreating enemy; and one German diary recorded that "the night was terrible. The English bombers came in full force and dropped their eggs. We had no cover, not a hole, not a building. When they had dropped their bombs, they made low-flying attacks and shot us up. So it goes on night after night." For Rommel's elusive strategy had its drawbacks for the participants, although his pursuers sometimes found it difficult to keep up with their quarry. But they concentrated on his air forces, dislocating the daily service of air transports from Athens (the last Axis convoy to reach Derna ran straight into the inhospitable arms of some waiting Sikhs, who had got there first and wrecked more than 100 grounded aircraft) and striking hard at airfields. When Derna fell, the captured aerodrome was a graveyard of abandoned aircraft, new wrecks wearing the *Luftwaffe*'s swastika and not the Roman emblem of an earlier defeat, though one trophy had been maliciously adorned with 27 unobtrusive sticks of gelignite (happily immobilised by an acquisitive airman, who removed the battery for other purposes). Although it still returned to make occasional attacks on British bombers operating over the green hillsides of the Jebel Akdar, the *Luftwaffe* was out of the race; and when the R.A.F. reached Benina, they found 63 abandoned aircraft round the wrecked buildings and 51 more at Berka.

Rain was beating on the empty farmhouses along the road as they came down once more to the green grass and the red earth and the white houses of Benghazi. This time the enemy's retreat had not been cut at Beda Fomm; and Rommel was still somewhere ahead of them in the great angle of the coast that turns towards El Agheila. But the grinning crew of a British armoured car was cooking their Christmas dinner on the muddy quayside of the capital of Cyrenaica under the disapproving silhouette of its cathedral. For they were in Benghazi once again, this time a little earlier than usual. The air campaign had ended in the destruction or damage of 1213 of their adversaries for the loss of 597 of their own; and it was significant that more than 200 aircraft had been abandoned by the retreating enemy on captured landing grounds. Air superiority had been the instrument of victory on land; and though the military situation lacked finality so long as Rommel was at large, "Crusader" seemed to have arrived at the destination of his long pilgrimage.

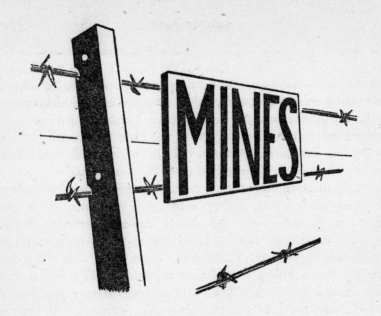

Chapter XV

THE DESERT: PARRY

AS A NEW YEAR OPENED in the first days of 1942, the pendulum of war was still swinging westward across Africa. It had swung that way less than a year ago, when they hunted Graziani to the west in Wavell's first offensive. Then, swinging in reverse, it swept them back to Egypt with Rommel at their heels; and now the pendulum had swung them forward to Benghazi once again. They were half-way to Tripoli; and if they were given time to gather strength for the next stage of their advance, to accumulate supplies and petrol in the forward areas, and to renew a good deal of their machinery, which was showing signs of wear after long weeks of activity in the air and on the ground, there was no reason why they should not go on to Tripoli and end the war in Africa. That had been prevented by the call to Greece in 1941; and now it was unfortunate to find the Far East competing with success for their limited resources. So far as concerned the R.A.F., whole squadrons, balloon units, maintenance echelons, and anti-aircraft equipment were leaving them for Asia, some transferred from the Middle East and others diverted from African destinations to reinforce the rather shaky line in Asia. (It was not surprising that an Empire whose resources just sufficed for war in Europe, Africa, and the Atlantic, was severely strained by this extension of its liabilities to Asia and the Pacific.) With the Germans half-way across Russia and the growing prospect of a Japanese advance after their successful efforts to paralyse American and British sea power in the Pacific, the war was entering upon a crisis comparable to the supreme emergency of 1940; and it was plain that British forces in the Middle East would have not only to rely on their own efforts, but to make substantial contributions to the war in Asia.

At the moment there was no reason to suppose them incapable of advancing further west, if they were only given time. That must depend on Rommel, who had already shown a marked preference for rapid movement, and on his ability to renew his strength by reinforcements from the Continent. These could only reach him over sea routes leading from Italian ports to Tripoli; and as these were incessantly attacked from Malta, Axis strategy appeared to realise somewhat belatedly the dangerous significance of that indomitable island, which was now subjected to prolonged attack by the *Luftwaffe* on a paralysing scale.

In the brown spaces of the Desert beyond Benghazi they were still going forward. The enemy withdrew behind Agedabia to positions of some strength at El Agheila. The new Kittyhawks were flown with effect by an Australian fighter squadron, dealing roughly with some German dive-bombers and taking heavy toll of Italian aircraft and their fighter escort; and a single Liberator, first of its majestic species in the Middle East, dropped a few bombs on Tripoli. Now they had leisure to dispose of the encircled garrisons behind them in the fortresses along the coast; and as there were not many targets in the forward areas for the light bombers, they were used on Bardia. This aid was welcome in the absence of a strong artillery by land or sea; and the subsequent bombardment, conducted under almost peace conditions without air opposition or effective anti-aircraft fire, gave some useful practice to new air crews and accelerated the capture of the place. Not long afterwards Halfaya succumbed to the same combination of bombing from the air and shelling by naval and land forces, and Sollum fell to a ground attack. Unlike Tobruk, the Axis fortresses had been unable to survive in hostile territory, since the sea was closed behind them and their fortitude was unequal to continuous attack from overhead. A German effort to drop supplies on Halfaya by transport aircraft from Crete was

insufficient for its needs; and six sacks of food, intended for con-
sumers on the other side and sent astray by a slight error in navigation, were gratefully received on the main landing ground of an R.A.F.
aerodrome 150 miles away in Egypt.

At Benghazi it was raining hard; and while the runways of the
captured airfields were reduced to an unpleasant sea of sticky chocolate,
German landing grounds on the sandy surface of the Desert further
west dried rapidly. The same fatality, which had worked in favour of
the R.A.F. on the first day of Auchinleck's offensive, now worked
against them, restricting their operations while their adversaries were
left free to fly. Rommel, who had been building up his strength
(nine large steamers were seen entering the port of Tripoli a fortnight
earlier), moved suddenly on January 21. Opening as a reconnaissance
in force, his tentative advance turned into an offensive as soon as its
initial purpose of testing the strength of the land forces in his immediate
vicinity had been attained by ascertaining that these failed to satisfy
the test. For their positions in the forward area beyond Benghazi
were insecurely held; and as the military screen in front of them collapsed abruptly, the main fighter force on a Desert aerodrome received
a sudden intimation that, as the enemy were coming, they had better
leave. It is not a simple matter to evacuate eight squadrons at short
notice from a waterlogged airfield. But they man-handled them
across the slough, six airmen to each wing; the aircraft were
manœuvred on to a single strip; and shells were dropping on the
landing ground as the last of them took off. There was no time for
them to move 6 unserviceable aircraft, which they had to leave
behind, as well as a good deal of petrol. But their rapid exodus
compared favourably with the large numbers of aircraft abandoned
by the *Luftwaffe* in the course of its retreat a few weeks earlier.

The pendulum was swinging once again; and the R.A.F. was soon
hard at work attacking an advancing enemy, some Hurricanes encountering a strong force of dive-bombers just as their own petrol
was running low, disposing of them, and then force-landing safely
with dry tanks. One week brought Rommel to Benghazi; and by
January 28 that elusive trophy was in Axis hands once more. As the
Eighth Army receded, the R.A.F. moved back to safety with their
armoured cars doing fine work in the defence of forward landing
grounds, one company exceeding its own duties in order to recover
some abandoned British tanks, which were delivered to their rightful

owners across 60 miles of desert by R.A.F. drivers who had never handled tanks before. At this stage Rommel elected to continue his advance at speed with bold unorthodoxy. Leaving his main force of armour halted and largely discarding air support, since it would take time to bring up all the petrol that they would require, he sent infantry in lorries racing eastward through the hill country of the Jebel Akdar. This decision, which left them entirely without air cover for five days, recalled his unprotected thrust through Cunningham's advancing columns, which had helped to disorganise the first impact of "Crusader" two months earlier. If the British contemplated a stand in the Desert to the south of him, they might find that he had got across the coast road at some point behind them. For his tastes always seemed to run in the direction of outflanking movements; and as he had outflanked them from the south in 1941, this time he preferred, if possible, to outflank them from the north. As for air support, he sometimes appeared to underrate it; and perhaps it might reasonably be dispensed with on this occasion, as the weather was still a formidable alternation of driving rain and sand-storms.

This swift manœuvre hustled the Eighth Army back; and though the advancing enemy afforded valuable targets to the R.A.F., it was not always easy to take advantage of them in a fluid military situation. For communications between units were impaired by rapid movement; friend was not always readily distinguishable from foe by aircraft overhead; and it was extremely difficult to fix a bomb line for their guidance. But as February passed, Ritchie stabilised his forces on a line slanting from Gazala deep into the Desert. The Jebel Akdar, where a single road wound over the green hills with their odd look of Devon at one end and Scotland at the other, had been left behind; and half the rungs of the long ladder by which they had climbed to Benghazi had slipped through their fingers. The small hotel at the corner beyond the citadel of Barce, where German eyes were offended by a fragment of antiquity bearing something that looked perilously like a Hebrew inscription, was left to other tenants; and their successors sunned themselves on the sandy beach of Apollonia. The enemy had flooded beyond Derna and the airfields of Martuba and Tmimi; and the Eighth Army was halted half-way from Benghazi to the Egyptian frontier.

February was nearly over, when the pendulum checked in its eastward swing and the two armies halted to face one another in the

empty *hinterland* of Gazala. The fighter squadrons, which had been
brought back to El Adem, found the neighbourhood a shade exposed
to enemy attack as well as far too dusty for convenience, and removed
themselves a little further off to Gambut. There a limitless horizon
framed the hard, brown soil of Desert airfields, where the scattered
tents resembled nothing so much as a vast show-ground. There was
an immense array of assorted caravans; runways seemed to take the
place of race-tracks; and amongst innumerable refreshment-tents
and their lesser satellites all that they seemed to lack was the music of
merry-go-rounds, for which the never-ending roar of aircraft engines
was the local substitute. In these surroundings the Western Desert
Air Force grew to maturity, ripening what Tedder used to call "the
old Desert squadrons who know not only the local dust, but also the
local Hun." For though the armies halted, air warfare was continuous.
Their strength in Africa had been impaired by the demands of the Far
East. Singapore had gone; Rangoon was going; and the drain of
aircraft towards India reduced Middle East Command to the uncomfortable expedient of "living on its fat," whilst ingenuity in maintenance became an unpleasant necessity. Malta's state was critical;
Egypt was exposed to hostile bombing; and Tedder faced the combined problems of home defence, a land campaign in the Desert, and
the naval needs of Malta convoys.

At Rome his adversary wielded Axis air power in the uneasy
equilibrium of an Allied headquarters. But Kesselring sometimes
appeared to be unequal to the divergent demands made upon *Luft-
lotte* 2 for simultaneous assaults on Malta and Egypt, as well as support
for Rommel in the Desert. German air power somehow lacked
independence since its glaring failure over Britain in 1940. There were
strong symptoms of subservience to purely military exigencies, and
opportunities were missed. Besides, the Russian front was paramount,
although the Marshal had the consolation that his Messerschmitt 109
was superior in performance to anything that could be flown against
it—Hurricanes, Tomahawks, and Kittyhawks—except the R.A.F.'s
half-dozen Spitfires. But Coningham was hard at work at weekly
conferences with his commanders in the shade of Desert caravans;
Kittyhawks were turning into fighter-bombers; resting air crews
learned to know the feel of army problems as the guests of troops in
forward areas; and a fair flow of new aircraft was reaching them
from home.

As spring deepened into summer, they continued to bomb Benghazi in a melancholy rhythm and with particular attention to three sunken ships employed as landing stages and known familiarly to their British visitors as "Harry," "George," and "Johnny." While night fighters from home fought defensive combats over Egypt, the chain of Axis airfields from Tmimi to Benghazi was assiduously bombed by Bostons; and transport on the roads was punished, until two officers of Bersaglieri reported to their captors that all drivers invariably jumped for shelter at the sound of aircraft overhead. This was no compliment to the *Luftwaffe*; and in May a German working on column of supply was painfully convinced that the best way of meeting low-level attacks was to dig a hole and stay there—"They came over us, wave after wave. One used to think, 'My God, how much longer?'" Besides, they had an irritating habit of bombing troops at hours appropriate for rest, one German diarist recording that "in the late afternoon Tommy came along with the bombs. Bombs were whistling through the air and bursting round us. We hit the ground, but were almost lifted off it by the force of the explosions. We wonder if we shall ever get out of this hell. We have had many attacks, but these bombs were the worst I have ever experienced."

This ascendancy was not maintained without its price; and though Tedder could congratulate his South Africans upon an "excellent start of the shooting season" and Smuts visited them in May, the Desert was an uncomfortable fighting ground, where pilots might alight 150 miles from home after combat or misadventure and then cover fantastic distances on foot through an inhospitable void of hostile territory before the "missing" men walked in to earn the winged boot of the "Late Arrivals' Club," worn (as the certificate of membership directed) upon the left breast of the flying suit. But in the last week of May enemy attacks were growing stronger. British aerodromes and railheads were significantly bombed. For strong air reinforcements had reached the enemy; his fighter screen endeavoured to obstruct observation of Axis troop movements; and it was plain that something more was stirring in the Desert.

Chapter XVI

THE DESERT: RETURN

THE ENEMY STRUCK FIRST in spite of a numerical inferiority
in tanks and guns. Numbers, in Rommel's view, might not
be everything; and what his armour and artillery appeared to lack
in quantity might be made up by their armament. His command
approached equality with the Eighth Army in infantry, though most
of his infantry was Italian; and in the air he could outnumber the
R.A.F. over Egypt and the Desert. But counting heads has never
been a satisfactory method of ascertaining relative strengths in air
warfare. For the decisive figure must always be the number of aircraft available to fly in the right way and at the right place; and in
arriving at this total mere arithmetic must be corrected by the factors
of leadership, morale, and training, to say nothing of the location and
serviceability of aircraft. Tedder's squadrons were just where they
were wanted; they now maintained a higher proportion of serviceable aircraft than their adversaries; and, in his view, they had sufficient
strength in spite of smaller numbers to support a ground offensive by
the Eighth Army. But after an initial blow at an Axis aerodrome on
May 21 they were not called upon to do so; for the enemy struck first.

His air offensive opened with a series of attacks on British airfields
and back areas, followed on May 26 by an outflanking movement in
the familiar manner. As Ritchie's forces were aligned from the sea
to Bir Hakim, Rommel passed his armour round their southern flank
and struck up behind them in an effort to take the Eighth Army in
rear. A series of attacks on Bir Hakim failed to dislodge the French,

while tanks and guns contended for days in a dun witches' sabbath of dust, gun flashes, and minefields nicknamed the "Cauldron" not far from El Adem. Coningham's fighter squadrons suspended their successful duel with the *Luftwaffe* to concentrate on close support of the land forces. In these operations Kittyhawks appeared as bombers, and aircraft operated dangerously near the ground. Their losses from this method were considerable; but results appeared to justify them, German diarists and prisoners testifying to its alarming efficacy and reviling the inadequate protection afforded by their own aircraft. Auchinleck recorded that "our own Air Force is co-operating magnificently as usual." But as the fighting swayed in the "Cauldron," it became evident that air superiority alone was not enough to win a battle on the ground.

Bir Hakim at the southern extremity of Ritchie's line was still in danger; and when the line was pierced some distance to the north of it, that danger was increased by isolation. For a week stray convoys reached them. But subsequently the beleaguered garrison was reduced to living on supplies dropped from aircraft; and the fighter squadrons adopted the defenders of Bir Hakim, whom they gratified with the spectacle of spirited attacks on Axis dive-bombers and gun positions. French gallantry, which was rejecting calls to surrender in language of increasing impropriety, responded gaily, "*Bravo. Merci pour la R.A.F.*"; and a laudable command of idiom inspired the R.A.F. to answer, "*Bravo à vous! Merci pour le sport.*" But the attack grew too strong to be resisted; and in the second week of June a brave remnant was withdrawn. The main position was in danger now. Things went badly in the "Cauldron" area, where Ritchie, after winning the first round, failed to win the second; and with Rommel's armoured thrusts flickering behind them in the direction of El Adem and still further to the west, there was nothing for it but a withdrawal from the Gazala line. June was half over; the squadrons had been in continuous employment over the battle area, a working force of less than 150 fighters making close on 5000 sorties in three weeks and earning Auchinleck's acknowledgment that "it should be made clear that R.A.F. support for the army has been unstinted at great sacrifice throughout the present campaign"; and it now became their business to cover the retreat.

For three long days the road from Gazala to Tobruk was a congested mass of slowly moving troops and transport, such a target as pilots' dreams are made of. But though the German fighter base was less than 50 miles away, the total casualties on the road from air attack were six men wounded and one lorry. For the fighter squadrons, still operating from Gambut, stood on guard, although a number of aircraft were diverted to protect a Malta convoy. Their airfields were a bare 20 miles from the enemy's land forces; and sometimes there was not much between them and the German tanks except a few of their own armoured cars. But the whole encampment with its multiplicity of tents and vehicles and its indubitable air of an immense country fair stood ready to move off at short notice. Landing grounds had been prepared behind them all the way back to the frontier; and the general notion was that they would move as soon as the advancing enemy got near enough for them to see their own bombs bursting on the target. That would not leave much time for a leisurely withdrawal. But the squadrons disliked being taken too far from the front; personnel in forward areas was systematically thinned out; the necessity of leaving absolutely nothing portable behind was inculcated at morning parades; and the whole apparatus of air warfare was ready to be moved at two hours' notice.

But the R.A.F. had more to think of than the pace and safety of their own withdrawal, although that was necessary for the preservation of a vital instrument of war. For it was now their duty to protect an army in retreat. Stripped of air cover, the Eighth Army on its way back across the Desert presented a target inviting annihilation by the pursuing air and ground forces; and it remained to be seen whether the air weapon could be so manipulated as to avert the worst consequences of a victorious pursuit. A limited degree of air superiority had not sufficed to win the land campaign; but if it could be maintained, there was a chance that aircraft operating as a novel form of rearguard might mitigate the failure of the land forces by preventing an oncoming enemy from converting his success into a final triumph. That was the service which Ney's handful had rendered to the *Grande Armée* by holding off the Cossacks at its heels; Craufurd had done something of the kind, as Moore's army dragged across the Spanish snow to Corunna; and cavalry had made a gallant effort to cover the retreat from Mons. Were aircraft now to appear in the ungrateful *rôle* of rearguard to a retreating army? Aircraft operating from fixed bases in Great Britain had covered the evacuation from Dunkirk with a large measure of success. But they had not been asked to operate from mobile bases as a part of the retreating army. Nothing like it had been seen in the succession of retreats that had swung to and fro across the Desert since 1940. Air superiority would not be easy to maintain under the conditions of a swift retreat, since air warfare entails a complicated apparatus, which might be dislocated by frequent changes of position at a rapid pace. For a high degree of accuracy can hardly be expected of marksmen distracted between shots by a vigorous game of leapfrog played in the opposite direction. Yet that was precisely what the Western Desert Air Force had to do, if it was to preserve its own existence while rendering its supreme service to the Eighth Army.

That was now their leading charge. As they fell back, their familiar targets at Benghazi receded out of range. But before they went, the heavy bombers found time to pay a final visit in the last week of June. More than 60 of them were out that night; and this time the Wellingtons were accompanied by some Liberators of the U.S. Army Air Corps. American aircraft had long ceased to be a novelty in the Middle East; but now they flew in their own right under American command. For that summer a detachment of the big blunt-nosed bombers *en route* for China had been detained in Egypt long enough to pay an unexpected visit to the oil refineries at Ploesti in Rumania 1000 miles away. The experiment was daring, though results were hardly up to expectation. But a few days later they performed with credit on some Italian warships at sea. Their heavy metal and long range formed a welcome addition to Tedder's bomber force; and shortly afterwards they were out with a few Flying Fortresses attacking Axis shipping off the further side of Greece.

But the pendulum of war was swinging once again across the Desert. They had lost Bir Hakim on June 10; and a week later the enemy were back at Sidi Rezegh and across the road to Egypt from Tobruk. That meant that the pendulum must swing still further, that there was no chance of holding any ground in Libya except the Tobruk defences, which were isolated once again in an unfriendly wilderness of Axis territory. The retirement had been miraculously free from air interference, one authority recording that the enemy's effort in this direction had been "practically nil." For his fighters had been fought to a standstill; an attempt to bring them forward to Gazala had been completely thwarted by two devastating raids of Kittybombers and Baltimores on their airfield; and for five days nothing more was seen of them. That precious interval, purchased by unceasing work on forward landing grounds, enabled the Eighth Army to get safely back to the frontier. Ground crews worked desperately all day long behind a light screen of R.A.F. armoured cars; and when they had to leave (they generally went when German armour was about 12 miles away), hurried men finished off last-minute jobs in the black-out by the light of a torch held underneath a blanket, pilots flew off aircraft in every prohibited degree of disrepair, all movables were packed, such petrol as could not be carted off was spilt on the thirsty ground, and the whole jolting caravan decamped.

But when they had to fall back from Gambut, there was no means of giving fighter cover to Tobruk. That fortress had once been held for months without protection from the air. But Rommel, anxious to avoid his former error, was disinclined to leave it in his rear; and once satisfied that there was no immediate risk of a counter-attack by his retreating adversaries, he turned back to dispose of it. This time a single day sufficed. His aircraft were free to use Gazala now; a combined land and air attack was launched on June 20; and Tobruk succumbed. Its elimination left him at liberty to sweep on towards Egypt, and four days later his forces reached the frontier. All Libya was clear once more; the last rungs of the ladder had slipped through their fingers; and for the third time since 1940 an invader looked down into Egypt from the Desert plateau. That week Auchinleck took over the command from Ritchie. Before Tobruk fell, there had been a notion that the invasion could be stopped half-way from the frontier to Alexandria in the stony *hinterland* of Mersa Matruh, which had been the limit of Wavell's withdrawal in 1940; and the R.A.F. prepared to work from forward landing grounds a few miles further back at their old Desert starting-point of Maaten Bagush, with fighter bases on the edge of the Delta and bombers to the rear in the Canal zone. Bostons, Beaufighters, Hurricanes, and Baltimores maintained a shuttle service over the advancing enemy. Heavy bombers pounded his back areas, whilst U.S. Liberators did their best to discourage the use of Tobruk harbour for his supplies. But too much had been lost in Cyrenaica. Matruh could not be held; and as the retreat went on deeper into Egypt at the end of June, a fighter force was kept in a perilously advanced position to cover the withdrawing columns. "Thank God," said General Freyberg, "you didn't let the Huns Stuka us, because we were an appalling target."

In their effort to protect the army in retreat air operations mounted to an intensity unequalled since the Battle of Britain. For one June day in the Desert saw the Bostons register 111 sorties, some pilots making 5 successive trips. The fighters were all based in the Nile valley now, with light bombers in the Canal zone and the heavier aircraft as far back as Palestine. Middle East Command was concentrated for a final stand over Egypt. Maintenance units were working twenty-four hours a day on repairs and belting ammunition; and the invaders complained bitterly of the exhaustion of their troops by continuous machine-gunning from British aircraft that "seem able to do what they like without interruption," pausing to denounce their own lack of air support. Had Rommel's swift advance outrun their strength? In the age of cavalry Allenby's pursuit of the defeated Turks after Beersheba became a classic on the strength of covering 50 miles in 10 days. But the pendulum of war swung faster now. For Rommel had not taken quite so long to advance 250 miles; and Alexandria gleamed 60 miles ahead of him across the bay. An army stood between him and the goal, besides an Air Force that had just executed an incomparable retreat. For though the *Luftwaffe* had abandoned 200 aircraft on evacuated landing grounds in its last withdrawal over the same course, all that the R.A.F. now left behind were 5 damaged aircraft. All its spares and nine-tenths of its petrol and ammunition had been brought off; and this triumph of mobility accompanied their greater triumph of covering the army's long retreat in their indefatigable rearguard action. As Mr. Churchill told the House of Commons, "When we retreated all those hundreds of miles from Tobruk at such speed, what saved us was superior air power." The price, from Rommel's sudden move in May to the close of the ensuing struggle in the first week of July, was a loss of 600 fighters and 136 bombers against Axis losses of 527 fighters and 215 bombers; and as the guns opened within hearing of a small railway station by the name of Alamein hull-down on the Desert, the Prime Minister telegraphed to Tedder that he was "watching with enthusiasm the brilliant, supreme exertions of the Royal Air Force in the battle now proceeding in Egypt. From every quarter the reports come in of the vital part which your officers and men are playing in the Homeric struggle for the Nile valley. The days of the Battle of Britain are being repeated far from home. We are sure you will be to our glorious Army the friend that endureth to the end."

Chapter XVII

MALTA AND THE NARROW SEAS

IF ONE THING HAD EMERGED SINCE 1940, it was that the result of naval and military operations anywhere except in mid-ocean is powerfully influenced, if not finally determined, by the control of airfields. This had been decisive in Norway, Greece, and Crete; it had closed the Mediterranean to through traffic since the arrival of the *Luftwaffe* at Sicilian bases; it had changed the balance of sea power in Malayan waters; a single aerodrome had saved Iraq; and when they had to fall back from the landing grounds within reach of Tobruk, leaving the enemy in a position to bring his bomber force to bear, the fortress fell. War, in fine, had now become a war for aerodromes. Syria had been invaded for the simple purpose of keeping German aircraft off French airfields; the only effective safeguard for sea traffic in the waters west of Alexandria was to hold air bases on the hump of Cyrenaica; and as the tide of war ebbed and flowed across Africa, the situation was transformed by the control of airfields. When the R.A.F. held Berka and Benina, they could sustain an advance of the land forces further to the west and strike at Tripoli; if they could be maintained in Cyrenaica, they were still in a position to strike Benghazi and to protect shipping in the strait between Africa and Crete; and when they receded into Egypt, the whole range of their activity contracted. These vicissitudes affected the whole course of the campaign on land and sea, as every airfield in the 500 miles between Daba and the Gulf of Sirte successively changed hands. But there was one air base on the chess-board of the Mediterranean of which they never lost control; and in the war for aerodromes Malta sustained the note of victory for three unbroken years.

That was now the significance of the island with grey cliffs, where the Knights Hospitallers had once held the gate for Christendom. For Malta was, above all, an aerodrome. The Knights had armed their island for defence with all the stateliness of military architecture, stern rectangles of blinding limestone enlivened with a dignified Baroque. It had been a fortress then, poised in the narrow sea-lane where Barbary creeps close to Europe. Bonaparte had grasped its value as a stepping-stone to Egypt; Nelson saw "a most important outwork to India"; and the enclosed waters of the Grand Harbour, where tiers of little houses look down across stone terraces and green palms to the blue beneath, became a link in the long chain of Britain's sea communications through the Mediterranean. As a naval base it had mattered greatly to Nelson, for whom "Malta, my dear Sir, is in my thoughts sleeping or waking," and to his successors in the exercise of Britain's sea power. But that phase was over now. For British fleets had been withdrawn to safety at either end of the Mediterranean, because Italian airfields were only 60 miles from Malta. It was plain that Gibraltar and Alexandria were both more secure as naval bases; and this wise precaution cost Malta much of its maritime significance. But if the Grand Harbour had largely ceased to count except as a submarine base, the little fields of Malta might still have a value of their own. For Malta, which had been in turn a fortress and a naval base, might become an aerodrome.

Its value as an air base had been lightly estimated a year or so before the war, when it was felt that Malta's limited accommodation in such close proximity to the Sicilian mainland afforded little prospect of successful air attacks on Italy. But this was not surprising at a time when British forecasts were founded on the axiom of an Anglo-French alliance and France was not expected to leave a European war before its end. With the aerodromes of Tunis at their command the directors of Allied air power could contemplate attacks on southern Italy delivered from the African mainland; and it would plainly be superfluous to maintain a forward landing ground in Malta, dangerously near the main Italian air force and isolated by the sea from petrol and supplies. But the situation changed completely, when Marshal Pétain withdrew his undefeated forces in North Africa and their uninvaded territory from the war. For Malta now became the only base from which the R.A.F. and Fleet Air Arm could operate in the 1700 miles of empty water and unfriendly land that lay between Gibraltar and the Western Desert. If hostile shipping was to be observed, it must be watched from Malta; and if Italian harbours were to be attacked, Malta was now the only airfield from which they could be bombed. It was already plain that an Italian invasion of Egypt was imminent; and if Malta could be held, it gave the R.A.F. an aerodrome in rear of the Italian armies, from which their bases and communications could be struck, to say nothing of a submarine base in convenient proximity to the sea routes by which they were supplied. But if the French surrender lent the island a new strategical significance, it multiplied its problems of defence. For it was now completely isolated, 800 miles from the nearest friendly territory and a few minutes' flying time from hostile airfields. Every ration, gun, bomb, round of ammunition, pint of petrol, and spare part must be brought to it in ships; even its fighter aircraft must come a great part of the way by sea; and it was anything but certain how far the needs of Malta could be supplied by convoys traversing the long sea routes from Gibraltar and Alexandria.

That summer and in the three years that followed Malta faced one more of the sieges that made up its indomitable history. But this time the significance was not in the defence, in the unbroken gallantry of its defenders and the dumb endurance of its shattered alleys, where the heaps of dusty limestone that had once been homes were piled into its monument. Endurance had always been their badge, when the Knights held off Suleiman and Dragut's galleys pulled round the little capes to put their men ashore and batter La Valette's outworks. Those had been defensive victories; but this time the defence of Malta meant more, far more, than the retention of a threatened island 60 miles from Sicily. For Malta was an aerodrome; and its air power, vital to its own defence, was put out in offensive operations of which the war in Africa felt the effect.

The tale of its defence was simple. No island can maintain itself against attack without fighter cover. Fighter Command had been Britain's first line of defence against invasion; Crete could not be defended, when it receded out of fighter range of Desert airfields; and the same lesson was later learnt by Pantelleria and Sicily. Malta's fighter cover against the Italian air offensive was at first a gay and gallant improvisation of four borrowed Sea Gladiators (soon reduced in number to Faith, Hope, and Charity), hopefully put into the air by Maynard and shortly supplemented by Longmore's welcome loan of a few Hurricanes. The long epic of innumerable air combats fought by indefatigable pilots from Malta's battered aerodromes opened, as they wheeled endlessly above the tiny fields with their pale walls and saw the long succession of their enemies come on above the little island, veined like an ivy leaf and pencilled with the pattern of its roads. Beneath them in the limestone glare untiring ground staffs worked on the tattered aircraft or patched gaping cavities in the bombed runways, while the stubborn island stood the last and longest of its sieges. The guns accounted for 236 hostile aircraft in the first eighteen months. But the fighters disposed of 893 at a cost of 568 aircraft to the R.A.F. For the defence of Malta was, in the main, a fighter epic.

The significance of its defence lay in the offensive which it rendered possible; and aircraft of the Fleet Air Arm were already busy over Sicilian targets in the first weeks of the war. That winter some heavy bombers favoured Italian harbours with a number of explosions and a few copies of Mr. Churchill's latest speech; and as Wavell moved forward in the Desert, bombers from Malta were at work far in the Italians' rear at Tripoli. But Malta had other uses. Kinglake had once called the island "our English stepping-stone"; and the term, applicable to its uses as a naval base, became strictly true of its new rôle in British air power. For it was now a useful port of call for long-range bombers outward-bound from home to Egypt; and these guests were apt to return Malta's hospitality by paying a few visits in the neighbourhood before going on their way. Besides, its reconnaissance aircraft were the Navy's principal resource for locating Italian warships; and that winter Cunningham bore witness to the vital contribution made by their long patrols to his destructive swoop on Taranto.

It was plain that the defence of Malta was more than a sentimental gesture. But if its activities were to be maintained, Malta convoys must be kept running with supplies. That was the Navy's contribution, made with unchanging gallantry through narrow waters exposed to air and under-sea attack. It had not been too difficult so long as Italy remained the sole belligerent in the Mediterranean. But early in 1941 the *Luftwaffe* came to Sicily; and one January afternoon they followed an aircraft carrier, which had been damaged before reaching Malta and limped in with its convoy, into the Grand Harbour. In the three days' engagement that ensued the dive-bombers came screeching through a sky that was three parts flying steel and drifting smoke to one part of falling water in an effort to destroy H.M.S. *Illustrious*; R.A.F. fighters plunged through their own barrage in pursuit; and a methodical attempt was made to wreck the island's airfields. But Malta and *Illustrious* both came through; and as the great ship steamed off to Alexandria, the island which a captured German general once termed "the unsinkable aircraft carrier" remained on guard in the Sicilian Channel.

It had reacted to the *Luftwaffe's* attack with considerable effect, as nine busy days in January, 1941, saw the destruction or damage of 196 Axis aircraft. Some were shot down over the island, where "the 'game' remained plentiful and enterprising"; and a rewarding visit paid to the new German air base at Catania by some bombers that were passing through *en route* for Egypt destroyed 35 aircraft on the ground. The arrival of the *Luftwaffe* accelerated the *tempo* of events at Malta, where Germans did the bombing now and their bomber crews seemed to prefer fighter escorts of their own nationality. Its fighter defences were maintained by reinforcement from Egypt and by aircraft flown off from aircraft carriers that steamed into range from Gibraltar; and the island's striking-power was vigorously used on Tripoli and Axis shipping. For the lonely aerodrome in rear of the Italian armies could make its contribution to the course of land campaigns in Africa, where victory depended ultimately on supplies, on each belligerent's ability to arm, transport, and feed his forces in a barren land. Axis armies operating overseas were totally dependent on supplies from Europe. Their ammunition, armoured vehicles, bombs, petrol, and motor transport were all bound to come in ships from Italy; and if these failed to arrive, there was nothing more that they could do. Shipping losses in the Mediterranean, if they reached a certain point, implied defeat in Africa, since an interruption of the sea routes in their rear had power to silence every gun they had, ground the *Luftwaffe*, and immobilise the *Afrika Korps*; and Malta's situation astride their communications was peculiarly menacing.

The Axis problem was to reach Tripoli with their transports from Naples and Palermo and their oil tankers from Taranto. If they went direct, they were exposed to Malta's aircraft and submarines; and if they deviated to the west at some cost in time and fuel, crossing the Sicilian Channel at its narrowest point opposite Cape Bon and creeping down the hospitable coast of Tunis, where Marshal Pétain's easy notions of neutrality prevailed, there was still a risk of meeting British submarines and aircraft, as they came into range of Malta. The remedy, so far as one existed, was to edge further to the east for safety, to elude the watchful island by keeping north of Sicily, crossing the mouth of the Adriatic, then heading for the shelter of Corfu, coasting the mainland of Greece, and running for Benghazi. Once in African waters, they could unload their cargo or steam back 360 miles across the gulf to Tripoli. It was a fantastic detour involving endless waste of time and fuel, imposed on them by Malta, where the busy submarines slipped in and out. Aircraft of the Fleet Air Arm (irreverently known as "goldfish" and at one stage awarded a precious bottle of Plymouth gin for each sinking) left their island base to bomb and torpedo shipping; and Blenheims came down to mast-height for unfriendly purposes far out at sea.

All through the summer months of 1941, as Rommel hung on the edge of Egypt, the sea routes behind him were assailed from Malta, where Maynard had been succeeded by Lloyd in May; and as Axis shipping edged eastwards out of range of Malta, a new menace dawned in that quarter. Hitherto the formidable island had been all they had to fear. But when No. 201 (Naval Co-operation) Group was reorganised at Alexandria that autumn, there was a threat of trouble in the sea-lanes further east. With duties similar to those assigned at home to Coastal Command, it worked from a combined operations room of the two Services; and when its personnel contrived to get the right training and equipment, Malta's striking-power would be duplicated by a powerful colleague in Egypt. This combination held a promise of eventual attacks on Axis sea routes, in which they might be ground between the upper and the nether millstone. But at the moment Alexandria was busy failing to persuade home experts that torpedoes could be launched from Wellingtons, a bold improvisation in which practice triumphed over theory; and anti-shipping operations were not without their complications for enthusiastic novices. One autumn morning a small unit of the Royal Navy off Tobruk was vigorously attacked by a Blenheim under the impression that it was an Axis coasting vessel off Bardia. For navigation and identification both present special difficulties at sea. But as the ship firmly identified its persecutor as a Ju. 88 (of whose painted swastikas its crew retained a vivid memory), the R.A.F. was not alone in its misconception; and since a German fighter on the scene put up a chivalrous defence of the British ship, which it had mistaken for a friend, it will be seen that errors can occur at sea.

The attack on Axis sea communications developed with success; and as the year drew on, it was estimated that not more than half his sea-borne cargoes were reaching Rommel owing to the combined attentions of the Navy and the R.A.F. It was a highly economical form of war, as a few bombs or torpedoes expended in sinking two 6000-ton transports and a 3000-ton oil tanker disposed at one blow of more than 40 tanks, 130 guns, 5000 tons of ammunition, 1000 bowsers full of petrol, and other fascinating targets which, if once dispersed across the Desert, could not be reached in less than 3000 bombing sorties; and it was plain that, if their pressure could only be increased, Malta and No. 201 Group might one day function as the two arms of an immense pair of shears cutting Rommel's communications.

At the moment they were busy with assaults upon his bases and sea routes in preparation for Auchinleck's advance; and as that proceeded, they covered the movements of British shipping with supplies for Malta and Tobruk. For a time Malta was the base of large-scale naval operations by a cruiser squadron, which sank an entire Axis convoy in the Tripoli sea-lane. The island's aircraft were a constant threat to enemy communications; the western route to Tripoli was now completely closed; and as Rommel hurriedly withdrew a starving force to El Agheila in the last days of 1941, it was plain that, if he was to survive, Malta's ability to interfere with his supplies must be eliminated. The limestone aircraft carrier, in fact, must be put out of action. For with the British in control of Cyrenaica he was now forced to draw all his supplies through Tripoli; and if they were to reach him, the wasps' nest at Malta would have to be burnt out.

That was Kesselring's affair; and this decision opened a flaming chapter in the island's story, as the *Luftwaffe* returned to Sicily in force. Aircraft were hastily transferred from the Russian front; and some 600 German bombers with a stronger force of German fighters to escort them assembled to dispose of Malta. Its fighter defence consisted at the moment of 3 squadrons and a flight of Hurricanes with a few Beaufighters. Hitherto no more than 70 aircraft had been operating weekly against Malta, and they rarely came more than 20 at a time. But in December the weekly number rose to 200, and the weight of bombs dropped on the island was multiplied by ten. This was doubled in the first eight weeks of 1942 and quadrupled in March. By April, as the Axis shipping lanes were crowded with supplies for Rommel's next advance in Libya, the air attack on Malta mounted to a *crescendo*; and the island's ability to influence events in Africa, which had still been exercised against shipping at Palermo early in March, was practically paralysed. For April saw Malta fighting for its life. Their Hurricanes were quite outclassed; and though some Spitfires had reached them in March, they were too few to redress the balance. Their own supplies were running desperately short. One convoy had failed to reach them in February; and though Vian brought another through in March, they needed all that they had got in April. That month more than 6000 tons of bombs fell on the island; and as the limestone dust settled on 10,000 shattered buildings, Malta entered a new order of chivalry. Hostile aircraft were perpetually overhead; bombing shifted from the airfields to the docks and painted churches and little alleys of Valletta, where angry citizens scrawled "Bomb Rome" on broken walls. On the battered airfields soldiers working in twelve-hour shifts were building them new runways and dispersal pens; for the Services were never in a closer partnership. Overhead the fighters wheeled in uninterrupted combat; and as they mounted in the sky to meet an endless stream of German aircraft, they saw the dim Sicilian shore and the distant shape of Etna and the smoking, flashing island at their feet. Their own strength was running low, with 129 Spitfires and Hurricanes out of the race. But the rationed anti-aircraft guns expended their daily 15 rounds with formidable skill, destroying 122 aircraft in the month. The fight in April cost the *Luftwaffe* 379 aircraft lost or damaged; and though it was known that they must get more fighters, anti-aircraft ammunition and flour in the next few weeks in order to survive, Malta had contrived to live through April, 1942.

By May they were reviving fast, as 50 Spitfires, flown in from a U.S. aircraft carrier on the further side of Tunis, landed safely on the island in the middle of a raid, promptly took off again with Malta pilots, and after witnessing a few more raids that afternoon disposed of 55 hostile aircraft on the next day. For U.S.S. *Wasp* had reinforced the threatened wasps' nest; and that morning so many German bombers seemed to have a Spitfire close behind them that one fighter pilot was forced to go 7 miles out to sea in order to find one to shoot down, while cheering ground crews flung rifles, helmets, tools, anything that they could find to throw into the air at the sudden spectacle of victory, as all Valletta stood to watch the fight over the Grand Harbour and cheered and cheered again. Malta was recovering its tone; and as the defence began to rally, the *Luftwaffe's* attack fell away. Now there was other work for German aircraft in the Desert, where Rommel was about to launch a fresh attack; and Malta's striking-power was put out again in May with grave consequences to the Messina train ferry. The lonely aerodrome in the Sicilian Channel had proved its value; and Mr. Churchill expressed the view that its loss would be "fatal in the long run to the defence of the Nile valley." That was in danger now, with Rommel in full cry after the Eighth Army and his advancing columns almost in sight of Alexandria. But before the situation on the mainland deteriorated too far (for when the airfields on the hump of Cyrenaica were lost, it became intolerably difficult to cover shipping between Alexandria and Malta), they made a supreme effort to run supplies into Malta.

The island's torpedo-carrying Wellingtons and Beauforts were now operating with success once more against Axis shipping; and this offensive, even when it failed to sink much-needed cargoes, prolonged their voyage to unconscionable lengths. For it was taking Axis steamers as long as 16 days to reach Benghazi from Taranto round the long detour by way of Greece; and soon the Germans were reduced to flying oil supplies for Libya from Crete in preference to risking it in tankers. But though Malta's aircraft were active in the sea-lanes, fuel shortage denied them longer flights to mainland targets; and in June there was a concerted effort to reach the island with two simultaneous convoys from east and west. The convoy from Alexandria was turned back to its starting-point by a formidable force of two Italian battleships with escorting cruisers and smaller vessels, which sustained loss and damage from an attacking force of Beauforts and U.S. Liberators, as well as by the pressure of German aircraft based at Crete. But the Gibraltar convoy passed its two surviving freighters into Malta after the island's aircraft had disposed of two Italian cruisers in its path, and a running fight with hostile bombers ended in the destruction or damage of 26 Axis aircraft for the loss of 6 Spitfires. For naval pertinacity in "Bomb Alley," where Royal and Merchant Navy displayed equal heroism under air and submarine attack, was the sole condition of Malta's continued existence as an effective force. But so long as the island's fighters could be kept flying, the fight went on; and when supplies permitted, Malta's aircraft reached out again at the long line of Rommel's communications.

That was his vital problem now, as he confronted the Eighth Army 60 miles from Alexandria; and if Malta, where Park succeeded Lloyd in July, could maintain its striking-power, the island's contribution to the war in Africa might be decisive. For where Nelson had once seen "a most important outwork to India," Malta was now the foremost bastion of Egypt. But this time it was an aerodrome.

Chapter XVIII

MAINTENANCE AND REPAIR

SUCCESS IN AIR WARFARE depends upon the presence of efficient aircraft in sufficient numbers; and in this respect R.A.F., Middle East Command, was unevenly matched against its adversaries. For while the Germans and Italians fought in close proximity to their own countries and could bring aircraft to the Mediterranean direct from Continental production lines and aircraft parks, the R.A.F. was based in Egypt and had to fight with aircraft manufactured in an island 2000 miles away or on the further side of the Atlantic. The *Regia Aeronautica* in Africa could renew its strength direct from factories and stores in Italy, while the *Luftwaffe's* reinforcement route was almost as simple. German aircraft required for use in Africa or Sicily were delivered to depots near Munich, flown to Foggia or Bari, and collected by their units, while those intended for operations based further east in Greece or Crete were concentrated near Vienna and flown to Athens. Nothing could be simpler than their journey from the factory across populous and friendly territory. But before

British and American aircraft could operate from Egypt, the more formidable obstacles of a far longer journey had to be overcome. For their destination lay on the further side of the next continent; and a broad belt of hostile territory intervened. Direct approach from Britain was impracticable except for long-range aircraft, which could use Malta as a stepping-stone; and the sole alternative was to make a complete circuit of Africa, arriving at a Red Sea port, or else to cross the continent by air. Before this stage was reached, each crated aircraft in its ship must have traversed the long sea-lanes, where German submarines and bombers were at work; and air warfare could hardly be conducted in the Mediterranean, unless the Battle of the Atlantic was going reasonably well. For shipping losses might mean the loss of aircraft which had never flown at all, a risk to which the *Luftwaffe* was not exposed.

But once in Africa, they were no more than half-way to the fighting line. For the Gold Coast is a long way from Egypt; and the route from Takoradi to the Nile valley lay across 2000 miles of an unwelcoming continent, where the weather was uniformly un-accountable and forced landings offered an agreeable choice between impenetrable forest and empty wilderness. This journey had been shrewdly contemplated by official foresight some years before the war, when Italian truculence seemed likely to bar the Mediterranean to British traffic; and the first convoy of Bristol Blenheims was flown over it in September, 1940. As the months went by, its difficulties were surveyed and surmounted; fresh landing grounds appeared on the long trail; a miscellany of pilots of all ages and assorted nation-alities sampled its discomforts and dangers; and by 1942 1455 new aircraft flew over it to Egypt in seven months, earning Tedder's commendation of the unwearied pilots and ground crews at their endless task in the steamy heat of the West Coast and the dusty glare of the Sudan. All the way from Nigeria to the Nile valley they fed new aircraft to his hungry squadrons; and "without their loyal, ever-willing, and tireless assistance our recent successes would have been impossible." For victory in Egypt came by the Takoradi Route.

But no aircraft last for ever. Mere numbers are no criterion of air power, since aircraft which cannot fly have ceased to count; and it follows that battle strengths are in direct relation to the prolongation of their effective life by efficient maintenance. Maintenance, in fine, is the key to victory. For air battles are lost and won by ground staffs. Faulty maintenance had kept large numbers of Italian aircraft on the ground in 1940, when Longmore drove them from the skies of Africa. That year the air campaign over Britain had been largely won by aircraft replacements due to rapid salvage and repair; and at home the total of salvaged aircraft was rising to a figure that was not far below that of new production. Such things were possible at home, where air battles were fought on the doorstep of the aircraft industry and the Ministry of Aircraft Production was only a few yards away. But aircraft maintenance in Egypt, where the Industrial Revolution had not yet arrived, was a more exacting problem. There was no aircraft industry in the Nile valley; and squadrons in the Western Desert could not afford to "write off" damaged aircraft in the easy manner of home units based a few score miles from Coventry or Bristol. For Egypt was, from the supply point of view, an island; and, what was worse, it was for most industrial purposes a desert island.

In that case the only thing for them to do was to make the most of every fragment of material on which they could lay hands; and the result was a ramifying system of aircraft recovery, salvage, repair, and maintenance, which kept Tedder's squadrons at the highest battle strength of which their mechanical equipment was capable. The chief practitioner was Air Vice-Marshal Dawson, who took charge in the course of 1941; and his arrival from England in a salvaged Catalina flying-boat was a parable of what they had to do. The enemy had problems of his own that year, when losses on the Russian front bit deep into his reserves of aircraft; and the *Luftwaffe* was soon reduced to more cautious methods, husbanding its aircraft and conserving all its strength for special efforts at Sebastopol, Tobruk, and Stalingrad. But if Middle East Command was to prevail in the Mediterranean, they could not hope to win without practising a desperate economy. That was now the business of the Chief Maintenance and Supply Officer and his splendid miscellany of establishments, ranging from Repair Depots and Aircraft Replacement Pools of impressive magnitude to back streets in Cairo, where a cheerful clatter came from coal-yards that forgot their humble office in the loftier functions of No. 1 Engine Repair Section. For under R.A.F. tuition the swarming alleys of Bûlâk stepped straight out of the naughtier tales of the Thousand and One Nights into the machine age. Carpenters passed direct from wood to metal; stray garage hands, accustomed to the engine troubles of Egyptian motorists, graduated in sleeve valves; R.A.F. sergeants were foremen ready-made; and as Bûlâk met and succumbed to the Industrial Revolution, engines that Bristol and California had made and the Desert spoilt renewed their youth under the busy fingers of the East. Some of their labour had been in R.A.F. employ for years. But most of it was a bold improvisation; and when alleys which had long been viewed by the police with dark misgivings turned out to cheer a royal visitor from England, it was an extra triumph. Beyond the city, where there was more room to work, the delicate skeletons of flayed and disembowelled aircraft were displayed in rows, ready for the strange surgery of engineers; and each tangle of battered metal-work yielded to the patient searchers something which would otherwise have had to come 12,000 miles by sea and might, if anything untoward happened on the way, never come at all.

These mechanical refinements were often strangely housed in the Nile valley. Deep in a brown cliff-face that stares eternally across the river and its broad green verge to a horizon neatly punched with the triangles of distant pyramids, a line of caves accommodated No. 111 Maintenance Unit, "A" Echelon. Once the quarry from which Cheops' workmen had hewn limestone blocks to build his pyramid, it was explored by eager tourists, respectful of the cautious Baedeker's advice to take "a guide and candles." But candles were no longer necessary, as enterprising British officers had seen its possibilities before the war; and now the tool-marks of Pharaoh's workmen looked down in the white electric glare on a strange blend of one of Piranesi's cavernous fancies and the shops of Coventry, where six-foot cases stood piled like a child's bricks beneath vast arches of rough-hewn Mokattam limestone. Not far away reposed enough explosives to blow up, as its custodians lovingly believed, the whole continent of Africa. But the Tura caves were safer than the open country, where at least one depot had been bombed with serious results.

As the tide of aircraft and supplies rose slowly in the Middle East, it was distributed with care and methodically husbanded. Delicate machinery is not improved by Desert warfare, where a tank's engine is apt to collect 20 lb. of sand (one spoonful is enough to ruin it) in 100 miles. Observers had been baffled by the spectacle of large numbers of Italian aircraft and motor transport stationary on the ground in Wavell's first offensive. But they soon learned the reason, when they looked inside their engines. For Italian planning of the Desert war had failed to notice that they would encounter sand as well as enemies. Air filters are the first requisite of victory in Africa; and British aircraft engines, instruments, gun turrets, and under-carriages were carefully protected.

The leading service of the maintenance establishments was to keep the squadrons up to strength. It was not easy, as a stream of damaged aircraft came back to them from the front line. But in the course of the winter campaign of 1941 they recovered some 1000 damaged aircraft and sent back more than 800 to fight again; and then, as afterwards, the whole fabric of British air power in the Middle East rested upon their unromantic efforts.

Chapter XIX

EGYPT

I

As the pendulum of war swung over Africa, it seemed to gather speed. Its movement had a longer sweep than in the days when Graziani took three months to creep half-way to Alexandria from the frontier. The recoil swung him back with O'Connor at his heels beyond the further edge of Cyrenaica; and it had paused there for a few weeks in 1941, until Rommel caught its rhythm and the *Afrika Korps* swung back to the Egyptian frontier. It checked there all that summer and then swung back beyond Benghazi once again in Auchinleck's offensive. But that always seemed to be the limit of its westward swing; and now the fatal rhythm had brought them back once more to Egypt with Rommel in pursuit.

This time the pendulum swung through a longer curve, taking them almost beyond the Western Desert to the green edge of the Delta; and anxious watchers began to wonder whether the interminable see-saw of the Desert war would ever end. But few wars in history have been a swift, unbroken catalogue of victories, although the names of victories are often all that history retains. Judged by the battle-honours on their colours, British regiments marched through the Peninsula from Vimeiro to the Pyrenees by way of Talavera,

Salamanca, and Vitoria. But as the war swung up and down a barren country for five long years, this splendid sequence of remembered names had not been quite so smooth. For they had climbed the ladder more than once; and more than once its rungs had all slipped through their fingers, leaving them at its foot with the whole ladder to climb again. The first attempt had ended on the evacuation beaches of Corunna; the second, which had brought them near Madrid, left them entrenched in the lines of Torres Vedras with their backs to their last Portuguese seaport; and the third swing of the pendulum, which took them more than half-way to France, had dropped them back from Burgos into Portugal again. Close on five years had passed in these alternations of success and failure before they succeeded at the fourth attempt; and if final victory had come on these dilatory terms in the Peninsula, there was no reason to despair of its eventual arrival in the Desert war.

Indeed, the two wars had much in common. Each was initiated in an outlying theatre of operations at a time when Europe in defeat had left Great Britain to fight on alone. Both wars employed her limited resources in arms and men at the end of a long line of sea communications against the full weight of military monarchies; and there was a strong resemblance between the regions in which each was fought. For French condescension always held that Africa begins south of the Pyrenees; and it was undeniable that war in Spain, where the wide spaces of an empty country left them room to fight, was not unlike the Desert war. Spain, it had been said by Wellington quoting Henri IV, was a country where small armies were defeated and large armies starved; and one German described the Western Desert as "the tactician's paradise and the quartermaster's hell." Both were areas in which it was impossible for armies to live on the country, since the country scarcely lived itself. A historian of the Peninsular War had written that "Spain was a desert, and in desert warfare supply and transport are the only wings upon which armies can rise into motion." For victory depended ultimately upon each belligerent's ability to solve his problems of supply. That was perhaps the reason why success in the Peninsula had come to a Sepoy general, accustomed to think at least as much of commissariat bullocks as of the enemy; and where Wellington reiterated that "if I had rice and bullocks I had men, and if I had men I knew I could beat the enemy," commanders in the Desert were no less aware that victory depended in the last resort on water and oil fuel. For unless men could drink, fly aircraft and drive vehicles, there could be no fighting, and the pendulum of war must jar slowly to a standstill.

Its swift momentum had brought them all into a region where the navigable Desert narrowed to a width of 35 miles to pass between the sea and the impenetrable Qattara Depression. Road and rail crept towards Alexandria across the brown infinity; a little station bore the name of Alamein; and there the British turned to fight. The swarming streets of Alexandria were a bare 60 miles behind them now; and if the pendulum swung further to the east, they might lose Egypt. For that week Mr. Churchill told the House of Commons that "we are at this moment in the presence of a recession of our hopes and prospects in the Middle East and in the Mediterranean unequalled since the fall of France." The dark days of 1940 were returning with the darker shadow of advancing German armies on the north shore of the Black Sea and the Japanese swarming towards the further side of India. If the British barrier in the Middle East collapsed, a German thrust through Egypt might take the Caucasus in rear. For Egypt guarded the left flank of the Russian front; and a German victory in Egypt, followed by a northward sweep, might involve the loss of Russia's oil supplies and the paralysis of Russian armies. A more distant peril lurked in the shadows of 1942, since Egypt was half-way to Persia; and if the German thrust could reach the Persian Gulf, they would be half-way on the long road towards a meeting with the Japanese, which would spell complete disaster.

All this depended on events along a narrow front at the gates of Alexandria, where Axis victory would bring a Roman triumph; and that summer Mussolini made his preparations for a triumphal entry into Egypt in the wake of his advancing legions. The uniform, the charger, and the medal all, it was believed, awaited the event; the imperial brow was bared for Egyptian laurels; and in the outcome it was tragic for a man, who mistook himself for Caesar, to find that he was only Pompey. For Pompey's end came on an Egyptian beach at Alexandria; and Mussolini's was appointed not far away at Alamein.

2

A single battle failed to decide the issue, since First Alamein, which opened on July 1, merely showed that Rommel's forces were unequal at the moment to continuing their race across the Desert into Alexandria. It was a holding battle in which Auchinleck, who had taken command of the Eighth Army, maintained his chosen ground. The running fight was over now; and as they turned to hold the 35-mile front, their oncoming assailants felt the full weight of British air superiority. Collaboration between ground and air had been perfected, until the interval between a call from the land forces and the arrival of the bombers was frequently reduced to 35 minutes; and Auchinleck reported that "the R.A.F. effort is truly remarkable." Now their whole strength was available, Coningham's command of Western Desert fighters, fighter-bombers, and light bombers attending to the tactical requirements of the battle, and the heavy bombers turning their weight on less immediate objectives at longer range. All day long the Bostons, "going out every hour" (as one war diary recorded) "with the regularity of seaside excursion trains in August," maintained a "shuttle service"; and it was not long before troops below learned to recognise affectionately the pattern, which no anti-aircraft fire seemed to affect, of the "Eighteen Imperturbables" on the sky. Passing overhead, they left a corresponding pattern of bomb-craters on ground occupied by Axis forces, which reduced them to nerve-shattered misery. Deafened and sleepless, they were showing signs of shaken morale; and when some captured Germans wished to escape, they were outvoted in the little party by refusals to return to the "bombing hell." Escaping British prisoners reported uncomfortable nights passed under R.A.F. bombing; and a German diary recorded that machine-gunning was followed by *Flucht-Psychose.*" Small wonder that when General Navarini's Order of the Day assured his army corps that "final victory is within your grasp," it added with pardonable caution that his men should not let themselves "be over-awed by some momentary predominance of enemy aviation."

The moment, though the German wireless averred that Rommel would be at Alexandria in three days, was prolonged; nor was air superiority confined in its effects to forces on the ground. For the *Luftwaffe* was effectively prevented from intervening in the battle; and when 15 German dive-bombers appeared at dusk one evening and were just starting to peel off for their attack on the troops below, they were so discouraged by the arrival of No. 1 Squadron, S.A.A.F., with No. 274 Squadron R.A.F. as top cover, that they jettisoned their bombs and ran for safety near the ground. The squadron leader, after shooting down one of them, withdrew to a commanding height from which he directed the battle with one eye on the German fighters overhead, until his Hurricanes had disposed of 14 dive-bombers and 1 fighter without loss and (as one pilot said) "we ran out of Stukas." This "Stuka party," which gave immense satisfaction to a fighter squadron on its first full day of operations in the Desert battle and with many pilots new to its peculiarities, was an interesting contribution to the current controversy on the value of dive-bombers; and its vivid demonstration of their weakness in face of effective air opposition impelled many local witnesses, whom Mr. Churchill asked a few weeks later, "What do you think of the dive-bombers?" to answer the Prime Minister with the eloquent enquiry, "Which dive-bombers?"

The battle lasted for four days, while Rommel's infantry and armour played round the front, inland flank, and rear of Auchinleck's position. But the troops fought stubbornly; and by July 4 they had fought the invaders to a standstill. The long pursuit was over; the last rearguard action (for First Alamein was little more) had been definitely won; and it was clear that Alexandria could not be rushed. The contribution of air power to this result had been decisive; and it was largely made by the light bombers and by the ground crews, who had serviced and refuelled them from dawn to dusk. A few days later Coningham signalled his admiration of No. 3 S.A.A.F. Wing, intimating that "the Eighth Army, the Press and the B.B.C. have all wondered at your work, but in due course the best testimony will come from the enemy." He added the good news that the question of leave had been reconsidered, that the curfew in Cairo and Alexandria was lifted, and that 25 per cent. of all personnel were free to go to town on each of the next four nights, if they were back in camp by midnight. A cautious postscript emphasised that "the importance of good behaviour is stressed." When the Wing celebrated their 1000th sortie with a seven-course dinner (there were advantages in fighting close to Egyptian cities), Coningham addressed the banquet at some length, congratulating one Boston squadron on keeping its aircraft serviceable with over 20 sorties daily. That figure, if maintained for four days, was the peak by peace-time standards; but No. 24 Squadron had kept it up for more than seven weeks "uninterruptedly and in spite of an odd spot of sand here and there, as well as considerable inconvenience caused through their having to travel hundreds of miles during the period. The enemy, too, had not failed to show them some attention on occasion." Then the orator paid tribute to the fighter squadrons; and a chronicler recorded that "the fighter pilots who were present (many of them with long moustaches carefully tended) proceeded to look quite uncomfortable." His closing passages dealt in becoming terms with the admirable qualities of their American aircraft and of the ground crews by whom they were enabled to fly them. For First Alamein, like the retreat which it concluded, had been a notable performance on the part of R.A.F., Middle East Command.

3

They had made consummate use of the air weapon to avert defeat. That stage, it might be hoped, was over; and it now remained to employ air power as an instrument of victory. Their adversaries showed little tendency to do so. Rommel's swift advance owed nothing to the *Luftwaffe*; and now there was no serious attempt on their part to exploit the advantageous position in which it had placed them by initiating a sustained air attack on Egypt. For the whole country lay within range of German bombers. Its crowded cities were now a few minutes' flying time from the front line; the British bases with their vast accumulations of inflammable and irreplaceable stores lay in the same area; and the disembarkation points at the Red Sea end of the Canal zone, through which all reinforcements and supplies arrived from overseas, were only a few miles further on. But this immense and tempting target area was relatively undisturbed except for a few small-scale attacks by German bombers based in Greece and Crete on forward areas, airfields, and the ports of Alexandria and Suez. All through the summer reinforcements continued to arrive in Egypt unmolested from the air; the elaborate machinery of aircraft replacement worked at high pressure; and the long, dun vista of the Desert road from Cairo to Alexandria, crowded with military traffic and flanked on either side with camps and landing grounds, was rarely visited except by a few German fighter-bombers. If victory depended on supply, the *Luftwaffe* seemed to neglect a golden opportunity for offensive action, as Kesselring apparently preferred the defensive *rôle* and used his bombers to escort Axis convoys across the Mediterranean. His use of the air weapon had never been particularly enterprising; but he was not alone in this omission to strike at vital targets, since

German air power was never seriously used against the Russian nexus of communications and supply round Moscow; and a similar inertia was subsequently to permit the free use of Algiers as a base for Allied operations in North Africa. The truth, indeed, appeared to be that the R.A.F. took a more active view of the air weapon.

The fighting of First Alamein had ended just a week, when Tedder announced that "enemy supplies are my main preoccupation." That was how air power might ensure victory over an adversary who was forced to fight at the end of long lines of communication. If the land and sea routes behind Rommel could be cut, his advanced position would become a greater menace to his own forces than to Egypt. But that was not so easy as it had been when Cyrenaica was in British hands. Malta was not yet in a position to send aircraft far afield; and the recession of the front line effectively reduced the range of No. 201 Group, whose headquarters were still in Alexandria. Benghazi lay beyond the reach of Wellingtons; but Liberators paid the port some useful visits. The enemy, however, had now brought Tobruk into use as his principal supply base; and the harbour was assiduously bombed. The difficulty was to reach his shipping, since Axis sea-lanes between Europe and the hump of Cyrenaica were now inaccessible for short-range aircraft based on Egypt, although admirable work continued to be done by submarines. But in at least one instance they made daring use of a bold expedient, flying petrol and ground staff to a landing ground deep in the Desert nearly 150 miles behind the enemy's front line. A force of Albacore torpedo-bombers met them in the night, refuelled on the open Desert, and took off again to surprise an Axis convoy as it steamed through safe waters out of range, as they believed, of air attack from Egypt. The stealthy party in the Desert watched the lights of enemy motor transport pass securely down a track within two miles of their secret landing ground. Indeed, one Axis lorry appeared to break down; and its headlights bore them company for some time. But the trespassers were undiscovered; and as the participants flew safely back to Egypt, Operation "Chocolate" remained a striking proof of the strange mobility of air power.

The problem of mobility, indeed, was still engaging them that summer. For it was no part of British strategy to stand on the defensive for ever. The R.A.F. expected to be moving through the Desert once again; and although their performance in the course of the retreat showed that they had learnt to be nomadic in a high degree, improvements were still possible. A complete Wing could now get on the move in 15 minutes; squadron personnel, in the case of single-engined fighters, were reduced to a strength of 200 men; and the unit's mobility was maintained by a leapfrog system, under which one ground party went ahead by road, whilst its counterpart remained behind to operate the squadron until their forerunners had prepared a landing ground with all the necessary services, an alternating process that could be repeated indefinitely in the course of an advance. Further to the rear mobile aircraft depots and salvage units were ready to move forward with their cranes and workshops and a fleet of those impressive vehicles that earned the title of "Queen Mary" by their ability to ship entire aircraft.

But they could not move before the battle-front left Alamein; and at the moment it displayed a tendency to stay there. Their ascendancy was still maintained in spite of the superior qualities of some German aircraft; and when two Stuka pilots encountered far behind their own line were moved to land without a shot and run for cover, leaving their aircraft behind to be destroyed at leisure on the ground, it was plain that air superiority had not departed from the R.A.F. In the third week of July Auchinleck landed an offensive. But though the fighting swayed for some days along the dusty shoulder of Ruweisat and Tedder's squadrons played an effective part, the land forces failed to make much progress; and Second Alamein ended where it had begun.

This was discouraging. In spite of constant air superiority the Eighth Army had been fighting unsuccessfully since May with inferior equipment against approximately equal numbers of the enemy. True, they had spent a few weeks in Benghazi earlier that year; but their stay had been shorter than usual, and the ensuing campaign was hardly calculated to inspire them with confidence. The tank battles in the "Cauldron" had gone seriously wrong; the loss of Tobruk had been a most unpleasant shock; and the retreat was an unhappy memory. They had fought under three army commanders in seven months; and when their latest effort failed to break the deadlock at Alamein, it was clear that something more was needed. It was administered in August by a familiar figure in an unfamiliar hat, when the Prime Minister appeared in Egypt, at Cairo, in the Western Desert, asking questions and pronouncing judgment. Tedder diagnosed the visit as "a grand

Royal Air Force and
Axis Air Forces Range
July-October, 1942.

Royal Air Force
and Axis Air Forces Range.

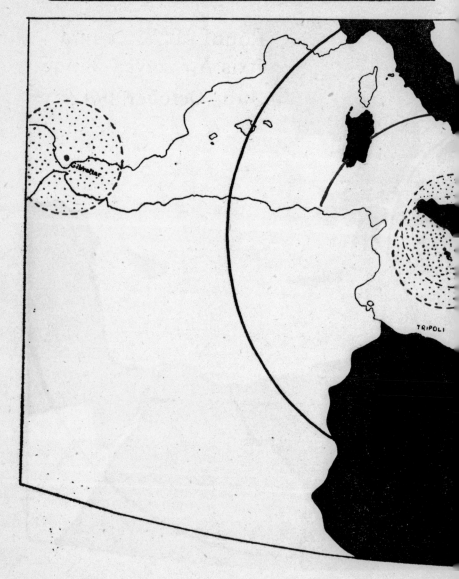

O German Bomber Cover

O Allied Bomber Cover

July-October 1942

German Fighter Cover ⬤

Allied Fighter Cover ⬤

German Fighter Cover
Allied Fighter Cover

tonic for everybody." Smuts met him there; and presently Auchinleck was succeeded by Alexander with instructions from Mr. Churchill,
which had an ample ring in the straitened circumstances of that
summer.

"1. Your prime and main duty will be to take or destroy at the
earliest opportunity the German-Italian army commanded by
Field-Marshal Rommel, together with all its supplies and establishments in Egypt and Libya.

"2. You will discharge, or cause to be discharged, such other
duties as appertain to your Command without prejudice to the
task described in paragraph 1, which must be considered paramount
in His Majesty's interests."

At the same time the Eighth Army passed to General Gott and, after
his tragic death on the next day, to General Montgomery, under
whom it found itself. There were no changes in the R.A.F. commands.

4

Before the end of August air reinforcements continued to arrive,
although there was not much prospect of building up a force of heavy
bombers in the immediate future, and their fighter strength in types
comparable to the latest German aircraft caused some misgivings.
But they had 3 squadrons of Spitfires, although their Hurricanes were
overworked and they were short of Kittyhawks. Axis airfields in
Egypt were attacked with a steady hail of bombs and spikes, Baltimores proving highly effective; and a fine contribution was made
by the U.S. squadrons, whose Liberators were employed in long-
range attacks on Rommel's supply route. Starting from Greece and
Crete, this had its terminus in Africa at Tobruk and further forward
at Mersa Matruh; and his shipping was attacked in transit and at both
ends of its journey by aircraft based in Egypt. If Malta was to make a
contribution, its supplies must be maintained by another convoy,
since it was now eight weeks since the last had reached them; and
that month 14 merchantmen, escorted by 2 battleships, 4 aircraft
carriers, 7 cruisers and 24 destroyers, left Gibraltar for the east. The
island had been reinforced with Spitfires, which had repelled a renewed
air offensive in July with the loss of 95 Axis aircraft; and it was
capable of defending shipping in its own waters. But before this

relatively safe area was reached, the convoy was heavily attacked by submarines and aircraft; H.M.S. *Eagle*, 9 freighters, and 3 warships were lost; and the sheer bastions of the Grand Harbour saw 4 merchantmen arrive, followed by the indomitable tanker *Ohio* towed in by two destroyers. That was the last convoy to reach Malta for three months.

In Egypt Rommel was preparing to attack at the full moon. That would be on August 25; and as he had no time to lose, his convoys were unloading at Tobruk, which brought the shipping within range of submarines and aircraft based in Egypt. His first petrol convoy failed completely to arrive; and this mishap postponed the offensive. But at the next attempt some tankers managed to get through; and on the night of August 30 he attacked. Before Third Alamein began, the *Luftwaffe* had been raiding R.A.F. airfields (including some thoughtfully devised for the purpose, complete with fires, to gratify the visitors); and his armour groped round Alexander's inland flank in the old manner. The Eighth Army fought back; and the light bombers made a vital contribution to the battle. R.A.F. Baltimores, S.A.A.F. Bostons, and U.S. Mitchells were active against targets described appreciatively as "magnificent M.T. and armoured concentrations" in spite of heavy anti-aircraft fire and unsuccessful efforts on the part of Axis fighters to break up their formations; and these activities, which continued all through the five days of Third Alamein, were known collectively as the "Boston Tea Party." A vigorous defensive on the ground and in the air checked Rommel's onslaught, which died away by September 5; and its termination was not unassisted by the loss at sea of one more of his convoys under air attack.

The German push had failed to move the British line, which still held in front of Alexandria; and on the fourth day of the battle Coningham was informed by Montgomery that "we know quite well that the results so far attained could not have been achieved unless the R.A.F. had put forth so great and so sustained an effort. . . . It is quite clear to me that such a magnificent co-operation can produce only one result—a victorious end to the campaign in North Africa. Let our motto be: 'United we stand, divided we fall, and let nothing divide us.'" The price was not negligible, since it had cost them the loss or damage of 20 bombers, although the enemy had lost 26 bombers with 7 damaged and 5 "probables." But the brunt had been borne by the fighters, whose casualties amounted to 43 aircraft shot down and 27 badly damaged as compared with Axis fighter casualties of 22 aircraft lost with 18 "probables" and 39 damaged. It had been supremely worth it, though; since Rommel had been decisively checked at the gates of Egypt.

5

It had been convenient to hold the bottleneck of Alamein, where the whole outcome of the war in Africa could be made to depend upon events along a 35-mile front and the defenders had little to fear either from surprise or from those wide outflanking movements which were familiar in Desert warfare. But its brevity became an adverse factor, when the *rôles* were changed and the defenders turned to attack, since Rommel's front was just as narrow. For it might become as formidable as Montgomery's had proved; and his ability to hold it would depend upon the weight and skill with which it was attacked.

That was the problem now confronting them; and it was solved by a new integration of air power with the land forces. The Prime Minister, who looked in again on his way home from Russia, had already seen "the Army and Air commanders in the field live and camp together in the same moving headquarters"; and something of the first importance was brewing in that "little circle of lorries, wagons and tents" where the commands of the Eighth Army and the Western Desert Air Force lived and worked side by side. Tedder was already noting a commander who put co-operation with the R.A.F. first in his order of priority of things to be done; and it was plain that they were moving into a new era.

It was all stated afterwards by General Montgomery:

"I believe that the first and great principle of war is that you must first win your air battle before you fight your land and sea battle. If you examine the conduct of the campaign from Alamein through Tunisia, Sicily and Italy—and we have now got 700 miles up here—you will find I have never fought a land battle until the air battle has been won. We never had to bother about the enemy air, because we won the air battle first.

"The second great principle is that Army plus Air—the Eighth Army and the Desert Air Force, if you like—has to be so knitted that the two together form one entity. If you do that, the resultant military effort will be so great that nothing will be able to stand up against it.

"The third great principle is that the Air Force side of this fighting machine must be centralised and kept under Air Force command. I hold that it is quite wrong for the soldier to want to exercise command over the air striking forces. The handling of an Air Force is a life-study, and therefore the air part must be kept under Air Force command.

"The next principle is that the Army Commander directs the military effort of Army plus Air, and the Air Force Commander who is with him applies the air effort in accordance with the combined plan. There are not two plans, Army and Air, but one plan, Army-Air, which is made by me and the Air Vice-Marshal together.

"Next, the Army and Air Staff must sit together at the same headquarters. There must be between them complete mutual confidence and trust. Each has to understand the problems and difficulties of the other. My headquarters and the headquarters of the Air Support Force must be together. When I go forward with a small headquarters, there must be good telephonic communication back to our combined headquarters.

"The confidence, trust, and integration of the two staffs is quite remarkable. The S.A.S.O. and the Chief of Staff have to be great friends. If there is any friction there, you will be done. You have to be great friends, not merely to work together. And so it must go downwards. The machine is so delicate that it can be thrown out of gear very quickly. That mutual confidence and trust, starting with the Air Vice-Marshal and myself, must go right down.

"Each side has to realise the other's difficulties. A soldier has to realise that the Air has certain problems. The Air cannot operate without good landing grounds, and the getting of landing grounds always forms part of the army plan. Across Africa and through Sicily we fought for airfields. The air aspect dominates the plan. The soldier has to realise it is not sufficient just to hand over the airfields. Proper communication must be established. It is our job to protect the airfields, and the soldier has to realise the airman is very sensitive about them. If we let up, at once there will be repercussions.

Air Marshal
SIR ARTHUR CONINGHAM, K.C.B., D.S.O., D.F.C., A.F.C.
From a drawing by H. A. Freeth

"The airman must realise that the soldier is sensitive about things too. We take a tremendous interest in our 'recco' wing, which is almost our life-blood. We are always very anxious that it shall be properly equipped. . . .

"As regards the striking power of the Air, we have developed a system whereby the Air definitely takes part in the land battle. It has been brought to a very high pitch. We got to the stage in the Battle of the Sangro where we had a group captain with us at the forward headquarters directing fighter-bombers to targets which required immediate treatment. The participation of the fighter-bombers is an important part of the set-piece of a land battle.

"Fighting against a good enemy—and the German is extremely good, a first-class soldier—you cannot operate successfully unless you have the full support of the air. If you do not win the air battle first, you will probably lose the land battle. I would go further. There used to be an accepted term of 'army co-operation.' We never talk about that now. The Desert Air Force and the Eighth Army are one. We do not understand the meaning of 'army co-operation.' When you are one entity you cannot co-operate. If you can knit together the power of the Army on the land and the power of the Air in the sky, then nothing will stand against you and you will never lose a battle. I would never dream of going into battle without the Desert Air Force behind me. Every soldier and airman here knows that. . . .

"The integration of Army-Air has been closely followed by us, and you see the result. I doubt if you will find such close integration anywhere else—certainly not in the German army. They have not got it at all—they are not even beginning to get it. Here we have brought it to a very fine pitch, and we realise we cannot fight successfully without it."

That was the secret, worlds removed from Kesselring's 1941 ideal of a *Luftwaffe* "working within the *Wehrmacht* framework." Now they no longer talked about army co-operation, because (as Coningham said) "the difference in the Eighth Army is that there has been as much air co-operation by the army as army co-operation by the air, and the natural result is that we have now passed beyond that stage into a unit or team which automatically helps the other."

It was freely recognised that the land and air forces both retained their own commands, each qualified to face its special problems and operating under a combined plan; and as the soldier no longer wished to control the air striking force, there was no danger now of dissipating air power in small instalments at the will of ground formations whose vision was limited to a few attractive targets on their own immediate front. For, as Coningham said, "penny packets of air are a luxury which can only be afforded at certain times . . . judgment on the question of targets is the result of agreement between the Army and Air Commanders." That was reached in the light of the situation as a whole; and it might well lead them to disappoint a section of their front by declining to use the bombers on one particular hostile concentration, which was troublesome that afternoon, in order to dispose of a more formidable mass 20 miles away, whose safe arrival at its destination might affect a whole week's fighting on the entire front.

"The Air front," as Coningham said, "is indivisible." That was one more reason for centralising its control under R.A.F. command that could direct the fighter force, by which the front was governed. The only difference was that "an Army has one battle to fight, the land battle. The Air has two. It has first of all to beat the enemy Air, so that it may go into the land battle against the enemy land forces with the maximum possible hitting power." That was the sequence of events. For if the Germans had devised a method of operating aircraft with ground forces which swept the Continent in 1940, R.A.F., Middle East Command, and the Eighth Army were perfecting a broader road to victory in 1942. For now an entire Air Force worked with an army in a way the world had never seen.

6

It was September now; and they were to attack in the last week of October. That left six weeks, an interval which Alexander and Montgomery devoted to intensive training, to that exacting process by which the Eighth Army was forged into an offensive weapon of the first order. All its doubts evaporated before hard training and new equipment in comparative profusion. They were fast becoming, as Wellington had once reported before an operation that required his army's confidence, "*an unanimous army*"; and it was not long before Montgomery could say with his predecessor, "They will do for me what perhaps no one else can make them do." The R.A.F. rested, trained, and reorganised their squadrons. Fresh arrivals from America were initiated; a new fighter Wing of Kittyhawks was formed; and the Mitchells were attached to a light bomber Wing. But now the flow of aircraft to the Middle East was diverted towards a destination further west. For an Anglo-American invasion of Morocco and Algiers had been timed to open just a fortnight after their attack on Rommel.

That paladin, who had been far from well, was recuperating on the Continent; and when his convalescence was assured one sunny autumn day in Berlin by his Führer's kindly act in tendering a Field-Marshal's *bâton* before a company of press photographers, he reciprocated with a cheerful intimation that Alexandria was not far off. Indeed, it was a good deal nearer than the bases from which his supplies had all to come; and there was no interruption of the air attack on his Achilles' heel. For Rommel's weakness lay behind him, where Malta's aircraft hunted shipping, U.S. Liberators flew from Egypt to afflict Benghazi, Beaufighters attacked trains and lorries in the Desert, and Wellingtons haunted the night sky over Tobruk. There was an attempt to fend off the attack from Malta, when the *Luftwaffe* concentrated half its local bomber force at Sicilian airfields in October for one more effort to eliminate the limestone aircraft carrier. But the island was well supplied with Spitfires now; and the attack was beaten off with the loss or damage of 255 aircraft and 50 "probables" at the devastating rate of 15 members of Axis air crews for each R.A.F. pilot lost. It had been a poor return for the operations of 600 bombers; and having taken heavy toll of German bombers, who might have been more usefully employed elsewhere, Malta lived to fight another day.

As October passed, the supply war went on over and beneath the Mediterranean; and it was estimated that one-third of Axis shipping failed to reach any port. Its lot was scarcely brighter when it did, since Tobruk was an uncomfortable landfall in spite of an impressive anti-aircraft barrage. But hardly a ship reached it now, and not one of them was an oil tanker. That was the crux, since oil fuel was the life-blood of Desert warfare; and the Axis forces in front of Alamein were running dangerously short. The autumn rain drove down on the melancholy spaces of the Daba landing grounds, where the *Luft-waffe* had its forward bases; and as reconnaissance photographs disclosed a morass from which Axis aircraft would be unable to take off, the R.A.F. did not disdain a providential target. Breaking off their training, fighters, fighter-bombers, and light bombers were launched to the attack on October 9 with destructive consequences; night bombers followed up with an attack on Fuka a few miles further on; and this happy chance enabled them to strike a blow from which the *Luftwaffe* never rallied. The air offensive was reopened with more formality on October 19, when the airfields at Daba and Fuka were attacked again; and from that instant they were never unmolested. Tedder was impressed by the "Hendon precision" with which formations moved against the German fighter aerodromes. It was estimated that more than half the *Luftwaffe's* effective strength had been disabled by the end of the next three days' operations; and with the air battle safely won, the land battle was ready to begin.

A little before ten o'clock that Friday night (it was October 23) the guns opened Fourth Alamein with the heaviest artillery barrage that Africa had heard; and twenty minutes later the infantry went forward in the flaming darkness on a 6-mile front, with 4 S.A.A.F. Bostons laying a smoke screen in front of them, to clear a passage for the tanks. Heavy bombers and night-flying Hurricanes added to the night's entertainment; and on Saturday the light bombers entered the land battle with a succession of 14 consecutive attacks that reached the highest number of sorties which they had yet achieved. As Bostons, Baltimores, and Mitchells concentrated on Axis vehicles at a cost of 12 aircraft destroyed and 4 damaged, the landing grounds at Daba were attacked twice more in the day to discourage fighter intervention, whilst Hurricanes provided cover for the waiting tanks. In the night infantry went through, supported by a force of tanks; and on Sunday morning the light bombers dealt so adequately with hostile motor transport that they could find no more targets in the afternoon. Axis fighters showed few signs of life; but though some air combats developed on the next day, they were quite unable to prevent the light bombers from dissipating concentrations on the ground, where Axis land forces were gathering for a counter-attack.

Rommel was not far away. Hurriedly recalled to Africa, he was on the grey cliffs of Tobruk that Monday (if a prisoner could be believed) just in time to see a most unpleasant spectacle. An Axis convoy had been creeping up the coast towards the harbour. Its safe passage was assured by the close proximity of shore-based fighters, to say nothing of the Tobruk defences. But in the afternoon an intrepid striking force of R.A.F. Beauforts and S.A.A.F. Bisleys attacked the convoy and left its only tanker blazing, although their gallantry cost them 4 aircraft. One large freighter still survived; and in the failing light it limped towards Tobruk, watched by the Field-Marshal on the cliffs, until he saw it hunted by 3 Wellingtons. They caught it with torpedoes just outside the harbour; and after an explosion there was nothing more for him to see.

He had returned to an unprepossessing situation. His deputy, Stumme, had been killed; his line was in considerable danger; and no more convoys reached him, as three consecutive attempts in the next few days were unsuccessful. His supply ships were uniformly sunk; he was reduced to flying petrol in from Crete, to the great disgust of bomber crews relegated to these humble duties; and it was evident he would have to fight it out with what supplies he had. Would they suffice? He had just enough, as it turned out, to last for one more week after that unpleasant Monday at Tobruk—one more week of desperate manœuvre under unremitting air attack in the bronze wilderness of Alamein, with his armour plunging at the advancing enemy and his aircraft out of the race. Whenever his vehicles gathered together, they became a target for implacable waves of light bombers; and his Stukas had grown so ineffective that they were developing an unpleasant habit of jettisoning their bombs over their own troops in order to escape the fighters. One afternoon his armour began to concentrate for an attack. But the light bombers struck first; Baltimores, Bostons, and Mitchells with strong fighter escort came over seven times; and after that day his land forces never took the initiative.

They were providing a more scattered target now; and the fighter-bombers took up the tale over the whole battle area, whilst low-flying fighters ranged at large behind him. On the night of November 1 the Eighth Army struck again. There was heavy fighting on the ground next day, with the light bombers operating their "shuttle service" once more and fighters working harder than ever overhead. That evening a German diarist wrote indignantly, "Where are our fighters, our Stukas and A.A.? Can't see a thing of them. Tommy comes every quarter of an hour with eighteen heavy bombers."

(This was a rare compliment to the Baltimores.) They were bombed all night long; and when daylight crept across the bay from Alexandria, the dawn patrols observed that traffic on the Desert road was all moving west. For by November 3 Fourth Alamein—air battle, land battle and all—had been safely won.

Chapter XX

TRIPOLI

WHEN THE GERMANS CAME OUT OF EGYPT, they were moving at a higher velocity than the Chosen People and in the opposite direction. The Promised Land was far behind them; there was no arm of the sea to interpose between their fleeing columns and a pursuing enemy; and Providence showed little tendency (apart from a downpour of rain) to interfere with the pursuit. But they were preceded in the customary manner by a pillar of cloud, turning after dark to flame (one observer counted thirty fires on the first night), where the R.A.F. swept down the road in front of them. For the pursuit from Alamein, which ended twelve weeks later just 1000 miles away, was one of the most remarkable in history.

Rommel was in full retreat; and as Alexander announced the victory (with General von Thoma, commanding the *Afrika Korps*, as one of its trophies), Coningham issued his directions for the pursuit:

"There they go. The enemy ground forces have cracked on the eleventh day and are starting to run. When this occurred previously, the German fighter force acted as rearguard and was most effective when we were rash or careless. With our air power we can pulverise the enemy, but it must be controlled power. I shall call on you for every effort by officers and airmen, and that includes cooks, postmen, orderlies, and the padre and M.O.s. But pilots and air crews must rigidly conform to the tactical rules of their present excellent work, and, though working at an exhausting pace, they must not relax or show any fighting indiscipline. My orders for ground attack are to be given careful attention and obeyed. I want this job done efficiently and with a minimum wastage. Be calm and ruthless but respect the Red Cross. Avoid capture. Good luck."

This was a rousing send-off; and all down the Desert road they meted out to German transport what the *Luftwaffe* had once inflicted on civilian traffic in the dust of 1940 down the crowded roads of France. For the transport was mainly German now, although it might have been Italian once. But the Italians were often left to walk or to surrender in the thirsty wilderness. Their air force, though, was leading in the race, as it got away before the *Luftwaffe*; and few Italian aircraft or air personnel were captured. German infantry and armour tried to make a stand at Fuka. But they had no success; and the pursuit went on.

The pace was rapid, as the Daba landing grounds were scarcely mined; and three German fighters almost intact on the ground appeared to show that the enemy had left unexpectedly or was short of petrol. The same signs of haste were visible all the way back to the frontier and beyond; and it was not until they got to Derna that the retreating enemy had found time to leave any quantity of mines behind him. Tedder's aim in the pursuit was to "get the fighters right forward quickly in long bounds"; and now the apparatus of mobility began to work, although heavy rain that bogged the landing grounds did not assist their progress. All the familiar landmarks were seen passing in reverse, as they looked down on the land-locked bay of Matruh with its sunken Axis steamers and saw the last of Rommel's lorries winding slowly up the steep shoulder of the Desert beyond Sollum. When Egypt fell behind them, the Eighth Army could look back as Wellington, borne forward into Spain by the last swing of the pendulum, had once turned his horse on the frontier to ejaculate with a lift of his hat, "Farewell, Portugal! I shall never see you again."

The R.A.F. kept up with the advance, descending on deserted airfields as fast as the retreating enemy abandoned them. R.A.F. Aerodrome Reconnaissance parties with the forward troops pro-

Royal Air Force and
Axis Air Forces Range
February, 1943.

Royal Air Force
and Axis Air Forces Range.

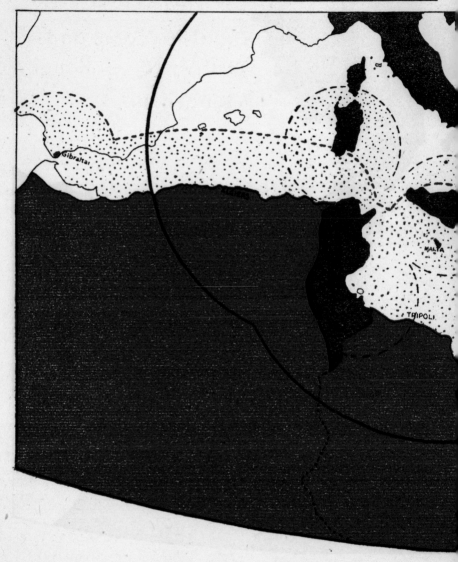

O German Bomber Cover
◉ German Fighter Cover
● R.A.F. Fighter Cover

February 1943

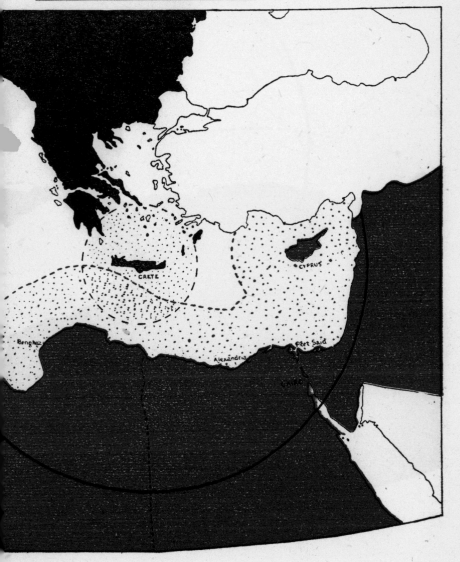

Territory in Axis hands ■

Territory in Allied hands ■

spected for R.E. Aerodrome Construction parties, whose sappers
cleared the ground; and when the site was ready, R.A.F. ground
parties moved in to receive and operate the squadrons. Fighters and
fighter-bombers were now doing all the work by day, as they provided
the ideal harriers of a routed army. Besides, they were more rapidly
established and more easily maintained than light bombers on an
advancing line of landing grounds. They were at Daba, where the
army was a few miles ahead of them at Fuka. A week later the head
of the advance looked at a broken town of empty windows backed
against a grey escarpment, where the harbour held a fleet of sunken
ships that had made their last landfall at Tobruk; and the fighter
squadrons were not far behind. For on the next day they were
working from Gambut a short drive away.

If life was arduous for the pursuers, it was more exacting for the
pursued under the lash of Coningham's controlled air power. They
were desperately short of petrol; and it was prohibitive to leave the
road for a long detour in the Desert that might take them further
from the watchful fighters overhead. One German major said they
used to come "so low you'd have thought they wanted to look down
our throats"; Italian drivers stopped their vehicles and ran whenever
they heard aircraft; their anti-aircraft guns were not used for fear
of drawing fire; and the Beaufighters were known by the alarming
title of the "Order of Dread." It was disconcerting when Hurricanes
appeared over their leading columns far beyond Benghazi three days
before the Axis rearguard came in sight of its cathedral domes. For
two squadrons had moved forward with their ground staff, who
preceded them by air; and as they were not expected in the neighbourhood, they managed to destroy or damage 300 vehicles and 14
aircraft before resistance stiffened and they were withdrawn to a safe
distance. The retreating enemy reached Benghazi in time for
Rommel's birthday; and as road transport was getting scarce, aircraft
were freely used for the next stage in their exodus, R.A.F. fighters
destroying 37 transport aircraft in two November days. But now a
fresh anxiety clouded the western sky, since four days after the collapse
at Alamein a fleet of Allied transports had appeared off Africa.
American and British troops landed in Morocco and Algeria; and
as they made for Tunis, it was plain that Axis forces in Africa were
caught between the hammer and the anvil, although these were at
present 800 miles apart. For the Eighth Army had now become

one jaw of the enormous pincers, which must eventually close on Rommel.

They were close behind him now, although his retreat from Fuka to Mersa Brega in 18 days was a record for the course. This year the British reached Benghazi some weeks earlier than usual and for a longer stay. Their advance was not so easy now, since the abandoned airfields had been liberally mined, and hostile ingenuity had gone so far at Berka as to fit a handsome coffee urn with explosive consequences. But Tripoli, the last port through which the retreating enemy could draw supplies, was coming within reach of long-range bombers; and with the hump of Cyrenaica safely occupied behind them shore-based aircraft could now cover convoys bound for Malta practically all the way from Alexandria. In November fighters operating from the Desert saw 4 freighters and their escorting warships safely through to the island; and the long siege was over. It was the first convoy to unload in the Grand Harbour since August; and this welcome supplement to Malta's rations, ammunition, and supplies of petrol, which could now be maintained without further difficulty, promised a brisk renewal of the island's hitting power. Indeed, the value of the lonely aerodrome in the Sicilian Channel was rising fast, as the war in Africa converged on Tripoli and Tunis; and it was not long before a large proportion of the Wellingtons from Egypt were transferred to Malta with a liberal provision of Beaufighters, Beauforts, and aircraft of the Fleet Air Arm. As the war came nearer, Malta struck vigorously at the rear of Axis armies on the mainland and at their supplies from Europe; and as the next phase opened, it became a stepping-stone to Sicily.

But Rommel was still hunted across Africa, and one of his pursuers had a superstitious feeling that they would not know how it was going to end until they were past El Agheila. For the pendulum had never swung so far to the west before. After a short pause in the last weeks of 1942 it swung still further, with Rommel somewhere beyond Sirte. When they reached the aerodrome at Marble Arch (which startled Londoners by being about 250 miles west of Knightsbridge), the army cleared the ground of mines and booby-traps with some loss of life; for inter-Service collaboration was now complete. Further down the road 2000 fighting troops were detailed by the New Zealanders to pick up stones and make a landing ground; and there were cases where a whole brigade performed this service for the R.A.F. The retreating enemy was now developing a new technique of ploughing up abandoned airfields. One craftsman, in particular, impaired their surface with enormous furrowed whorls of rich complexity and individual design, until a burst of cannon fire from a fighter overhead turned him from the plough. His touch was never seen again; and his successors worked more hastily in meagre patterns infelicitously borrowed from the Union Jack.

As Rommel turned to face them once again at Buerat, the heavy bombers were pounding Tripoli behind him, where they found the Spanish Mole agreeably conspicuous. But no more Axis shipping reached the harbour after January 2; and a fortnight later the Eighth Army struck again. Kittyhawks and U.S. Warhawks were prominent in the attack; and the *Luftwaffe* showed no appetite for air combat. Its strength in Africa had been reinforced by large withdrawals of aircraft from Russia, where their absence had been influential on operations at Stalingrad and elsewhere since October. But German strategy was always reconciled to sacrifices of Italian territory; and with Tunisia in danger the defence of Tripoli was secondary.

The pursuit went on towards Tripoli; and now they were capable of strange feats of mobility. One evening an advance party located a landing ground. The armoured troops moved on at dawn, leaving some Bofors guns and ground staff; and by nine o'clock the strip was ready. All that day transport aircraft were arriving with petrol, ammunition, and personnel, while fighters based on the new airfield were at work 80 miles ahead, and the transport aircraft flew back to base with army casualties. By the next morning work had started on two more landing grounds, and that day the whole fighter force was operating 80 miles beyond its starting-point. That was the standard of mobility attained by the Western Desert Air Force. Soon their bombs were falling among targets in Tunisia; and as they reached out beyond Tripoli, it was plain that the pincers had begun to close on Rommel. That would be achieved when the two Allied forces in Africa finally converged; and this event came appreciably nearer when the whole air war was centralised in one command. Tedder, under whom the U.S. Army Ninth Air Force had worked in Egypt, left Cairo to wield Allied air power over the whole Mediterranean from Algiers. He had left Anglo-American co-operation "working like clockwork" in the Desert; and the same mechanism was needed elsewhere.

But R.A.F., Middle East Command, had shown the way to victory. Egypt was saved; the waters east of Malta were clear for sea traffic; and the Eighth Army was knocking at the gates of Tripoli. The long, brown shore was safe behind them now; the great airfield at Castel Benito with all its dainty buildings was full of wreckage; and the harbour mouth was blocked with sunken ships. A little after dawn on January 23 the wide streets beyond the ochre dunes saw them arrive. It was three months to a day since the guns opened at Alamein; and they had come through. The Desert war was over; and, two thousand miles from end to end, the Mediterranean danced in the winter sunshine of 1943.

El Adem, March, 1943–*Little Easton, February,* 1944.

AIRCRAFT WHO'S WHO

BEAUFIGHTER.—Bristol: maximum speed 323 m.p.h.; cruising speed 257 m.p.h.; effective range 900 miles; service ceiling 30,000 feet; armament four 20-mm. cannon, six ·303 machine-guns. Intruders carry one ·303 free gun and occasionally two ·303 backward-firing guns. Especially suitable for ground strafing. First used in Middle East May 1941.

BLENHEIM I.—Bristol: maximum speed 265 m.p.h.; cruising speed 230 m.p.h.; effective range 678 miles; service ceiling 27,280 ft.; armament five ·303 machine-guns, two ·303 defensive machine-guns; after May 1941 carried one 20-mm. cannon (offensive). First used in Middle East (Egypt) July 1940.

BUFFALO.—Brewster: maximum speed 313 m.p.h.; cruising speed 255 m.p.h.; effective range 520 miles; service ceiling 30,650 ft.; armament four ·50 machine-guns.

FULMAR (F.A.A.).—Fairey: maximum speed 253 m.p.h.; cruising speed 228 m.p.h.; effective range 625 miles; armament eight ·303 machine-guns; convoy escort duties. First used in Middle East (Malta) January 1941.

FURY I & II.—Hawker: maximum speed (I) 205 m.p.h., (II) 223 m.p.h.; cruising speed (I) 186 m.p.h., (II) 217 m.p.h.; effective range (I) 283 miles, (II) 259 miles; armament two ·303 machine-guns. First used in Middle East (Abyssinia) October 1940.

GAUNTLET.—Gloster: maximum speed 223 m.p.h.; cruising speed 187 m.p.h.; effective range 424 miles; armament two ·303 machine-guns. First used in Middle East (Abyssinia) August 1940.

GLADIATOR.—Gloster: maximum speed 242 m.p.h.; cruising speed 214 m.p.h.; effective range 328 miles; service ceiling 32,800 ft.; armament four ·303 machine-guns. This aircraft carried all the early Middle East work. First used (Egypt) June 1940.

HURRICANE I.—Hawker: maximum speed 320 m.p.h.; cruising speed 275 m.p.h.; effective range 340 miles; service ceiling 36,000 ft.; armament eight ·303 machine-guns. Hurricanes, very manœuvrable aircraft, stood the brunt of the Middle East fighting. First used (Western Desert) August 1940.

HURRICANE II A & II B.—Hawker: maximum speed 335 m.p.h.; cruising speed 281 m.p.h.; effective range 314 miles; service ceiling 40,000 ft.; armament eight (Hurricane II B twelve) ·303 machine-guns. First used in Middle East 1941.

HURRICANE II C.—Hawker: maximum speed 332 m.p.h.; cruising speed 278 m.p.h.; effective range 311 miles; service ceiling 36,000 ft.; armament four 20-mm. cannon. First used in Middle East 1942.

KITTYHAWK.—Curtiss: maximum speed 350 m.p.h.; cruising speed 280 m.p.h.; service ceiling 29,100 ft.; armament at first four, then six ·50 machine-guns. First used in Middle East (Western Desert) December 1941.

MARTLET (F.A.A.).—Gruman: maximum speed 310 m.p.h.; cruising speed 257 m.p.h.; effective range 690 miles; service ceiling 28,000 ft.; armament varies—two or four ·303 and two ·50 machine-guns, or four or six ·50 machine-guns; convoy escort duties. First used in Middle East (Western Desert) October 1941.

MOHAWK (F.A.A.).—Curtiss: maximum speed 302 m.p.h.; cruising speed 248 m.p.h.; effective range 345 miles; armament six ·303 machine-guns.

SPITFIRE I & II.—Vickers-Armstrong: maximum speed (I) 355 m.p.h., (II) 363 m.p.h.; cruising speed (I) 304 m.p.h., (II) 314 m.p.h.; effective range (I) 415 miles, (II) 335 miles; service ceiling 36,000 ft.; armament eight ·303 machine-guns. First used in Middle East (Malta) spring 1942, (Western Desert) summer 1942.

SPITFIRE V.—Vickers-Armstrong: maximum speed 375 m.p.h.; cruising speed 310 m.p.h.; effective range 335 miles; armament four ·303 machine-guns, two 20-mm. cannon. First used in Middle East June 1942, four aircraft being specially adapted for Photographic Reconnaissance.

SPITFIRE IX.—Armament four ·303 machine-guns, two 20-mm. cannon.

TOMAHAWK.—Curtiss: maximum speed 345 m.p.h.; cruising speed 278 m.p.h.; effective range 485 miles; service ceiling 30,000 ft.; armament four ·303 machine-guns, two ·50 cannon. First used in Middle East (Egypt) May 1941.

BRITISH FIGHTER BOMBERS

BEAUFIGHTER.—Bristol: maximum speed 323 m.p.h.; cruising speed 257 m.p.h.; effective range 900 miles; service ceiling 30,000 ft.; armament four 20-mm. cannon, six ·303 machine-guns, four 250-lb. bombs. First used in Middle East autumn 1942.

HURRICANE I.—Hawker: maximum speed 320 m.p.h.; cruising speed 275 m.p.h.; effective range 340 miles; service ceiling 36,000 ft.; armament eight ·303 machine-guns, eight 40-lb. bombs. First used in Middle East (Western Desert) November 1941.

HURRICANE II B.—Hawker: maximum speed 335 m.p.h.; cruising speed 281 m.p.h.; effective range 314 miles; service ceiling 40,000 ft.; armament twelve ·303 machine-guns, two 250-lb. bombs. First used in Middle East (Malta) June 1942.

KITTYHAWK (A).—Curtiss: maximum speed 350 m.p.h.; cruising speed 280 m.p.h.; service ceiling 29,100 ft.; armament six ·50 machine-guns, one 250-lb. bomb. First used in Middle East April 1942.

KITTYHAWK (B) (American type).—Armament six ·50 machine-guns, one 500-lb. bomb. First used in Middle East June 1942.

KITTYHAWK (C) (American type).—Armament six ·50 machine-guns, one 250-lb. bomb, six 40-lb. bombs. · First used in Middle East November 1942.

SPITFIRE V.—Vickers-Armstrong: maximum speed 375 m.p.h.; cruising speed 310 m.p.h.; effective range 335 miles; armament four ·303 machine-guns, two 20-mm. cannon, two 250-lb. bombs. First used in Middle East (Malta only) autumn 1942.

GERMAN FIGHTER AIRCRAFT

FOCKE-WULF 190 A.3.—Maximum speed 390 m.p.h.; cruising speed 335 m.p.h.; effective range 380 miles; armament two 7·92-mm. machine-guns, two 20-mm. Mauser cannon, two 20-mm. Oerlikon cannon; with maximum fuel load cruising speed 220 m.p.h., range 820 miles; service ceiling 36,000-38,000 ft.

MESSERSCHMITT 109 E.—Maximum speed 355 m.p.h.; cruising speed 300 m.p.h.; effective range 450 miles; with maximum fuel load cruising speed 200 m.p.h., range 660 miles; service ceiling 35,000-36,500 ft.; armament two 7·7-mm. machine-guns, two 20-mm. Oerlikon cannon.

MESSERSCHMITT 109 F.4.—Maximum speed 375 m.p.h.; cruising speed 320 m.p.h.; effective range 360 miles; with maximum fuel load cruising speed 200 m.p.h., range 600 miles; service ceiling 38,000-40,000 ft.; armament one 20-mm. Mauser cannon, two 7·92-mm. machine-guns.

MESSERSCHMITT 109 G.2.—Maximum speed 395 m.p.h.; cruising speed 316 m.p.h.; effective range 415 miles; with maximum fuel load cruising speed 210 m.p.h., range 568 miles; service ceiling 37,500-39,000 ft.; armament two 7·92-mm. machine-guns, three 20-mm. Mauser cannon.

MESSERSCHMITT 110 E.1.—Maximum speed 340 m.p.h.; cruising speed 285 m.p.h.; effective range 740 miles; with maximum fuel load cruising speed 200 m.p.h., range 2100 miles; service ceiling 32,000-34,000 ft.; armament two 20-mm. Oerlikon cannon, four 7·9-mm. machine-guns and one movable machine-gun in rear.

MESSERSCHMITT 210 C.—Maximum speed 368 m.p.h.; cruising speed 325 m.p.h.; effective range 1300 miles; with maximum fuel load cruising speed 227 m.p.h., range 1500 miles; service ceiling 28,500-33,000 ft.; armament two 7·9-mm. machine-guns, two 20-mm. cannon, two 23-mm. machine-guns port and starboard.

GERMAN FIGHTER BOMBERS

FOCKE-WULF 190 A.4/U.8.—Maximum speed 367 m.p.h.; cruising speed, with bombs, 320 m.p.h.; effective range 320 miles; with maximum fuel load cruising speed 220 m.p.h., range 420 miles; service ceiling 28,500-34,500 ft.; armament one 550-lb. bomb (maximum 1100 lb.), two 7·92-mm. machine-guns, two 20-mm. Mauser and two 20-mm. Oerlikon cannon.

HENSCHEL 129 B.2.—Maximum speed 240 m.p.h.; cruising speed with bombs 210 m.p.h.; effective range 240 miles; with maximum fuel load cruising speed 173 m.p.h., range 314 miles; service ceiling 24,500-29,500 ft.; armament one 220-lb. bomb (maximum 770 lb.), one 30-mm. cannon, two 15-mm. cannon, two 7·9-mm. machine-guns.

MESSERSCHMITT 109 E.—Maximum speed 320 m.p.h.; cruising speed with bombs 285 m.p.h.; effective range 410 miles; service ceiling 33,000-36,500 ft.; armament one 550-lb. bomb, two 7·7-mm. machine-guns, two 20-mm. Oerlikon cannon.

MESSERSCHMITT 109 F.4.—Maximum speed 360 m.p.h.; cruising speed with bombs 295 m.p.h.; effective range 460 miles; service ceiling 33,000-40,000 ft.; armament one 550-lb. bomb, one 20-mm. Mauser, two 7·92-mm. machine-guns.

MESSERSCHMITT 109 G.2.—Maximum speed 367 m.p.h.; cruising speed with bombs 306 m.p.h.; effective range 400 miles; service ceiling 35,000-39,000 ft.; armament one 550-lb. bomb, two 7·92-mm. machine-guns, three 20-mm. Mauser cannon.

MESSERSCHMITT 110 E.1.—Maximum speed 325 m.p.h.; cruising speed with bombs 253 m.p.h.; effective range 600 miles; with maximum fuel load cruising speed 215 m.p.h., range 1320 miles; service ceiling 23,000-34,000 ft.; armament 1540-lb. bombs (maximum 4400 lb.), two 20-mm. Oerlikon cannon, four 7·9-mm. machine-guns, one movable machine-gun in rear.

MESSERSCHMITT 210 C.—Maximum speed 355 m.p.h.; cruising speed with bombs 290 m.p.h.; effective range 1050 miles; with maximum fuel load cruising speed 230 m.p.h., range 1400 miles; service ceiling 27,000-33,000 ft.; armament 1540-lb. bombs (maximum 2200 lb.), two 7·9-mm. machine-guns, two 20-mm. cannon, two 13-mm. machine-guns port and starboard.

ITALIAN FIGHTER AIRCRAFT

MACCHI 205.—Maximum speed 390 m.p.h.; cruising speed 320 m.p.h.; effective range 400 miles; with maximum fuel load cruising speed 200 miles, range 500 miles; service ceiling 36,000-38,000 ft.; armament two 12·7-mm. machine-guns.

ITALIAN FIGHTER BOMBERS

FIAT .C.R. 42.—Maximum speed with bombs, 260 m.p.h.; cruising speed 223 m.p.h.; effective range 400 miles; with maximum fuel load cruising speed 150 m.p.h., range 575 miles; service ceiling 32,000-34,000 ft.; armament one 12·7-mm. and one 7·7-mm. or two 12·7-mm. machine-guns. Obsolete by March 1941, but still in service January 1943.

FIAT G. 50.—Maximum speed with bombs 290 m.p.h.; cruising speed 257 m.p.h.; effective range 250 miles; with maximum fuel load cruising speed 170 m.p.h., range 510 miles; service ceiling 31,500-34,000 ft.; armament 36 3-kg. bombs, two 12·7-mm. and two 7·7-mm. machine-guns. Obsolete by June 1941, but still in service January 1943.

MACCHI 200.—Maximum speed with bombs 295 m.p.h., cruising speed 255 m.p.h.; effective range 380 miles; with maximum fuel load cruising speed 170 m.p.h., range 570 miles; service ceiling 31,000-34,000 ft.; armament two 12·7-mm. and two 7·7-mm. machine-guns. Obsolete by June 1941, but still in service January 1943.

MACCHI 202.—Maximum speed with bombs 340 m.p.h.; cruising speed 290 m.p.h.; effective range 400 miles; with maximum fuel load cruising speed 195 m.p.h., range 550 miles; service ceiling 33,000-36,000 ft.; armament two 12·7-mm. machine-guns. Introduced November 1941.

REGGIANE, RE. 2001.—Maximum speed with bombs 325 m.p.h.; cruising speed 280 m.p.h.; effective range 680 miles; with maximum fuel load cruising speed 195 m.p.h., range 920 miles; service ceiling 34,000-36,000 ft.; armament two fixed forward-firing machine-guns. Introduced May 1942.

BRITISH LIGHT BOMBERS

ANSON.—A. V. Roe: maximum speed 178 m.p.h.; cruising speed 154 m.p.h.; effective range 540 miles; service ceiling 19,500 ft.; armament one offensive and one defensive ·303 machine-gun, 500-lb. bombs. First used in Middle East (Abyssinia) November 1940.

BALTIMORE I, II & III.—Douglas: armament four ·30 machine-guns (offensive), eight ·30 or ·303 machine-guns (defensive), 2000-lb. bombs. First used in Middle East summer 1942.

BALTIMORE II.—Douglas: armament four ·30 machine-guns (offensive), ten ·30 or ·303 machine-guns (defensive), 2000-lb. bombs. First used in Middle East summer 1942.

BALTIMORE III A.—Douglas: armament four ·30 machine-guns (offensive), two ·50 and six ·30 or ·303 machine-guns (defensive), 2000-lb. bombs. First used in Middle East summer 1942.

BLENHEIM I.—Bristol: maximum speed 265 m.p.h.; cruising speed 230 m.p.h.; effective range 678 miles; service ceiling 27,280 ft.; armament originally one ·303 per. machine-gun, later two ·303 backward-firing guns also, 1000-lb. bombs. First used in Middle East (Libya) June 1940.

BLENHEIM IV.—Bristol: maximum speed 266 m.p.h.; effective range approximately 1200 miles; service ceiling 27,000 ft.; armament one ·303 machine-gun (offensive), two ·303 (defensive), 1000-lb. bombs.

BLENHEIM V (Bisley).—Bristol: armament one ·303 machine-gun (offensive), four ·303 (defensive), 1000-lb. bombs. First used in Middle East summer 1942.

BOSTON I, II & III.—Douglas: maximum speed 312 m.p.h.; cruising speed 245 m.p.h.; effective range 360 miles; armament four ·303 machine-guns (offensive), three or four ·303 (defensive), 1500-lb. bombs. First used in Middle East for Tactical Reconnaissance (Western Desert) November 1941, as a Bomber (Western Desert) December 1941.

HARDY.—Hawker: maximum speed 156 m.p.h.; cruising speed 135 m.p.h.; effective range 452 miles; armament one offensive and one defensive ·303 machine-gun, 500-lb. bombs. First used in Middle East (Abyssinia) November 1940.

HUDSON.—Lockheed: armament two ·303 machine-guns (offensive), five ·303 (defensive), 1000-lb. bombs. Used on anti-submarine and shipping convoy work.

MARAUDER.—Glenn Martin: armament six ·30 and three ·50 machine-guns (defensive), 3500-lb. bombs. First used in Middle East autumn 1942, and used also as a Torpedo-Bomber.

MARYLAND.—Glenn Martin: maximum speed 294 m.p.h.; cruising speed 240 m.p.h.; effective range 1040 miles; armament four ·303 machine-guns (offensive), six ·303 (defensive), 1000-lb. bombs. First used in Middle East (Malta) May 1941, (Cyrenaica) August 1941.

MOSQUITO.—De Havilland: the fastest light bomber in use; armament four 20-mm. cannon, four ·303 machine-guns (offensive) or 2000-lb. bombs. First used in Middle East January 1943.

VINCENT.—Vickers-Aviation: maximum speed 139 m.p.h.; cruising speed 116 m.p.h.; effective range 618 miles; armament one offensive and one defensive ·303 machine-gun, 1000-lb. bombs. First used in Middle East (Eritrea) June 1940.

WELLESLEY.—Vickers-Aviation: maximum speed 206 m.p.h.; cruising speed 180 m.p.h.; effective range 1320 miles; service ceiling 35,250 ft.; armament one ·303 machine-gun (offensive), two ·303 (defensive), 1000-lb. bombs. First used in Middle East (Eritrea) June 1940.

BRITISH HEAVY AND MEDIUM BOMBERS

BOMBAY.—Bristol: maximum speed 174 m.p.h.; cruising speed 152 m.p.h.; effective range 745 miles; service ceiling 25,000 ft.; armament two ·303 machine-guns (defensive), 2000-lb. bombs (load increased indefinitely by carrying 20-lb. bombs inside fuselage). First used in Middle East (Libya) June 1940.

CATALINA FLYING BOAT.—Consolidated: maximum speed 190 m.p.h.; maximum range 4000 miles; service ceiling 21,900 ft.; armament six ·303 machine-guns (defensive), 2000-lb. bombs. Coastal reconnaissance duties.

FORTRESS.—Boeing: maximum speed 300 m.p.h.; effective range 2100 miles; service ceiling 29,300 ft.; armament six ·50 machine-guns, one ·30 (defensive), 5000-lb. bombs. First used in Middle East November 1941, more successfully during winter 1942.

HALIFAX.—Handley-Page : maximum speed 262 m.p.h. ; maximum range 3000 miles ; armament twelve ·303 machine-guns (defensive), 9000-lb. bombs. First used in Middle East (Cyrenaica) July 1942.

LIBERATOR.—Consolidated : armament fourteen ·303 machine-guns (defensive), 7000-lb. bombs. First used in Middle East November 1941 more successfully during winter 1942.

SUNDERLAND FLYING BOAT.—Short : maximum speed 204 m.p.h. ; cruising speed 174 m.p.h. ; effective range 1650 miles ; service ceiling 16,000 ft. ; armament nine ·303 machine-guns (defensive), 2000-lb. bombs. Coastal reconnaissance duties. First used in Middle East (Mediterranean) June 1940.

WELLINGTON I, II & III.—Vickers-Armstrong : maximum speed (I) 259 m.p.h. ; cruising speed 213 m.p.h., (II) maximum speed 244 m.p.h. ; effective range 1365 miles ; service ceiling 16,500 ft. ; armament six ·303 machine-guns (defensive), 4500-lb. bombs. The Middle East stand-by for night bombing, (III) maximum range 2120 miles ; service ceiling 19,000 ft. ; armament eight ·303 machine-guns (defensive), 4500-lb. bombs.

WELLINGTON V, VI, VII & VIII.—Armament four ·303 machine-guns (defensive), 4500-lb. bombs. Employed increasingly against shipping, in addition to attacks on land targets. Wellington V used as a Torpedo-Bomber, VIII on anti-surface vessel duties.

GERMAN BOMBERS

DORNIER, DO. 217 E.4.—Maximum speed with bombs 290 m.p.h. ; cruising speed 250 m.p.h. ; effective range 960 miles ; service ceiling 22,500-29,000 feet ; armament 4400-lb. (maximum 6600-lb.) bombs, one 15-mm. and one 20-mm. cannon, seven 7·92-mm. machine-guns.

FOCKE-WULF, F.-W. 200 K.—Maximum speed with bombs 235 m.p.h. ; cruising speed 215 m.p.h. ; effective range 2250 miles ; service ceiling 21,500-30,000 feet ; armament 4400-lb. (maximum 11,000-lb.) bombs.

HEINKEL, HE. 111 H.6.—Maximum speed with bombs 250 m.p.h. ; cruising speed 215 m.p.h. ; effective range 1580 miles ; service ceiling 26,500-32,500 feet ; armament 4400-lb. (maximum 7000-lb.) bombs, eight 7·9-mm. machine-guns, one 20-mm. cannon.

JUNKERS, JU. 86 P.1.—Maximum speed with bombs 215 m.p.h. ; cruising speed 195 m.p.h. ; effective range 900 miles ; service ceiling 36,000-45,000 feet ; armament 1760-lb. (maximum 2200-lb.) bombs.

JUNKERS, JU. 87 D.1.—Maximum speed with bombs 245 m.p.h. ; cruising speed 200 m.p.h. ; effective range 750 miles ; service ceiling 18,000-27,000 feet ; armament 2600-lb. (maximum 4000-lb.) bombs, four 7·9-mm. machine-guns.

JUNKERS, JU. 88 A.4.—Maximum speed with bombs 285 m.p.h. ; cruising speed 250 m.p.h. ; effective range 1200 miles ; service ceiling 22,000-30,000 feet ; armament 4400-lb. (maximum 6400-lb.) bombs, one 15-mm. cannon, four 7·92-mm. machine-guns.

ITALIAN BOMBERS

CANT., Z. 1007.—Maximum speed with bombs 270 m.p.h.; cruising speed 235 m.p.h.; effective range 920 miles; service ceiling 26,500-31,500 feet; armament 2640-lb. (maximum 4850-lb.) bombs; two 12·7-mm. and two 7·7-mm. machine-guns.

FIAT, B.R. 20 M.—Maximum speed with bombs 245 m.p.h.; cruising speed 217 m.p.h.; effective range 1210 miles; service ceiling 25,000-31,500 feet; armament 2200-lb. (maximum 3500-lb.) bombs, one 12·7-mm. and two 7·7-mm. machine-guns.

PIAGGIO, P. 108.—Maximum speed with bombs 260 m.p.h.; cruising speed 230 m.p.h.; effective range 1550 miles; service ceiling 23,000-30,000 feet; armament 4400-lb. (maximum 10,000-lb.) bombs.

SAVOIA MARCHETTI, S.M. 79.—Maximum speed with bombs 245 m.p.h.; cruising speed 211 m.p.h.; effective range 900 miles; service ceiling 23,000-28,000 feet; armament 2750-lb. (maximum 3960-lb.) bombs, four machine-guns.

SAVOIA MARCHETTI, S.M. 81.—Maximum speed 211 m.p.h.; effective range 930 miles; service ceiling 22,960 feet; armament five 12-mm. machine-guns, and bombs. Although obsolete at the outbreak of war, used in Italian East Africa and Libya; converted to transport June 1941.

SAVOIA MARCHETTI, S.M. 84.—Maximum speed with bombs 280 m.p.h.; cruising speed 250 m.p.h.; effective range 950 miles; service ceiling 24,000-29,500 feet; armament 2750-lb. (maximum 3960-lb.) bombs.

BRITISH TORPEDO CARRIERS

ALBACORE.—Fairey: maximum speed 163 m.p.h; cruising speed 138 m.p.h.; effective range 521 miles; armament one ·303 (offensive) and one ·303 machine-gun (defensive), 1500-lb. bombs. Normally carries one torpedo; used also for flare-dropping over targets for Wellingtons. First used in Middle East (Libya) March 1941.

BEAUFORT.—Bristol: maximum speed 275 m.p.h.; effective range 2000 miles; armament two ·303 machine-guns (offensive), four ·303 (defensive), 1500-lb. bombs. Normally carries one torpedo. First used in Middle East (Eastern Mediterranean) October 1941.

SWORDFISH.—Fairey: maximum speed 129 m.p.h.; cruising speed 116 m.p.h.; effective range 380 miles; service ceiling 19,250 feet; armament one ·303 (offensive), one ·303 machine-gun (defensive), 1500-lb. bombs. Employed on anti-shipping strikes. First used in Middle East (Tobruk and off Sicily) July 1940.

WELLINGTON I.—Vickers-Armstrong: maximum speed 232 m.p.h.; cruising speed 219 m.p.h.; maximum range 2440 miles; service ceiling 16,500 feet; armament six ·303 machine-guns (defensive), 2000-lb. bombs. First used in Middle East March 1942.

ITALIAN MARINE AIRCRAFT (SHIPBORNE)

MERIDIONALI, RO. 43 SEAPLANE (Recce).—Maximum speed 186 m.p.h.; cruising speed 160 m.p.h.; range with maximum fuel load 880 miles; service ceiling 23,000-26,000 ft.

MERIDIONALI, RO. 44 SEAPLANE (Fighter).—Maximum speed 189 m.p.h.; cruising speed 163 m.p.h.; range with maximum fuel load 760 miles; service ceiling 26,000-28,000 ft.

ITALIAN RECONNAISSANCE AND LIGHT BOMBING AIRCRAFT

CAPRONI, CA. 312 BIS.—Maximum speed 260 m.p.h.; cruising speed 222 m.p.h.; range with maximum fuel load 1585 miles; service ceiling 27,000-32,000 ft.; maximum bomb load 880 lb.

FIAT.—Maximum speed 286 m.p.h.; cruising speed 242 m.p.h.; range with maximum fuel load 1440 miles; service ceiling 28,500-32,000 ft.; bomb load 660 lb. (maximum 1100 lb.).

ITALIAN RECONNAISSANCE AIRCRAFT

CANT., Z. 1007 BIS.—Maximum speed 280 m.p.h.; cruising speed 235 m.p.h.; range with maximum fuel load 1925 miles; service ceiling 26,000-31,500 ft.

SAVOIA MARCHETTI, S.M. 79.—Maximum speed 255 m.p.h.; cruising speed 211 m.p.h.; range with maximum fuel load 2470 miles; service ceiling 23,000-28,000 ft.

BRITISH TRANSPORT AIRCRAFT

BOMBAY.—Bristol: maximum speed 186 m.p.h.; cruising speed 159 m.p.h.; effective range 790 miles; service ceiling 25,000 ft.; armament two ·303 machine-guns (defensive). First used in Middle East November 1940.

HUDSON I, II & III.—Lockheed; maximum speed (I) 222 m.p.h., (II) 225 m.p.h., (III) 252 m.p.h.; armament two ·303 machine-guns (offensive). First used in Middle East November 1941.

LODESTAR.—Lockheed: maximum speed 272 m.p.h.; cruising speed 251 m.p.h.; range 1890 miles; service ceiling 27,200 ft.

VALENTIA.—Vickers-Aviation: maximum speed 111 m.p.h.; cruising speed 104 m.p.h.; effective range 367 miles; armament one ·303 machine-gun (offensive), one ·303 (defensive). Used in Middle East before June 1940.

GERMAN TRANSPORT AIRCRAFT

BLOHM & VOSS, B.V. 222 TRANSPORT SEAPLANE.—Maximum speed 200-240 m.p.h.; cruising speed 150 m.p.h.; range with maximum fuel load 4000 miles; service ceiling 18,000 ft.; maximum load 22,000 lb., or 80 troops.

JUNKERS, JU. 52.—Maximum speed 170 m.p.h.; cruising speed 140 m.p.h.; range with maximum fuel load 1100 miles; service ceiling 27,000 ft.; load 5000 lb.

JUNKERS, JU. 290.—Maximum speed 240 m.p.h.; cruising speed 210 m.p.h.; range with maximum fuel load 1850 miles; service ceiling 23,000-27,000 ft.; load 18,700 lb. (maximum 25,000 lb.).

MESSERSCHMITT, M.E. 323.—Maximum speed 165 m.p.h.; cruising speed 135 m.p.h.; service ceiling 13,000 ft.; load 26,500 lb. (maximum 35,000 lb.).

ITALIAN TRANSPORT AIRCRAFT

GHIBLI, G. 12.—Maximum speed 255 m.p.h.; cruising speed 213 m.p.h.; effective range 875 miles; service ceiling 27,500-32,500 ft.; load 3075 lb.

SAVOIA MARCHETTI, S.M. 82.—Maximum speed 205 m.p.h.; cruising speed 172 m.p.h.; effective range 1160 miles; service ceiling 17,000-20,500 ft.; load 6600 lb. (maximum 8240 lb.).

ITALIAN ARMY CO-OPERATION AIRCRAFT

MERIDIONALI, RO. 37 BIS.—Maximum speed 200 m.p.h.; cruising speed 172 m.p.h.; range with maximum fuel load 1190 miles; service ceiling 25,500-30,000 ft.

GERMAN SEA RECONNAISSANCE AND LIGHT BOMBING AIRCRAFT

ARADO, AR. 196.—Maximum speed 195 m.p.h.; cruising speed 160 m.p.h.; range with maximum fuel load 900 miles; service ceiling 17,000-23,000 ft.; maximum load 220-lb. bombs.

BLOHM & VOSS, B.V. 138.—Maximum speed 180 m.p.h.; cruising speed 152 m.p.h.; range with maximum fuel load 3500 miles; service ceiling 18,000 ft.; load 1000-lb. bombs.

DORNIER, DO. 18.—Maximum speed 155 m.p.h.; cruising speed 139 m.p.h.; range with maximum fuel load 2500 miles; service ceiling 17,000-20,000 ft.; maximum load 1100-lb. bombs.

DORNIER, DO. 24.—Maximum speed 210 m.p.h.; cruising speed 180 m.p.h.; range with maximum fuel load 1710 miles; service ceiling 21,000-27,000 ft.; maximum load 3300-lb. bombs.

GERMAN RECONNAISSANCE AIRCRAFT

JUNKERS, JU. 86 P.2.—Maximum speed 230 m.p.h.; cruising speed 195 m.p.h.; range with maximum fuel load 1350 miles; service ceiling 40,000–45,000 ft.

JUNKERS, JU. 88 D.1.—Maximum speed 310 m.p.h.; cruising speed 265 m.p.h.; range with maximum fuel load 2200 miles; service ceiling 24,000–30,000 ft.

ITALIAN MARINE AIRCRAFT

CANT., C.Z. 501 FLYING-BOAT.—Maximum speed 165 m.p.h.; cruising speed 130 m.p.h.; range with maximum fuel load 2850 miles; service ceiling 16,000–22,000 ft.; maximum bomb load 1100 lb.

CANT., C.Z. 506 SEAPLANE.—Maximum speed 240 m.p.h.; cruising speed 198 m.p.h.; range with normal fuel load 1310 miles; service ceiling 24,500–27,500 ft.; maximum bomb load 2200 lb.

FIAT, R.S.14 SEAPLANE.—Maximum speed 247 m.p.h.; cruising speed 204 m.p.h.; range with maximum fuel load 1440 miles; service ceiling 27,000–30,000 ft.; maximum bomb load 1700 lb.

BRITISH COMMUNICATION AIRCRAFT

AUDAX.—Hawker: maximum speed 162 m.p.h.; cruising speed 143 m.p.h.; effective range 475 miles; armament one ·303 (offensive) and one ·303 machine-gun (defensive). First used in Middle East (Iraq) May 1941; obsolete by 1943.

HART.—Hawker: maximum speed 169 m.p.h.; cruising speed 147 m.p.h.; effective range 457 miles; armament one ·303 (offensive), one ·303 machine-gun (defensive). First used in Middle East (Abyssinia) June 1940; obsolete by 1943.

HIND.—Hawker: maximum speed 188 m.p.h.; cruising speed 158 m.p.h.; effective range 421 miles; armament one ·303 (offensive), one ·303 machine-gun (defensive). In use in Middle East 1940; obsolete by 1943.

MAGISTER.—Phillip & Powis: maximum speed 132 m.p.h.; cruising speed 123; effective range 250 miles. In use in Middle East 1940; obsolete by 1943.

PROCTOR.—Percival: maximum speed 174 m.p.h.; cruising speed 160 m.p.h.; effective range 540 miles. In use in Middle East 1940; obsolete by 1943.

BRITISH MISCELLANEOUS TYPES

GORDON.—Armament one ·303 machine-gun (offensive), one ·303 (defensive). Employed for target towing only.

HARVARD.—North American: maximum speed 210 m.p.h.; cruising speed 186 m.p.h.; effective range 610 miles; service ceiling 23,000 ft.; armament one ·303 machine-gun (offensive). Training duties.

HURRICANE II D.—Hawker: armament, two 40-mm. cannon, four ·303 machine-guns (offensive); tank buster. First used in Middle East (Western Desert) June 1942.

LYSANDER I & II.—Westland: maximum speed (I) 224 m.p.h., (II) 225 m.p.h.; cruising speed (I) 192 m.p.h., (II) 193 m.p.h.; effective range (I) 405 miles, (II) 445 miles; service ceiling 26,000 ft.; armament two ·303 machine-guns (offensive), one ·303 (defensive), 500-lb. bombs. A few aircraft carried 20-mm. cannon in place of two (offensive) machine-guns, but were not a success. Employed on Army Co-operation work. First used in Middle East (Egypt and Western Desert) July 1940.

OXFORD.—Airspeed: maximum speed 184 m.p.h.; cruising speed 159 m.p.h.; effective range 795 miles; service ceiling 23,500 ft.; armament one ·303 machine-gun (offensive), one ·303 (defensive), 200-lb. bombs. Trainer, used operationally in Iraq, May 1941.

WALRUS.—Vickers-Supermarine: maximum speed 135 m.p.h.; cruising speed 118 m.p.h.; effective range 350 miles; service ceiling 18,500 ft.; armament one ·303 machine-gun (offensive), one ·303 (defensive), 500-lb. bombs. Sea rescue and coastal reconnaissance work. First used in Middle East (Somaliland) November 1940.

INDEX

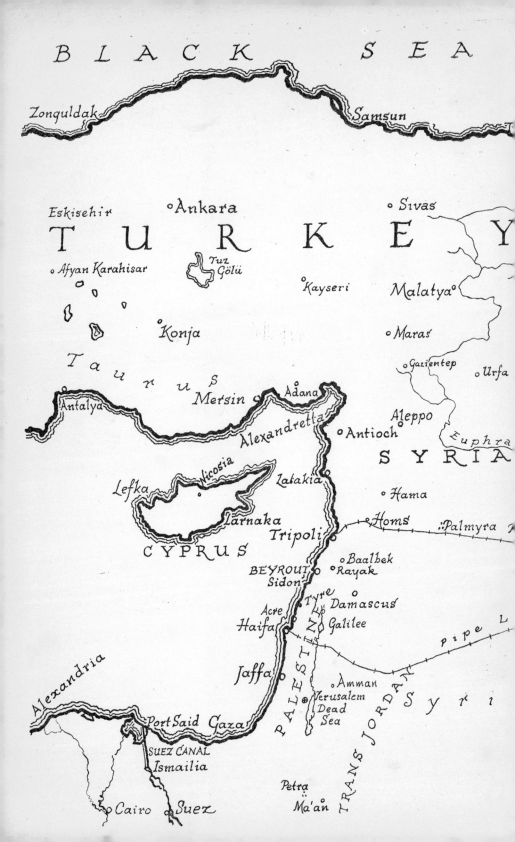